Should Britain Leave the EU?

Dedicated to the memory of Sir Julian Hodge (1904–2004)

Should Britain Leave the EU?

An Economic Analysis of a Troubled Relationship

Patrick Minford
Professor of Economics, Cardiff Business School,
Cardiff University, UK

Vidya Mahambare
Research Associate, Cardiff Business School,
Cardiff University, UK

Eric Nowell
Research Associate, Cardiff Business School,
Cardiff University, UK and Honorary Fellow,
Liverpool University Management School,
Liverpool University, UK

Edward Elgar in association with the
Institute of Economic Affairs

Edward Elgar
Cheltenham, UK • Northampton, MA, USA

Published by
Edward Elgar Publishing Limited
Glensanda House
Montpellier Parade
Cheltenham
Glos GL50 1UA
UK

Edward Elgar Publishing, Inc.
136 West Street
Suite 202
Northampton
Massachusetts 01060
USA

A catalogue record for this book
is available from the British Library

ISBN 1 84542 136 1 (cased)
    1 84542 379 8 (paperback)

Printed and bound in Great Britain by MPG Books Ltd, Bodmin, Cornwall

Contents

List of Figures

List of Tables

Author Biographies

Patrick Minford is professor of economics at Cardiff Business School, Cardiff University, where he has been since October 1997. Between 1967 and 1976 he held economic positions in the Ministry of Finance, Malawi; Directors' staff, Courtaulds Limited; H M Treasury; H M Treasury's Delegation to Washington, DC; Manchester University; and The National Institute for Economic and Social Research. From 1976 to 1997 he was professor of economics at the University of Liverpool. He was a member of the Monopolies and Mergers Commission from 1990 to 1996; and one of H M Treasury's Panel of Forecasters ('6 Wise Men') from January 1993 until December 1996.He was awarded the C.B.E. for services to economics in 1996. He has published books, articles and journalism on exchange rates, unemployment, housing, trade and macroeconomics. He founded and directs the Liverpool Research Group in Macroeconomics, which has published forecasts based on the Liverpool Model of the UK since 1979; the group is now very largely based within the Julian Hodge Institute of Applied Macroeconomics at Cardiff Business School.

Vidya Mahambare holds a BA in economics from the University of Bombay, and masters degrees in economics from Gokhale Institute of Politics and Economics and in International Trade and Finance from Lancaster University, where she later also obtained a doctorate in international economics. Her main areas of research and publication are in the economics of liberalisation and corporate finance issues in developing countries. She is a research associate at Cardiff Business School, Cardiff University.

Eric Nowell obtained his BA in Physics and his M.Sc. in Applied Statistics and Random Processes from U.M.I.S.T; and later an M.Sc. in Audiology from the University of Salford. He has worked as a researcher in applied medicine, in plasma physics, in computer-aided design engineering and in diesel combustion processes. Since October 1983 he has worked with Patrick Minford in developing economic models. He is based in the Management School of the University of Liverpool, where he is an honorary research fellow.

Preface

Europe – that is, the EEC or Common Market at first, most recently to become the European Union – has been a major issue of British political discussion since the Second World War, and since UK accession to the EEC in 1973 it has become arguably the dominant issue. For the first two decades of membership the basic assumption of most British politicians was that it was overall a good thing, even if particular elements in it (such as notoriously the Common Agricultural Policy) gave trouble. In the last decade, as the Franco-German programme for European integration has been pushed forward relentlessly, that basic assumption has come to be widely questioned. That questioning and with it the awareness of the difficulties created by membership was intensified by the debate over whether Britain should join the euro; though that debate was narrowly confined to the effects of euro membership, and for practical purposes took for granted that EU membership itself was beneficial, the arguments over the euro inevitably overlapped with wider issues – for example, those of harmonisation and budgetary discipline (especially pensions). In this book my co-authors and I have reviewed earlier work on the euro, harmonisation and budgetary issues, much of it by now familiar to informed British readers; but our main focus has been on trade, where the assumption of net benefit has been barely questioned and little serious work has taken place. That is the reason why, even though many of the worst problems for Britain in its European relationships lie in the areas of harmonisation, budgets and monetary affairs including the euro, the preponderance of material in this book is on trade. It has been startling to us to discover, as we worked on it, how little we or others have previously known or understood about this murky and complex area.

This book would not have been possible without the moral and financial support provided by Sir Julian Hodge, who died a few months ago in his hundredth year and to whose memory it is most warmly dedicated. With his support Cardiff University, its Business School and I set up the Julian Hodge Institute of Applied Macroeconomics in 1998; one of its key objectives was to examine the economics of Britain's relationship with the rest of Europe. Earlier work within the Institute covered the euro, harmonisation and budgetary issues; this latest book extends it to include trade. I am also grateful to Jonathan Hodge, Sir Julian's son, and to Eric Hammonds, for a long time chairman of the Julian Hodge Bank, for their enthusiastic and robust personal support of the Institute's efforts.

Edward Elgar and his staff, who are publishing this book in association with the IEA, have shown their usual efficiency and goodwill in seeing this project through. Bruce Webb typeset the book in LATEX to his usual high standards. He and David Meenagh at the Institute also kindly assisted us with the tables, figures and also the simulations of the Liverpool Model. My co-authors and I are grateful to them all.

Patrick Minford
February 2005

List of Abbreviations

ABARE	Australian Bureau of Agriculture and Research Economics
AD	Anti-dumping
AFTA	ASEAN Free Trade Area
ALM	Active labour market measures
AMS	Aggregate measure of support
ASEAN	Association of South East Asian Nations
AVE	Ad valorem equivalent
BOP	Balance of Payments
CAP	Common Agricultural Policy
CEEC	Central and Eastern European Countries
CGE	Computational general equilibrium
CITAC	Consuming Industries Trade Action Coalition
CMO	Common Market Organisation
CSE	Consumer subsidy equivalent
CV	Countervailing
DEFRA	Department for the Environment, Farming and Rural Affairs
EC	European Commission
EEP	Export enhancement programme
EFTA	European Free Trade Area
EIU	Economist Intelligence Unit
EMU	European Monetary Union EU European Union
FATS	Foreign Affiliates Trade in Services
FDI	Foreign Direct Investment
FOB	Free-on-Board
FSA	Financial Services Agreement
FSAP	Financial Services Action Plan
GATS	General Agreement on Trade in Services
GATT	General Agreement on Tariffs and Trade

GDP	Gross domestic product
GE	General equilibrium
GMO	Genetically modified organism
GTAP	Global trade analysis project
ICT	Information and communication technologies
IMF	International Monetary Fund
M&A	Mergers and acquisitions
MPA	Multi-Fibre Agreement
MFN	Most favoured nation
MMPT	Michigan Model of World Production and Trade
NAFTA	North American Free Trade Area
NATO	North American Treaty Organisation
NIESR	National Institute of Economic and Social Research
NTB	Non-tariff barrier
OECD	Organisation for Economic Co-operation and Development
PPP	Purchasing power parity
PSE	Producer support estimate
QR	Quantitative restrictions
REU	Rest of the European Union
ROW	Rest of the world
SMP	Single Market Action Plan
SMPS	Single Market Programme in Services
SPS	Sanitary and phytosanitary standards
SSG	Special safeguard regime (WTO)
TMNP	Temporary movement of natural persons
TRIPS	Trade Related Aspects of International Property Rights
TRQ	Tariff-rate quota
TSE	Total support estimate
TUPE	Transfer of Undertakings (Protection of Unemployment) Regulations
UN	United Nations
USITC	United States International Trade Commission
VER	Voluntary export restraint
WTO	World Trade Organisation

Part 1

COSTS AND BENEFITS OF UK MEMBERSHIP OF THE EU – A POLICY ANALYSIS

1 Introduction, Summary and Conclusions: Why the UK should Renegotiate or Leave the EU

The UK joined the EU – or the European Common Market as it then was – in 1973, under Edward Heath's Conservative government. Labour at that time was opposed and promised a referendum on withdrawal if it came to power. When it did so and the referendum was duly held in 1975, Labour had changed its mind; hence both Labour and Conservative parties campaigned for staying in. It was left to a minority in each party and to others to oppose and lose. Ever since there has been a shifting body of opinion opposed to EU membership, and both major parties have been seriously split on the issue, even though the official position of both has consistently been in favour of continued membership, as has been that of the Liberal Democrats.

It is not the purpose of this book to revisit the issues voted on in the 1975 referendum. Nor is it to speculate on, for example, what would have happened to the EU had we joined at the start; or indeed on a variety of 'what if?' questions of great interest. A great many things have happened since 1975, both politically and economically. Politically there has been most importantly the fall of the Berlin Wall and the steady expansion of the EU with the stated objective of underpinning peace in Europe and the world. Given the ferocious history of our continent in the twentieth century, there is no doubt that this is a crucial aim. The expansion of the EU to include the ex-Soviet countries of eastern Europe is a major contribution to this aim. The EU is therefore part of the emergence of a world community of nations and powers, with powerful centres of legitimacy such as the UN, the WTO and the IMF/World Bank. Economically, there has been a widespread liberalisation of markets and an almost universal restoration of monetary stability; the UK itself, perhaps because it was in such a mess in the 1970s, has been a pioneer of such programmes, whereas market liberalisation in major parts of the rest of the EU has made modest, faltering progress. Thus, in the favourite phrase of some politicians, the UK, the world and the EU have 'moved on' since 1975; the aim of this book is accordingly to evaluate the UK's relationship with the EU in the conditions of today, markedly different as they are from those of 1975.

Some people will be impatient with such an evaluation. They will say that this relationship is a given, a commitment, and it should be left alone to develop, with all partners contributing to the process – much as in a marriage or a nation. Talk of divorce, emigration or exit is simply counter-productive: instead one should focus on making it work.

The difficulty with this approach is that the EU treaty that the UK joined in 1973 has been under continuous change while, as we have seen, the surrounding political and economic circumstances have also been changing dramatically. Treaties come and go in the history of nations, as their interests change; and the EU relationship is just another treaty. It is not an indissoluble commitment; it was not for example a dissolution of the nation into a wider political union, such as a federation. If it was a marriage, then it was not a pledge to permanent union but rather to cohabit for convenience of cooperation in various important dimensions. It might be rejoined that the preamble of the Rome Treaty we signed in 1973 spoke of 'ever-closer' union and related ideas; however, UK politicians at the time stressed that such phrases were non-binding rhetoric and that the treaty merely committed us to certain key areas of practical cooperation, including – and especially in – trade. Look at the treaty commitments, they said, not at non-binding protestations of future intentions. And so we have; and so indeed the treaty has remained just that – a treaty.

The nations currently in the EU have different views about how the EU treaty (technically still the Rome Treaty as subsequently amended) should evolve. A majority, led by France and Germany, want greater central power, as exemplified by the draft EU constitution produced by M. Giscard d'Estaing's Convention. Most UK citizens, it seems fair to say on the basis of the opinion polls, do not want this: hence the UK negotiating position, even under the current Labour government, which has taken an enthusiastic stance on EU integration, has, on the whole, been one of reluctance in a series of areas. It has drawn up 'red lines', detailing points beyond which further central EU power would be unacceptable to the UK, including tax, defence, foreign policy, and legal process. It has also agreed to put any finally-negotiated proposed EU constitution to a UK referendum. It is simply not clear where this process will lead. Will the EU majority give up on centralisation? Will the UK agree after a referendum to a federal Europe with strong central powers? Or will both sides agree to differ, with some centralisation and with a separate relationship for the UK?

These are important questions and they are now at the centre of political debate in the UK and to a large extent also in other countries of the EU. There is rightly a demand for facts and analysis to help UK and EU citizens to reach well-informed views about what to do at this important watershed in EU affairs. This book aims to help satisfy this demand. It is primarily designed for UK citizens; but there is plenty of material that will be useful for citizens of other EU countries and also of those countries in the rest of the world, especially the Cairns group and the USA, for whom EU trade policies are of vital interest.

In the rest of this chapter we sketch out the lines of our investigation. Our main focus is on the economics of the UK's relationship with the EU. The reason for this is two-fold. First, in the UK the economics have supposedly been the main benefit to Britain of EU membership, and we believe they have been far from well-understood. Second, the political benefits of the EU for the UK are quite hard to define, as compared with being outside the EU and politically collaborative (like Norway, Iceland, the US and many others), whether in the UN, NATO, the WTO, the IMF or simply in specific multilateral and bilateral relationships. We do however consider the political arrangements after we have sorted through the very specific details of the economics.

In considering the economics of the EU, we interpret the thrust of future EU policy in the light of recent policy actions by the EU (for example the decision by France and Germany to scrap reform of the CAP) and of the general thrust (in favour of protectionism and social rights) of proposed new policies, such as those envisaged in the new draft constitution. We emphasise that the EU does not have to be this way; one can envisage an alternative, liberal set-up in which the CAP would be drastically reformed, free trade announced as the EU's commercial objective, and market forces as its guiding light in internal economic policy. But this, unfortunately, is not the EU we are currently asked to contend with. This book takes the EU as we find it and must accept it will develop, barring some currently unforeseen policy development.

We identify six areas in which economic issues arise. These are in turn the three major sectors of the economy – agriculture, manufacturing and services each of which is shielded by a variety of protective regimes; monetary policy and the euro; pressure to harmonise UK tax, regulation and social policy with other EU countries; and lastly public finances and the question of 'bail-out'. The chapters that follow deal carefully with all these questions. Here we give a brief summary of the arguments and of our conclusions.

First of all, there are the well-known costs of agricultural protectionism in the form of the Common Agricultural Policy (Chapters 2, 4 and 7). We put this at some 0.3–0.5 per cent of national income – a fairly typical estimate from the range available (1 per cent of national income is £10 billion per year). The sums involved vary with the state of the world market in agricultural products. But this estimate would correspond to an average year for relative world prices of food. The way in which the Common Agricultural Policy works is that it boosts the prices paid to farmers by consumers from across Europe by about 50 per cent above world prices and therefore, since we are big net importers of food in this country, that means that our consumers are basically paying a lot more for their imports than they need and therefore generally for their food. Furthermore they are paying this excess not in the main to UK farmers but rather to continental farmers, especially French ones.

The second cost is not so well known: the protectionism of manufacturing (Chapters 2, 5 and 6). Now again we were told that it is very important for us to be in the European Union because it would be good for our manufacturing industry. The truth of the matter is again we import more manufactures from the European Union than we export and therefore what is happening in manufacturing is very much like what is happening in food.

Manufacturing is a declining industry in the West: it is uncompetitive for obvious reasons, because we have emerging markets like China that undercut it so massively. What is left is in specialised, high-tech and niche areas. In our economy we have largely let market forces take effect, with generally favourable results for employment and growth; as a result we have let manufacturing go where it was essentially uneconomic. That has not happened to the same extent on the continent. As a result we find there a great deal of protectionist pressure. The EU is accordingly a customs union: for raising tariffs externally on manufactured imports, so that prices are kept up inside the European Union for manufactures. In addition to tariffs the European Union protects manufacturing through quotas in certain areas like textiles, but mainly through informal agreements (as in cars) and anti-dumping measures. Anti-dumping operates both through explicit duties and more generally through the threat of levying them, which results in importers raising their prices instead. (For some estimates of the effects of tariffs and non-tariff barriers in raising EU prices above world prices see Tables 1.1 and 1.2.) The latter action is more costly to us because not only do our consumers pay higher prices, the excess revenues resulting do not go to EU governments, including the UK, but rather to foreign non-EU producers. However, because it is not the result of an explicit action but rather of a threat, it is convenient to a protectionist bureaucracy both in its ease of imposition and in its non-transparency to the general public.

Now we are net importers so that this protectionism is costly to us in just the same way that the CAP is; it is, if you like, a 'Common Manufacturing Policy'. Our estimates below put the analogous cost at 2–3 per cent of GDP.

We now come to the third area of EU economics – services trade (Chapters 2, 6 and 7). British traded service producers are generally efficient and the UK has a comparative advantage in services, of which we are net exporters on a large scale. We are talking of such industries as insurance, banking, airlines, ground transportation, communication and electricity. It is often argued that, therefore, the UK stands to gain from the single market in services that is one aim of the EU. At present the services environment in Europe is one of national protection, mostly very high. According to available estimates of services protection the UK and the US both operate fairly unrestricted regimes, whereas EU countries

Table 1.1: Effects of EU manufacturing trade barriers on prices
– deviation from the US price (%)

	PCs[a]	Brown goods[b]	White goods[c]	Small domestic appliances[d]
US Price (£)	647	799	854	103
UK	24.0	66.3	11.2	55.3
Belgium	69.6	102.3	36.4	23.3
Sweden	38.9	118.8	47.3	14.6
France	27.0	74.1	18.9	68.0
Germany	8.2	77.0	32.9	37.9
Italy	38.9	65.8	−0.4	9.7
Spain	−3.2	64.6	0.1	5.8
European average	29.1	81.3	21.0	30.7

Notes:

[a]   PCs: notebooks and desktops.

[b]   Brown goods: audio home systems, cameras, camcorders, TVs and VCRs.

[c]   White goods: refrigerators, dishwashers and washing machines.

[d]   Small domestic appliances: irons, toasters, vacuum cleaners.

Source: The Arthur Andersen study reported in Haskel and Wolf (2002)

operate highly restrictive regimes at national level, presumably to protect their national companies (Table 1.3). The argument goes that if this national protection is replaced by an EU-wide protective regime of a customs union type, then Britain would gain greatly, in a mirror image of its losses on other trade.

Unfortunately there is a great difficulty with this argument. Why should the continental EU countries participate in a customs union for services that would retain high prices for their consumers while transferring service production from their own companies to UK companies that are more efficient? For these countries this would be like our opting for a CAP; they would be foolish to do it. (We only did it in the early 1970s because it was the price of

Table 1.2: Estimates of tariff-equivalents on manufactured goods due to all trade barriers (%)

	1990	1996	1999
Belgium	42	65	42
Germany	39	60	29
Italy	38	36	21
Netherlands	42	58	41
UK	41	41	50
US	16	14	15

Note: Data are expenditure-weighted average ratios of imputed producer prices to the landed prices of goods from the country with the lowest level of price in the sample.

Source: Bradford and Lawrence (2004)

Table 1.3: Survey indicators of service barriers (Scale 0–6 from least to most restrictive)

	1978	1988	1998
UK	4.3	3.5	1.0
REU	5.4	5.1	3.4
US	4.0	2.5	1.4
Australia	4.5	4.2	1.6
Canada	4.2	2.8	2.4
Japan	5.2	3.9	2.9
Switzerland	4.5	4.5	3.9

Note: Simple averages of indicators for seven industries – gas, electricity, post, telecoms, air transport, railways and road freight. Depending on the industry the following dimensions have been included: barriers to entry, public ownership, market structure, vertical integration, price controls. For the Rest of the EU, simple averages of individual EU countries.

Source: Nicoletti and Scarpetta (2001)

joining the EU and our politicians at that time felt there were compensating benefits.) It seems that instead they would be rational to opt for one of two alternative outcomes: either full deregulation or no change. No change would keep their own producers' privileges while continuing to penalise their consumers; the difficulties of achieving service liberalisation bear testimony to the tenacity of these producers' lobbying. If on the other hand liberalisation, as in the Single Market agenda, is effective, then full deregulation would give each country large gains to their consumers that would more than offset the losses of their producers. These countries would then if they chose be able to sweeten the pill for their producers by some transfer programme, at least for a transitional period.

From the UK viewpoint either outcome means that UK service firms would make no gains. Under no change they cannot enter the continental markets except at world prices – no attraction in doing so relative to any other world market. Under full deregulation the same applies, as EU prices would drop to world levels. (Under partial national deregulation, the same applies again; UK firms would still only get world prices.)

The whole point about the single market in services, if it were ever to happen, is that it gives a great benefit to continental consumers by dragging down prices of services across Europe. But it would not benefit British consumers because we have already got a highly competitive market in services and it would not benefit British producers of services because they would not get better profits in Europe than they can get anywhere else in the world. Therefore, there is no benefit. The only qualification to this is that if the EU deregulates services, this (by contracting EU production and expanding EU consumption) would drive up world prices of services and so improve the UK's terms of trade. But of course this benefit accrues to the UK whether she is in or out of the EU. Services therefore will not provide an area of gain that can offset the losses we make in our other trade with the EU.

We must emphasise that these 'costs' we have so far identified, in connection with the EU's arrangements for trade in goods and services, compare being inside the EU customs union with being outside under free trade. Some people then ask whether we could not still have some trade arrangement with the EU, other than the normal WTO guarantees of non-discrimination. But of course this is to miss the point of a customs union in which there is horse-trading between the producers of different countries, paid for by their consumers; if a country refuses to trade by penalising its consumers it has nothing to offer! Were the UK to be outside and let its consumers receive world prices, continental EU countries would be mad to let UK producers have access to their markets at preferential customs union prices; this would amount to asking their own producers to transfer profits to UK firms with no quid pro quo.

This is a familiar enough point in the content of the CAP. No one would expect that, if we left the CAP, thus being able to once again to buy our food at low world prices from countries like New Zealand, our farmers would still be able to obtain much higher CAP prices from selling their food inside the EU to EU consumers. The CAP is an arrangement whereby our farmers obtain high prices from consumers across the EU and in return our consumers pay high prices to producers across the EU. Once our consumers buy elsewhere at low world prices we cannot expect EU consumers to pay high prices to our farmers. Exactly the same logic applies if we withdraw from the customs union in manufactured goods.

Thus it must be realised that ceasing to participate in EU customs union arrangements would be just that – free trade at world prices would be in its place, with no 'EU preferences'. From this though we gain that 2–3 per cent of GDP.

The fourth area in our EU relationship – joining the euro (Chapter 3) – has now been amply explored, not least by HM Treasury in its voluminous study of the Chancellor's 'Five Tests'. The debate of the last few years has now clearly revealed how costly it could be to us, in the form of increased economic volatility, 'boom and bust' in the Chancellor's phrase. The recent experiences of Germany and Ireland within the euro-zone have borne witness to the problems the UK would itself experience. As a trading nation with over half our trade (inclusive of services and investment earnings) with the dollar area, we would be particularly destabilised by the fluctuations of the euro against the dollar, over and above our inability to set our own interest rates. Ironically, we would not even achieve currency stability, the main aim of our membership, for this very reason: that by joining the euro we would increase instability against the dollar. Indeed we find that our overall currency instability remains about the same.

We come now to the fifth area, to which the draft constitution is particularly relevant – harmonisation. Here matters have taken a new and dangerous turn with the appearance of the draft new constitution produced by M. D'Estaing's Convention. This constitution embodies tendencies that have long been quite apparent, not merely in the actions of the Commission but also and perhaps more importantly in the judgements of the European Court which have favoured the centralising and socialising objectives written into the previous EU treaties' vague preambles. By including the Charter of Fundamental Rights, the constitution has handed these judges the power to extend this agenda very extensively. The Constitution emphasises rights. The Charter of Fundamental Rights incorporated in it could take the UK back to the 1970s in terms of rights of collective bargaining and the unions. This may well be its the most significant feature. There is also a great deal on workers' rights and social entitlements. One of the key achievements of the Conservative governments of 1979 onwards was to destroy union power as a way of holding back development in this country. All the evidence we have shows that this was most significant in terms of the effect on our growth. Another thing they did was to make benefits highly conditional on looking for a job. So the Benefits Agency would help people who could not find a job but otherwise enact penalties such as benefit withdrawal. All this is potentially rolled back by the constitution and the Charter of Fundamental Rights. Some try to maintain that the declarations in the charter could be somehow non-binding; but then why have them in the constitution at all? Either they are in and have some potential force in terms of the interpretation and development of laws; or they are out. The experience of law-making by the European Court shows in fact that use will very likely be made of any material agreed in the constitutional treaty; the European judges have acted quite deliberately to increase the power and scope of the EU jurisdiction.

This would be harmonisation of a particularly damaging sort for the UK. Using the Liverpool Model of the economy of the effects of such policy changes we examine in Chapter 3 what might be the effects of these policies, which amount to the reversal of the reforms brought in by the UK government from 1979. On the assumption of rather moderate changes (a minimum wage raised to 50 per cent of male median wages, union power restored to mid-1980s levels, social cost rises worth 20 per cent of current wages), the model

predicts that they would raise unemployment by 5.7 per cent –
that is 1.8 million – and cost us 6.4 per cent in reduced output.
It could of course be either more or less depending on just how
extensively this harmonisation was pursued; but the constitution
indicates clearly enough that what we have seen so far – including
the working time directive, the social chapter and the works council
directives – is just a beginning.

Finally, we come to the sixth area – the cost of potentially insolvent state pensions on the continent. Extensive estimates were
made of these pension deficits in an OECD study in the middle
1990s. Recent attempts to recompute these prospects suggest little change. If we take these 1995 OECD projections as illustrative
at least, the projected deficits as a percentage of GDP come out
at Germany 10 per cent of GDP by 2030, Italy about the same,
France a little bit less. Add up these deficits as a percentage of
UK GDP, which is of similar size to each of these countries, and
you come to some 30 per cent. If we were to pay a quarter of that,
suppose we were via some federal system to be asked to 'share the
burden fairly', then the bill would be some 7 per cent of GDP.
Again, like harmonisation, the extent of this is rather uncertain;
it could be a lot more or a lot less, depending on both the extent
of reforms undertaken by these countries and the extent to which
the progress of federalism enables burden-sharing between countries. But this is certainly a burden we do not want to share or
risk sharing, at even a modest level.

What we find therefore in these chapters is that the economic
cost of our current relationship with the EU is already high and
carries the prospect that it might escalate alarmingly under the
thrust of the sort of policies set out in the draft constitution, itself
a clear enough indication of what the dominant coalition of our
EU partners wishes to happen. Nor is there any likelihood from
this policy thrust that the existing costs from protectionism will
be alleviated. Briefly and brutally, this prospect amounts to little
less than ruin for the UK – a return to the awful 1970s and yet
worse again.

Summarising our findings, we have identified 3.2–3.7 per cent
of GDP in ongoing costs and additionally substantial potential
future costs of harmonisation, pension sharing and euro membership; these latter costs could escalate to very much larger sums
than those currently being faced.

Table 1.4: A conspectus of costs

	% of GDP
Net UK contribution	0.4
CAP costs	0.3
Manufacturing trade costs	2.5–3
Harmonisation	6–25
Pensions	2–9
Euro membership	doubling of macro volatility

When one asks what are the countervailing benefits, one finds that they are hard to identify on the economic side. Some might point to an easier flow of immigration (from the rest of the EU) perhaps or an absence of EU exchange controls and consequently wider capital markets. However, it would be easy for a UK outside the EU to allow immigration from anywhere it chose; and for it to access any part of the world capital markets similarly.

The Cecchini Report claimed that there would be large benefits in greater specialisation and exploitation of scale economies because of the Single Market: the logic was that lower barriers within the EU would encourage a better adjustment to market forces. The evidence has not supported gains on the scale predicted by Cecchini; our model by construction does not impute scale economies but it does include any gains (the majority according to studies of UK Cecchini-style effects) from greater competition within the Single Market, whatever in practice they may have been. Free trade with the whole world (facing whatever unilateral barriers each country chose to levy) would permit the UK to exploit the same processes but in a way consonant with its comparative advantage. The gains we have identified from leaving the EU relate to the UK's exploitation of its true comparative advantage in services essentially; most studies agreed that in services scale economies are unlikely.

The NIESR (see Chapter 3) claimed that there are gains of foreign direct investment (FDI) from membership of the EU. FDI (see Chapter 2) is related to technology transfer and *where* it occurs depends on the structure of the economy. As we see in Chapter 6, that structure changes dramatically if we leave the EU. Whether

FDI as a method of technology transfer is as needed when the economic structure shifts to its true comparative advantage, we simply do not know. But if it is, it will occur equally in the new structure. The essential point concerns whether the economy's technology is at its maximum in the new structure as compared with the old: given that all industries will be competing on a level with the best in the world, the pressure at least will be maximal. But of course we have no real way of measuring this matter in practice. Thus to summarise, the NIESR rightly observed that in the old structure there was a high FDI level, much of it in manufacturing; and it conjectured that there would be less FDI outside the EU and concluded that this would reduce productivity. However, as our argument indicates, this conclusion is a non-sequitur: less could occur because the technology level in the new structure is higher, in which case productivity too would still be higher.

1.1   WHAT IS TO BE DONE?

In Chapter 8 we consider this question, in the context of the politics of our relationship with the EU. Some people say that the overriding reason for our membership of the EU is political: to ensure the unity of Europe and to prevent future wars. There is no doubt, given the ferocious history of our continent in the twentieth century, that this is a crucial aim. The expansion of the EU to include the ex-Soviet countries of eastern Europe is a major contributor to this aim. The EU is therefore plainly an important institution alongside others that govern inter-country relations in the twenty-first century including NATO, the UN, the WTO, the IMF and the World Bank.

However, the political aims of the EU as a community of nations do not need to be achieved by the exaction of huge economic costs from members of that community. We argue in the following chapters that these costs are large also for other members of the EU, but that is a matter for them; our focus is the costs for the UK which are of great size, as we have seen. Indeed, quite obviously the costs are unacceptably high by a large margin. Hence inevitably the UK is being forced to a reconsideration of its relationship with the EU in such a way that the political aims of peace and amity in Europe are not jeopardised.

It is obvious from our analysis that were the EU to change its policies in the direction of free markets, free trade and an effective commitment to no bail-out of insolvent states, the economic problems for the UK we have identified would be essentially dealt with in a way that would be optimal. Provided political issues, such as the threat to habeas corpus and the unacceptability of EU control of our national defence, were also dealt with, the UK could then happily continue within the Rome Treaty. Let us call this the 'reform solution'. We must naturally hope for this but, as our analysis shows, the direction of EU policies has been away from such ideas and the prospects for this solution seem at best poor.

If this indeed turns out to be confirmed in the coming months and years, the logic of the resulting situation would point to the UK doing one of two things. It could renegotiate a relationship within the Rome Treaty, a 'UK protocol' let us call it. Or it could leave the Treaty altogether and achieve its political aims through other avenues – much as other friendly countries outside the EU, such as Norway or the US, do.

It may seem that the idea of renegotiation is a hopeless one, since why should other EU members agree to it? Yet in the present context where a dominant coalition of EU members is bent on creating a federal structure and the UK is largely isolated in its opposition to such a structure, the renegotiation offers an opportunity of universal progress. Under the terms of the Rome Treaty agreement on a new structure must be unanimous; thus the UK has the power of stalemate. This power has been greatly enhanced by this government's agreement to a UK referendum on the new draft EU constitution; it seems fairly unlikely that any structure remotely like the draft constitution would get UK popular assent in a referendum. However, by renegotiation the UK could agree to allow others who so wish, to proceed to a new federal structure within the treaty.

Of course, such a renegotiation would no doubt cause other countries unhappy with aspects of the treaty to consider asking for renegotiation also. This would be a matter for them; many would in all probability rather settle to join the dominant coalition for a variety of reasons of national interest.

Thus it seems reasonably likely that this coalition of the EU majority would be happy to agree on a UK protocol as the price of using the treaty to forge a federal union. However, one cannot be sure; such inter-national bargaining is inherently unpredictable. Suppose they refused and did one of two things. First, they could accept a stalemate and rely on the forces of gradual pressure to achieve the same federalist objectives over a longer period of time. Or second, they could decide to proceed en bloc to recreate the desired federal union outside the EU institutions, creating in effect a duplicate structure; though this would pose practical difficulties as well as difficulties in the process of obtaining a completely fresh agreement on all previously agreed areas, it is not to be ruled out.

What should the UK do in these two cases? In the second the UK would de facto have left the EU since the existing treaty would be without practical content. In the first, the UK could wait and see, meanwhile resisting the pressure from the federalist agenda. However, given the extensive and subtle powers conceded already to the EU's central bodies, this resistance would be likely to fail. It is likely that before long the same crisis as has currently arisen with the draft constitution would reappear. It would therefore be an attractive option in this stalemate case to leave, given the lack of desire for accommodation.

In all this it needs to be remembered that the other EU members could react to the genuine threat of UK departure by becoming more accommodating. This is possible precisely because these members see the EU primarily in political terms and the loss of the UK would diminish the political weight of the EU.

There is a further point: that the present policy arrangements of the EU damage the welfare of the other EU country citizens just as they do that of UK citizens. With the UK threatening to leave over these policies, there could be a strengthening of the voices of those demanding change within the rest of the EU. The EU could reform in the direction of free trade, non-interventionism and competition, removing the arguments with the UK. However, in this debate it is essential to be realistic. Time and again UK politicians have announced 'game, set and match' after EU negotiations, only to have it explained to them red-faced that they have been comprehensively duped and defeated. The fact is that our EU partners and the EU Commission show no sign of adopting an agenda to our tastes: indeed, if anything, it is the reverse.

Some people fear a different reaction: where either the EU as a whole or individual EU member states erect discriminatory barriers against UK exports, whether special tariffs or other arrangements such as onerous customs requirements – all in retaliation against what they see as our unreasonable departure or renegotiation. But such fears can be dismissed, for three main reasons. First of all, the changes the UK would ask for would not end a high degree of mutual cooperation in a variety of economic and political areas; any such retaliation would put such other areas of cooperation at risk and be against EU and individual EU members' interests. Second, the EU exports far more food and manufactures to the UK than the UK does to the EU; the UK is a net importer of both and a war of trade retaliation would be damaging to the EU. Third, once the UK had opted for free trade in food and manufactures, such barriers would not affect the prices we paid for our imports or obtained for our exports, they would merely lead to a diversion of trade elsewhere than the EU. (The same applies to services where in any case the UK faces high barriers). The only cost in this case would be temporary disruption as trade patterns were changed. But last and most important, such actions would be illegal under WTO trade law, since the EU is a signatory to the WTO by implication under EU law. It is absurd to imagine that the EU, which relies so heavily on WTO law for large numbers of trade disputes, would put itself at risk by ignoring WTO law in its dealings with the UK, a state involved with it in friendly cooperation across so many areas, including the development of the single market in services.

What form in that case should a renegotiation of the UK's relationship take? We suggest in our final chapter that it should be:

1. The UK should leave the EU's protective agreements altogether – the CAP, tariffs and anti-dumping and all else – and resume unilateral free trade. The agreement would place the UK outside the EU's protective arrangements; non-discrimination would be agreed, so that we would have the same access to the EU market as any WTO non-EU member and EU members would have the same free access to the UK market as any WTO member.

2. If there were genuine concern about the EU pursuing discriminatory trade policies against us, then the UK could also join NAFTA to create countervailing power in the event of trade disputes. NAFTA allows each member to pursue its

own trade agenda, providing it allows other NAFTA members free access in agreed trade areas. It would therefore be entirely consistent with the UK's free trade policy. However, as noted in our discussion just above, there should be no concern on this score: joining NAFTA is unnecessary.

3. In the area of services, the UK already largely has free trade and free market entry. Here the Single Market could bring about competition within the EU through the discussions going on area by area. The UK has nothing to lose by participating in these discussions; and to the extent that residual UK barriers could be dismantled in particular areas, the UK would actually gain. Therefore, the UK should stay in the discussions on the Single Market for services, cooperating on a case-by-case basis to create new agreements. Existing competition agreements, as for airlines, would be kept to.

4. Freedom of movement of capital and labour has already been established and brought about benefits. The UK should continue in these arrangements.

5. In other areas – such as competition policy, economic consultations, coordination of anti-terrorist policies – the UK would continue to participate, by specific agreements in each area.

6. The 'social dimension' of the EU, including the Working Time
   Directive imposed for 'health and safety' reasons under the Single Market laws, would be abrogated in the UK.

7. Finally, EU law would no longer be binding on the UK. Instead, only those agreements explicitly made with the EU would be, as any treaty obligation, incorporated into UK law.

As already extensively discussed above, the UK would under these circumstances be outside the EU's customs union in food and manufactures and would enjoy world prices. The EU could not reasonably be expected – nor would it be likely – to extend to the UK preferences in EU markets for UK food and manufactured exports. Instead the UK would be treated like any other world trading country outside the customs union. It would have to pay any tariffs and anti-dumping duties and be subject to any other non-tariff barriers imposed on external suppliers. In whatever markets EU prices are kept up by the operation of an implicit cartel forcing potential low-price exporters to raise their EU prices – an arrangement we have suggested could be the most widespread of all the non-tariff mechanisms in EU use – then UK exporters too would be subject to this cartel. Ironically, this would benefit them considerably, just as it benefits other low-price participants in the cartel, provided they have a good market share. UK exporters are well established in the EU market and could well find that they continue to do well in it after UK exit to free trade. Since this situation would be costly to the EU and would draw wide attention to the existence of such cartel arrangements, the result could be greater pressure for EU competition, which would be beneficial to EU members. Such a development would bring about greater harmony in the long term in relations between the UK and the EU, making possible closer cooperation in trade policy, a key area from which the UK would have withdrawn.

Inside the UK either this new relationship, or total departure from the EU, would lower the prices received by farmers and by manufacturers previously protected by the EU customs union barriers. Transitional assistance should be given to them by the UK taxpayer (who of course will reap substantial gains from the new set-up). The whole issue of farm support and support of the rural environment will have to be visited afresh; in broad terms a long-lasting package that rewarded farmers for preserving the rural environment and freed them to carry out entrepreneurial development of their business and their assets (especially their land) could be devised that would make sense for both farmers and the taxpayer. For manufacturers, however, any assistance should only be transitional, since the UK's comparative advantage implies that resources should be shifted from this sector into the service sector.

In conclusion, the UK and the EU have had a seriously troubled relationship for some two decades. These troubles have concerned not merely the obvious irritations of rising political interference by the EU in UK affairs but also the major costs of the EU's use of its steadily-increasing powers in economic affairs; the latter are the focus of this book since they are of a technical nature and therefore not at all widely understood and appreciated. Since our analysis suggests that the EU generally is damaged by current policies, we must hope that these policies would change in a way that would progressively also reduce the UK's costs arising from the EU, making formal changes in the UK's treaty with the EU unnecessary. However in the event that this does not occur, as the tendencies of the last two decades suggest it will not, then such formal changes are inevitable. We have shown that they are possible and highly beneficial to the UK. We have also argued that they are likely to help the forces of change within the EU since they will highlight the problems there by the very fact that they will no longer be present here; institutional competition between countries is a potent force in world affairs. Thus in the long term it is in all EU members' interests that the UK puts an end to what we have shown are the intolerable economic costs of its relationship with the EU.

2 Evaluating European Trading Arrangements

At the heart of trade theory lies the simplest of models. We assume there are homogeneous commodities whose prices in the absence of protection would be set domestically at the world price. Consider such a commodity whose market is shown in Figure 2.1. A tariff or equivalent trade barrier, t, would raise its domestic price above the world price to $P_W (1 + t)$. At this higher price domestic supply increases, domestic demand decreases, so imports fall; tariff revenue levied on the imports is the quadrilateral $abcd$, and foreign suppliers receive P_W.

In a customs union, where a group of countries levies the tariff and internal trade is free of protection, the country's supply and demand are the same, the difference is that either imports are supplied by customs union partners at the price $P_W (1 + t)$, or if non-EU imports are still required, the tariff revenue is payable to the customs union not to the government, so the government receives no tariff revenue.[1]

We may note that for the price to rise to $P_W (1 + t)$, it is necessary for the customs union either to be a net importer or if it is a net exporter, the customs union must also pay an export subsidy equal to the tariff. Under the terms of the Common Agricultural Policy export subsidies are payable as well as import tariffs so prices are

---

[1]The government may receive a share of the customs union revenue, according to some formula. However, this revenue accrues to the EU and we treat the resultant effect on the national government as part of the country's net budget contribution – accounted for separately. Thus in our trade calculations no revenues are recorded. We should also note that if the tariff equivalent is achieved by the *threat* of anti-dumping, there is no revenue at all accruing to the EU because foreign producers raise their prices to avoid the duty.

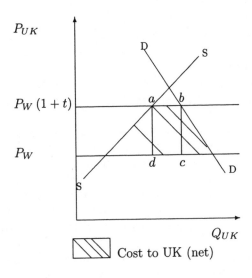

Figure 2.1: A customs union tariff on a commodity

held above world prices for all commodities covered by the CAP. In the case of manufactures no export subsidies are payable and therefore on goods where the EU has net exports prices would be at world price levels (because suppliers can only sell their output if they sell it on the world market and hence they must drop their prices to world levels). Prices only rise to $P_W(1+t)$ (with protection thereby being effective) in cases where the EU is a net importer. In the case of traded services import protection is at the level of the nation-state and there is no customs union; again for the protection to be effective the services involved must be imported.

This model refers to one market alone, in the given commodity; the rest of the economy's prices are taken as given or else some other ad hoc decision is made about how they will vary as this industry expands. However the model can be extended to general equilibrium by specifying the rest of the economy's equations and calculating the market-clearing prices everywhere in it, and also in the rest of the world if the country is 'not small' – that is its behaviour affects world prices. The famous Heckscher-Ohlin-

Samuelson model is attractive to use for this extension because it brings in the ultimate determinants of comparative advantage, factor endowments, with a minimum of complication, by assuming perfect competition in all markets.[2]

Besides its clarity and simplicity, the model has the further advantage – given our lack of detailed data – that it needs few parameters and data points.

A final, decisive, advantage is that it appears realistic in the long run we are here interested in to assume competition. Nowadays there are many trade models based on various sorts of imperfect competition. In the short run this seems realistic; modern industry aims to produce innovative non-homogeneous products so that it can attain super-normal profits for some period. However we know that such profits attract entrants and imitation; the most redoubtable monopoly power is subject to eventual annihilation. Competition driving profits to normality from peers either in the same economy or from other ones around the world is what we observe over some period which varies in length between products and over time and place.

If this is so then the super-normal profits are captured by factors in fixed supply. In a world of mobile capital and raw materials, these factors are the various types of labour, summarised here as skilled and unskilled, and land. In effect competition proceeds until the domestic prices of these immobile factors is driven up to where cost equals price.

Our interest here is in the long-run shape and behaviour of economies, that is, after this process is complete, the 'steady state'. Any actual economy will not be in this state of course, perhaps ever; but it is a benchmark that informs us about the eventual implication of its policies and factor structure.

Some authors have stressed 'path-dependence'. Thus for example a country that captured the dominant share of a market by first-mover advantage might then acquire skills in its labour force that perpetuated such dominance. One thinks of Boeing in Seattle or the Californian Silicon Valley. We do not wish to deny the possibility of such things though we can see no well-supported model to incorporate it as a general process; we do not pretend

---

[2] Also Cobb-Douglas production functions (that is, exhibiting constant returns to scale and a unit elasticity of substitution between factors of production).

fully to understand how countries acquire skilled labour of certain types – education, apprenticeship traditions, learning by doing, and much else no doubt contribute. A model must stop somewhere; our model treats the factor endowments as exogenous, the result of causes beyond. This of course leaves it open to others to argue that truly there is some feedback onto these, in justification of some proposed policies, perhaps of protection – along the lines of the 'infant industry' argument. We leave such arguments out in our analysis but they and the evidence for them can easily be considered at a later stage when evaluating policies. The model can in the presence of powerful ad hoc evidence be generalised for such feedback. The point is that we have a conceptual structure which can be used to analyse the problem whichever way the evidence points.

2.1 DEALING WITH FDI

Modern trade has now come to include goods and services delivered by foreign direct investment. Suppose that there is some tariff barrier; then this can apparently be circumvented by exporting capital, cooperating with some local factors of production to deliver the same product behind the tariff barrier. However note that in the HOS model capital is assumed to be mobile and tariffs cause immobile-factor rewards to capture the rents created by protection; thus a tariff changes relative prices and so the relative prices of immobile factors. Thus any excess returns to the mobile factor, capital, are eliminated.

We can think of FDI as being composed essentially of the movement of certain types of (usually skilled) labour and their associated technology which we assume can differ across countries – the capital from the world capital market simply flows in as required to accompany this movement. Thus we can think of FDI as consisting of migration of selected labour supplies and an accompanying rise in productivity. The migration of labour is motivated by differences of wages, that of technology by differences of productivity. If so one may then think of FDI as a process that is independent of tariffs. A tariff raises returns to an industry and this then raises immobile factor prices until marginal costs equal price. The overall incentive to transfer technology to the economy (which has a certain general level of technology creating attractions to inward investors) is then left unchanged; the only difference is that this industry is now larger than other unprotected industries and so part of the new technology flow will be diverted from other industries to this one. As for the incentive to migrate one would assume that the general levels of wages of such broad factors of production as unskilled and skilled wages would not be sufficiently affected to make much impact on migration flows; the rents one would expect to be captured by more specific factors (for example, particular types of land or labour).

On this argument one may naturally regard FDI and the stock of inward investment as exogenous to the trade policy decisions with which we are concerned here. The HOS model we use regards the size of an economy as determined by its stock of immobile factors and its available technology; its capital stock is then set by the size of output and its foreign-owned capital stock by the difference between required capital stock and available home savings. The country's technology we treat as exogenous; but clearly it in turn is determined by the availability of better technology elsewhere and the incentive to transfer that inwards by FDI and other means. Similarly stocks of labour are treated as determined by supply incentives operating on a fixed labour force of available work potential; migration is one factor in turn operating on that but we treat the resultant as exogenous here.

2.2   BLOCS TO BE CONSIDERED – PARTIAL AND GENERAL EQUILIBRIUM ANALYSIS

We have set up a world economy consisting of four blocs – NAFTA, the UK, the rest of the European customs union, and the rest of the world. Our sectors are Primary, Basic Manufacturing ('manufacturing' for short), Complex (hi-tech) manufacturing and traded services ('services' for short) and non-traded goods and services ('home' for short). Our aim is to inject our estimates of different trade policy regimes into this world model, to obtain general equilibrium estimates of the welfare costs. However, we also consider the facts of protection by sector, together with partial equilibrium estimates of their effects; this treatment allows us to obtain an initial benchmark on what we might expect at the general equilibrium level. GE estimates have the advantage of allowing for all simultaneous-feedback effects but the disadvantage that they are more aggregated; we hope to use the disaggregated material to ensure that the GE results are as good an average summary as possible of the disaggregated level. In our final GE results we can draw to some degree on other GE studies to compare and contrast.

2.3 ESTIMATES OF THE COSTS OF EU PROTECTION BY SECTOR

We now review the costs of EU protection in each sector, as if it alone were being protected and on the assumption that world prices remain unaffected. At a later stage we allow for a) the cross-effects of all protection on other sectors b) the effects on world prices. Furthermore, we make the assumption that the comparison is between the UK being in a protected EU market and having unilateral free trade outside a continuing EU trade barrier.

Agriculture

This sector has been well gone over in the past. The typical estimate of the costs of the EU's agricultural protection to the UK is generally set at about 0.5 per cent of GDP as a result of a tariff-equivalent typically of the order of 50 per cent. By withdrawing from this protective scheme therefore the UK would save this cost. There would be a loss to the REU of the tariff revenue it obtains on UK imports. If the UK left in this way there would be no sense from the REU's viewpoint in giving our farmers free preferential access to the REU market. This would simply mean that the REU's costs would be higher again by the transfer to UK farmers, made for no return favour.

There is often a misunderstanding of the effect of withdrawing from a customs union – an issue we consider at length in the Appendix. Thus one hears it said: we could leave and still maintain a trading arrangement giving us free access to the union market. However a moment's reflection shows this to be nonsense. A customs union reduces overall welfare compared with general

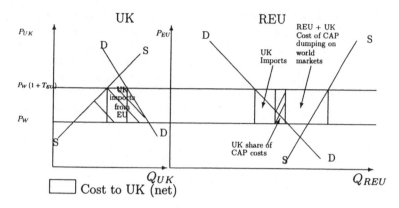

Figure 2.2: The CAP in outline

free trade but it gives producers in the joining countries extra net revenues at the expense of consumers across the union. Some countries' consumers pay more than others however so that one country (as in the case of the UK) pays a large share of the extra net revenues received by other countries' producers. Thus by withdrawing from this arrangement such a country is passing this cost to the other countries. They are hardly likely to reward this behaviour by offering still to transfer to the withdrawing country's producers the extra net revenues they previously received.

We can make the same point differently by asking: if the UK were to levy the same tariff as the REU, having withdrawn, and to offer REU producers free access to the UK market, would then the REU offer reciprocal free access? The answer is of course yes: because this would amount to exactly the same arrangement as the full customs union! In effect the UK would not be leaving; its domestic food prices would remain the same for both consumers and producers, while REU producers would obtain these prices for its exports to the UK. Thus if the UK relented and was willing to offer such an arrangement the REU would be very happy to carry on giving free access to UK producers.

One can make the same point about a diluted post-CAP situation. Suppose the UK had a modest tariff, one lower than the REU one, and offered the REU free access. Then the REU would gladly reciprocate because it would be like having a more modest customs union with the UK alone; not as good as the full one but better than nothing. However correspondingly the UK would be worse off than full withdrawal.

What one notices in this customs union situation where one partner is, like the UK, a net importer, is that it does not pay this partner to remain in the union or furthermore to enter into any sort of diluted arrangement.

Hence it is important to realise that withdrawal from the customs union in food means precisely that: operating outside it, including facing the barriers of the union from the outside. (All that this means is that our food producers would obtain world prices, unless assisted, as discussed below; while our food consumers would pay only world prices.) In such circumstances the UK would be best off under unilateral free trade since that eliminates the burden on UK consumers. As for the losses suffered by UK farmers from withdrawal, these can cheaply be compensated via direct subsidy from the Treasury, as under the old 'deficiency payments' scheme. Such a transfer between UK citizens has a cost in terms of the excess burden of the taxation needed to pay for it; but this is a small cost relative to the large gain of repatriating the 0.5 per cent of GDP spent on the CAP of the EU.

Manufacturing

While the cost to the UK of the customs union in food is well known, the same is not true of the customs union in manufacturing. No doubt when Britain joined the EU in the early 1970s the calculation of those in the Heath/Wilson governments that supported joining was that Britain was a great manufacturing nation which would benefit from the union by dint of being a major net exporter of manufactures. A union, though damaging to welfare in general relative to free trade, can be beneficial as we have seen in net terms to countries which are net exporters of the protected products.

Unfortunately for any such calculation, Britain has in the intervening period reduced massively the size of its manufacturing sector – a well-known trend, matched by a rise in its service sector. It is as a result a large net importer of manufactures.

At the same time the EU has proceeded to build up large protective barriers in manufacturing, responding to the demands of its manufacturing firms (such as Philips, Siemens and Renault, to name but a few in a few subsectors). The method by which it has done so has partly been tariffs but mainly, as these have been reduced in a succession of world tariff rounds, through anti-dumping duties or the threat of them and by quotas. Suffice it to say that they appear collectively to raise manufacturing prices at the border (Free-on-board) level by some 30–80 per cent above world levels.

Because of the inroads of low-cost competition from emerging market countries, the EU too, like the UK, is a net importer of most manufacturing subsectors. Where it is not, there is less or no protection. In effect the EU protects against the subsectors where there is world competition threatening the EU home markets of older high-cost domestic producers – often these are consumer sectors, but they also include input sectors such as computer chips and computer parts generally.

The analysis of the customs union in manufacturing exactly follows that of the union in food. The only difference is in the size of the estimates. We find an approximate cost of 2–3 per cent of GDP; this is rather similar to the findings of a recent study by Scott C. Bradford and Robert Z. Lawrence for the Institute of International Economics in Washington (Bradford and Lawrence, 2004).

Again we obtain this gain precisely by withdrawing from the customs union with the implication that we face world prices and the union's barriers to our exports. Again it would make no sense for us to erect a barrier of our own and give the REU free preferential access; the REU meanwhile would not offer us free access since that would mean they were transferring to us and our producers a share of their GDP, for nothing in return.

However, it would be possible (and perhaps politically necessary) to compensate our manufacturing producers directly for the loss of the higher prices they now receive – the analogy with our farmers is complete. The difference is that whereas farming is an area of political sensitivity and farmers, partly encouraged by social policy, do not adjust easily to new circumstances, the same is not true of manufacturers; they can contract capacity and withdraw resources from these markets, allowing other sectors to expand. Hence were there to be taxpayer support direct to them it would logically be transitory, to cover them for a period of adjustment only.

Services

Throughout the UK debate on the EU it has been implicitly assumed that somehow the UK would gain from the Single Market in services. We are after all large net exporters of services. It might therefore seem that we must benefit from a customs union in services where we are net exporters just as we lose from one in food and manufactures where we are net importers.

However there is little parallel between the arrangements in food and manufacturing on the one hand and services on the other. There is no EU customs union in the vast mass of service sectors. Instead there is a patchwork of national protectionism, with the UK having relatively free markets within it. The idea of the Single Market is to replace this patchwork with a free deregulated market across the EU; in principle this might be accompanied by some sort of barrier against non-EU service companies which could parallel the customs union in food and manufactures. However service markets within the EU are individually often penetrated by foreign (notably US) firms through FDI and other arrangements (especially in the UK which in practice has liberal access for US firms). Hence once there was EU-wide deregulation it would inevitably allow free access to foreign firms lodged in national markets which cannot be practically distinguished from their national counterparts, indeed in many cases have merged with them.

Moreover EU-wide deregulation would, independently of such penetration, unleash strong competition between a large swathe of European national firms. Such competition would be deliberately boosted by EU competition authorities whose aim would of course and rightly be to ensure that prices were pushed down to competitive levels. Indeed they would welcome any assistance in that regard from foreign competitors located in the EU.

Hence the prospects for services sectors would appear to consist of two main possibilities:

a. The Single Market fails to make much progress at all in the face of strong producer vested interests in national markets; national protection thus remains as now.

b. It is highly successful in the end and produces competitive price levels.

What of a third option where the EU established a customs union in services? Under this the Single Market would establish EU-wide regulative barriers which put EU-wide prices somewhere between the most liberal and the most restricted regimes currently in place – that is, typically somewhere between the restricted REU average and the current liberal UK regime. We find that such a service customs union would involve substantial transfers to the UK from the rest of the EU as UK service producers displaced REU home producers within the customs union. UK producers of services would receive higher than world prices, this amount on UK net exports being paid for by REU loss of tariff revenue. Such a transfer is unlikely to appeal to the REU majority within the EU's Council of Ministers. If protection is to fall, they would prefer it to fall without a customs union being formed.

Assessing the costs to the UK of these arrangements is rather easy in cases a) and b). Under both the UK's leaving would make no difference on the assumption the UK's regime is already liberal. Under a) the UK continues in its liberal regime if out just as when in; the REU too carry on as now. Under b) if the UK stays in it is part of a competitive market; but if it left it would also enjoy a competitive market – exactly the same situation for its consumers and producers. Thus contrary to the popular perception the UK faces no prospective gain from being within the EU Single Market in services; it would be as well off under free trade.

2.4   OVERALL EVALUATION OF THE UK COMMERCIAL INTEREST

What we have found can be put quite succinctly. The UK would gain from leaving the EU customs union in food and manufactures, to the tune of 2.5–3.5 per cent of GDP; it would also not lose from leaving the EU Single Market in services. In all cases if the UK left it would be on the basis of unilateral free trade. The reason for this is that it would not suit it to offer preference in food and manufactures, being a net importer of both; while it would not suit the REU to offer preference in services, being a net importer of these.

One can thus think of the overall EU commercial arrangements as a package deal in which all parties agree, expecting to get some net benefit overall. Without the package as a whole such expectations are unlikely to occur; with it they may. However, for the UK at least this expectation is plainly disappointed; the package yields a substantial net cost. While the UK would like a sub-package consisting of a services customs union alone, such a sub-package is costly to the REU and not on offer. Thus it is in the UK's interests to abandon the whole package in favour of unilateral free trade.

The EU consists of many other things than this commercial package; and no doubt many accommodations can be reached on these non-commercial aspects for the simple reason that they do not involve serious amounts of money. They may be political agreements or to do with visas or mutual acceptance of nationals for work purposes or mutual recognition of property rights of other nationals; or a host of other detailed arrangements for mutual benefit of modest monetary proportions. However, the central agreements of the EU concern commercial arrangements of major monetary value. These, we conclude, are no longer in the UK's interests, on a fairly substantial scale. The UK should abandon them.

It is sometimes suggested (for example, the Cecchini report in the late 1980s for the EU on the Single Market) that there are gains from the Single Market – understood as the elimination of barriers to trade *within* the EU – because of economies of scale. Thus with common prices production could relocate to achieve maximum production runs. The argument applies only to manufacturing. Estimates of the gains to the EU from this process differ: as it is not clear how far existing operations are away from optimal-sized runs.

However, the UK's manufacturing sector has declined substantially as the UK has become a service-based economy. Furthermore, were the UK to enjoy free trade, the sector would decline very considerably further, indeed it would according to our estimates become largely extinct; so that this gain would disappear also. Thus the 'Cecchini dividend' only accrues to the UK if its economy is distorted by protection; it is of no consequence in an efficient UK economy. It does not therefore affect our comparison of the status quo economy (in which the dividend exists) with the free trade economy, because the difference takes the loss of dividend into account.

Our evaluation of gains and losses from UK participation in the

EU's trading arrangements including the Single Market suggests a substantial net loss compared with free trade.

APPENDIX: MARKET ACCESS AND WELFARE ON LEAVING A CUSTOMS UNION

In popular discussion gains and losses in trade arrangements are often considered as to do with the extent of 'market access'. Thus it is assumed, for example, that it must be disastrous for a country to face a high trade barrier from the EU and therefore that this must be avoided at all costs.

However this is a misleading way to calculate trade gains and losses. Consider the situation of a trading country like the UK. It produces quantities of different goods and consumes certain quantities of them. Those goods of which it produces more than it consumes it exports the balance; those it consumes more than it produces it imports the balance. Two things concern us. The first is what are the (external) prices the UK faces for its exports and its imports: the 'terms of trade' is the ratio of the import prices to its export prices. Given the quantities available for export and required for import, the prices the UK gets and pays externally or internationally are crucial to its welfare.

The second matter of concern is the effect of available external prices and relevant trade barriers on the (internal) prices faced by UK producers and consumers and also the effects on the quantities produced and consumed by them. These quantities will affect the use of UK factors of production and, together with the prices charged, will affect the welfare of consumers and producers in the UK, and also government revenues.

With this information we can calculate UK welfare. Market access is merely one element in the determination of the prices the UK will face in international trade and internally.

Apply this now to the calculation of the effects of the UK withdrawing from the EU customs union in manufactures and adopting unilateral free trade. As we have seen the EU levies large external trade barriers on manufactures which raise its internal EU prices well above world prices. As the UK is a net importer of manufactures what happens is that EU exporters (within this trade wall) undercut other exporters within the UK market and thus all UK imports will tend to come from the rest of the EU. Similarly its exports will tend to go to the EU where prices are above world markets.

As we have seen this situation is damaging to the UK compared with free trade for two reasons. The external prices for UK imports are higher; as the UK is a net importer of manufactures this more than offsets the higher prices it gets on its exports. The second reason is that internal UK prices are far above world prices causing a misallocation of resources in the UK; consumption is reduced and production is expanded, both inefficiently.

Therefore the UK is better off under free trade, outside the EU trade barrier. Notice this is so even though the EU does levy its full trade barrier against the UK now it is outside. What is happening is that the UK is selling its goods now on world markets at world prices; if perchance some of them go to the EU they only get world prices in the EU market, just as they would get anywhere else. As for imports the UK is getting them at world prices from the cheapest producers worldwide. The UK is better off because its prices for imports are lower and this lowering more than offsets the lower prices on its exports because it exports less than it imports. Also its consumption increases at these lower prices and its production falls, causing increases in the efficiency of the economy. But of course all this is happening while (indeed because) it is 'excluded' from the (high-price) EU market. It is not in fact excluded exactly. It can sell as much as it likes to the EU but it will now only get world prices; the EU will slap extra protective charges on it and so it will sell inside the EU at high EU prices. The point is that the UK is better off precisely because it is outside this restrictive arrangement, and even though it does not have 'free market access to the EU'.

People then are tempted to say: should we not be able *also* to have 'free market access' to the EU market? But this question stems from a misunderstanding of the economics of this situation. Were the EU to give the UK free entry into the protected EU market, this would enable our UK producers to obtain high EU prices for their exports to the EU – a premium over world prices. (In principle UK producers could switch all their sales into the EU to obtain these high prices. Yet EU producers could not obtain such prices within the UK.) Notice this premium would be a transfer from EU consumers to UK producers, who would be displacing EU producers, previously receiving this transfer. Thus the EU would be transferring large amounts of money from EU producers to UK producers. Why should it do so when the UK has just withdrawn from the EU trading system (thus taking back the transfers the UK had been making to EU producers!)? Of course it would be a nice bonus for the UK to receive such access but it is hardly likely to please EU producers and therefore to obtain EU approval.

The important thing to realise is that the UK gains by moving to free trade even though this inevitably means that it will face the same trade barriers outside the EU as anyone else does. This comes about because of the effects on prices and quantities. It illustrates why market access is no guide to gains and losses from trade arrangements.

3 Other Issues: Currency, Regulation and Public Finance

In the past decade it has become apparent that most of our EU partners, led by France and Germany, are determined to establish a European Union involving far closer ties than the UK expected when it joined in 1973. In the 1990s began the drive to set up the euro, achieved in January 1999. At the same time pressures were exerted to harmonise regulations, taxes and social provisions both within the Single Market and more widely. Most recently the draft EU constitution, if enacted, would enable even faster and more complete integration both politically and economically. All this has occurred against the background of an alarming deterioration in the public finances of the major continental EU nations, France, Germany and Italy; the fact that their current budget deficits have breached the Stability and Growth Pact can be put down mainly to cyclical reasons – far more serious is the prospect of massive state pension deficits, rising to more than 5 per cent of GDP by around 2050. It is now rather plain, even to UK public opinion which has hitherto hoped that an integrationist agenda would be quietly forgotten, that the majority of our EU partners are set on rapid and considerable integration: the adoption of the euro has been followed by demands for policy coordination, harmonisation and burden-sharing. These demands are consistent with the generally interventionist and dirigiste ideas of EU policy makers discussed earlier. They pose serious potential risks for the UK.

We deal in turn with the euro, harmonisation and public finance problems.

3.1   THE EURO

The plan for the euro adopted by Kohl and Mitterrand was political in intent. When economic problems were referred to, these and other protagonists replied that they were secondary and indeed that they would act as a stimulus for further integration 'to make the euro work'. Such problems have become apparent since 1999; asymmetries between member countries have caused acute discomfort. For example, for Germany interest rates have been mostly too high while for Spain and Portugal on the other hand they have been mostly too low. There have been persistent and occasionally large inflation disparities implying equal disparities of real interest rates that have tended to reinforce the inappropriateness of nominal interest rates.

However, there is good reason to believe that these problems would be even more acute for the UK. Not only is the UK economic cycle very different from that of the euro-zone but also the UK's trade (including all-important services and other invisibles like overseas investment earnings) is less with the euro-zone than it is with the dollar area, that is – effectively – with the rest of the world. These two facts – themselves no doubt related – imply that for the UK to abandon its own interest rate and the floating pound would cause two main problems: first the euro interest rate would frequently be inappropriate for UK conditions and second the euro exchange rate would frequently imply an inappropriate dollar exchange rate for the UK, as the euro-dollar exchange rate has tended to fluctuate massively – Figure 3.1.

My colleagues and I have quantified these problems by using the method of stochastic simulations whereby a model of the economy is subjected repeatedly to historically-relevant shocks inside the euro on the one hand and on the other as now floating outside it. We found that under our central set of assumptions a general measure of UK economic variability ('boom and bust' as politicians sometimes call it) roughly doubled inside the euro compared with carrying on as now. We also found that under virtually no conceivable other set of assumptions, however favourable, would economic variability not increase materially. Table 3.1 shows some details of these calculations

What all this implies is that the UK would be worse off inside the euro: there would be greatly increased volatility and there

Table 3.1: The welfare losses (political cost) produced by EMU compared with floating (floating= 1.0)

ratio of variances (EMU/floating)	total[a]	output	unemployment	real interest rate	inflation[b]
The central case	2.21	1.24	1.18	4.32	20.17
No indexation	2.74	1.63	1.51	5.56	23.27
Low interest rate sensitivity	2.16	1.03	1.04	5.17	21.62
More labour market flexibility[c]	2.72	1.18	1.08	4.04	33.19
High unemployment	2.23	1.21	1.21	4.80	20.15
More exchange rate instability	2.04	1.23	1.18	3.27	17.48
Enhanced fiscal stabilisers[d]	2.29	1.20	1.12	5.50	21.64

Notes:

a. the weights used in the political cost are (all divided by the weights total of 2.2):1 for output and unemployment variance; 0.1 for inflation and real interest rate variances

b. under our Montecarlo sampling procedure with the number of draws at 12,078, the standard error of the floating regime's variance, VARF, is 0.013VARF (Wallis, 1995). Hence a ratio in excess of 1.026 indicates that the EMU regime's variance is higher than that of floating at the 95 per cent confidence level. Thus all the numbers in this table are statistically significant.

c. monetary policy response to inflation under floating raised by a third (to 1.3), to output lowered by a third (to 0.7), to counteract greater inflation volatility from greater wage volatility.

d. assumes no enhanced fiscal activism under floating

Figure 3.1: Euro–dollar exchange rate

would be no compensating benefits. Hence the UK's opt-out will continue to be essential. As far as one can tell, the opt-out is not specifically threatened by the draft constitution; however, it is not easy to tell as a variety of clauses about 'policy coordination' could be interpreted as implying that all EU members should be in the euro.

3.2   HARMONISATION

Harmonisation refers to the general approach which aims to make taxes, regulations and social provisions the same throughout the EU. This process – strongly espoused by Germany – has started under the Single Market and the Social Chapter. Under the Single Market examples are common industrial standards agreed industry by industry and the Working Time Directive (introduced under health and safety aspects of the single market). Under the Social Chapter examples are the Transfer of Undertakings (Protection of Employment) Regulations 1981 (TUPE) and workers' consultation councils and procedures. Tax harmonisation has occurred for VAT where rates are limited to a range of 15–25 per cent, otherwise it is still subject to unanimity, though a proposal to impose an EU-wide interest-withholding tax is still being debated and has so far been vetoed by the UK. The draft constitution, by incorporating the Charter of Fundamental Rights, appears to open the door wide to further harmonisation as well as rises in the general level of social provisions and hence of taxes

Harmonisation is a precise arrangement, in principle. It implies that taxes and regulative structures should become identical. Since the UK (with that other Anglo-Saxon outpost, Ireland) stands out within the EU as being subject to a generally lower level of taxation and a substantially lesser degree of regulation, harmonisation in effect means that UK levels will be raised to prevalent EU levels. This has already occurred with VAT where harmonisation became effective within a fairly tight range a decade or so ago. However the UK has used the opportunity of raising VAT to lower a variety of other taxes, including the local authority council tax and income tax.

In Table 3.2 we show where the UK stands relative to the EU average with respect to some major indicators of tax and regulation. This table is limited and illustrative only. But it does show how far out of line the UK is with current EU average practices. It is no wonder that there is such constant acrimony in relations between the UK and other EU members over these issues, whether it be the Social Charter, the Charter of Fundamental Rights (now written into the draft EU constitution), the level of social spending by the state or a host of other detailed areas of intervention. It should be stressed that the level of public spending as a percentage of GDP does not capture the full effects of state intervention; regulation is a form of concealed taxation and therefore adds substantially to the overt taxation required to pay for public expenditure. For example in the 'big 3' continental EU countries employers are forced to pay for their employees' numerous 'social entitlements' at the workplace, including pre-eminently their medical insurance; this does not show up as taxation since it is a regulated obligation of employers to transfer these benefits to their employees directly.

It must be conceded that prior to 1979 the UK was in many respects as regulated and as highly taxed as the EU average – even more so in some aspects (for example the top rate of income tax). When the UK joined the EU, these issues were not seen as problematic by officials since the EU appeared to be economically successful and the UK where different did not appear to have any economic advantage from it. However after 1979 this began to

Table 3.2: Indicators of tax and regulation

		UK	EU[a]
1	OECD index of regulation (0 least–5 most)		
	Product markets	1.0	3.5
	Labour markets	0.8	2.6
2	Unionisation (% of employees union members)	38	81[b]
3	Overall % of GDP devoted to public spending (= 'permanent' tax rate)	40	53
4	Employer social security contributions, 2003	9	24
5	All-in tax rate paid by employees, 2000 (income tax plus employee social security contribution)	32	36
6	Total tax take on labour, 2001[c]		
	Average income	22	40[d]
	Low paid	25	48[d]
7	Minimum wage (% of full-time median earnings)	40	48[e]
8	Unemployment benefit ratio to net labour income (replacement ratio), 1999	18	30[d]
9	Cost of establishing a business late 1990s		
	in euros	420	2333
	in weeks	1	11
10	Maximum working hours per week	48[f]	35[g]
11	Notice period (days) (for employees up to 4 years service)	28	50
12	Unemployment benefit duration (months)	6	4–60[g] 6–32[h]
13	Annual average holidays	28	33

Notes: a. Average of 3 large EU economies; b. Collective Bargaining Coverage, 2000 (% of wage contracts by collective bargaining process; 32.5% in UK). Union membership (23% in these 3 countries) does not represent union powers of control because of laws governing collective bargaining under which union settlements are generalised across the parts of the rest of the economy covered by collective bargaining which is therefore a better measure; c. difference between the total wage cost paid by business/production price and the net wage received by worker/consumption price; d. euro-zone average; e. average of Spain/ Portugal/ Netherlands/ Luxembourg/ Belgium/ Greece/ Ireland/ France; f. subject to voluntary abrogation; g. France; h. Germany

Sources: 1 – Nicoletti et al. (1999), 2, 8, 10, 11, 12 – OECD (2004a); 3, 4, 5, 6 – Forbes Global (2004c); 7 – OECD (2004b); 9 – OECD (2000a); 13 – TUC (2002a);

change and by the late 1990s the UK's level of tax and regulation had dropped markedly while that of the rest of the EU had if anything increased. At the same time it has become apparent that the UK's economy is markedly more successful at creating jobs and growth both relative to its own past and relative to the main continental EU economies; and that this is essentially due to its more laissez-faire environment.

In Table 3.3 we consider the extent of the damage to this success that could be done by various degrees of harmonisation; we use the Liverpool Model of the UK (which being estimated over the 1970s to 1990s has been able to capture the effects of deregulation). In practice of course harmonisation occurs by degrees, which is why it has proved so hard for the UK to resist within the EU to date. Examples of EU intrusion have included the Working Time Directive, TUPE, the Part-Time Workers Directive, as well as the whole gamut of worker consultation directives emanating from the Social Charter. On each occasion the UK has been forced to concede, usually because of qualified majority voting under the Single European Act and more recently the Maastricht Treaty (within which our opt-out from the Social Chapter was – short-sightedly – deleted by Labour). The draft EU constitution in effect however provides implicitly for the possibility of complete harmonisation, since the Charter of Fundamental Rights gives the European Court in Luxembourg the ultimate power as the final constitutional court to bring the UK structures into line with EU norms – via statute law.

We show two levels of harmonisation – 'partial' and 'total' – based on the four key supply-side variables of the Liverpool Model: the unionisation rate (UNR), the average direct tax rate on workers (LO), the tax and contribution rate paid by employers (BO), and the unemployment benefit rate (UB). In the case of full harmonisation we use the figures from the table of indicators (Table 3.2) for the three largest EU economies as the one the UK will be forced to adopt. There is just one exception; for UNR we use an upper ceiling of 57 per cent, which is where it peaked in the UK in 1980. We are therefore simulating a return to the worst period of UK union power in the late 1970s which would seem qualitatively on a par with the worst the EU could inflict on the UK in the way of union power.

These numbers are, to be blunt, nothing short of horrifying. Of

Table 3.3: Degrees of harmonisation and their long-run effects on output and unemployment

Partial	Unemployment (%)	Output (%)
UNR + 0.05	2.5	3.0
LO + 0.04	0.7	0.8
BO +0.05	1.0	1.2
UB +5%	1.0	1.3
Total combined*	5.7	6.4

Total	Unemployment (%)	Output (%)
UNR +0.19	30.0	10.9
LO +0.04	0.7	0.8
BO +0.15	3.8	3.4
UB +66%	46.0	12.4
Total combined*	‡	25.2

Notes:

The combined total effect is greater than the sum of individual effects because of the model's non-linearity.

‡The combined effect is explosively larger.

course British business opinion has become increasingly aware of the costs being loaded onto the UK economy by EU regulation. But these costs still only scratch the surface of harmonisation. The EU economy groans under a weight of intrusive intervention that is scarcely imaginable to modern British businessmen. Hence the extraordinary damage of even 'partial harmonisation' – under which UK unemployment would rise by 5.7 per cent, equivalent to 1.8 million people.

Supposing that the progress to total harmonisation took two decades, then these figures suggest that growth would decline by 1 per cent per annum over that period, while unemployment would rise by 0.75 per cent per annum (continental experience suggests that much of it would be concealed by devices such as early retirement, sickness and disability pensions, longer university training, and barriers to female participation).

3.3 PUBLIC FINANCES

A central concern of the Maastricht Treaty setting up the euro was to solve the 'bail-out' problem. Implicit in a single currency is the sharing of monetary risks, including those coming from the public finances. Should a government whose debts are denominated in the euro threaten a default, this would create a dilemma for other member governments. To allow the default would create spillover problems to other members' economies; confidence in the debts of other governments would inevitably be shaken. Yet to provide bail-out funds would be costly in itself. Prevention of the default threat is therefore highly desirable. The Maastricht Treaty laid down that bail-out would not occur; it also set out the Stability and Growth Pact whose aim was to prevent budget deficits from emerging.

Unfortunately this pact was at once highly rigid and yet ineffective in providing long-term discipline. The rigidity lay in not allowing deficits to exceed 3 per cent of GDP, though business cycle effects alone could produce deficits well in excess of this for a government pursuing responsible fiscal policy. The lack of long-term discipline came from neglecting 'off-budget' items, especially state pension commitments. Because these commitments and the taxes which finance them refer to the future, they escape the pact entirely. Yet they are likely to be more intractable than current taxes and spending since pension commitments are made to the powerful 'grey lobby'; while taxes must be raised mainly from the active working population which also constitutes a powerful voting coalition. The difficulty that arises is: how exactly will any elected government dare alienate either set of voters? If so, how can this problem be resolved?

In 1996 the OECD made projections of the state pension deficits implied by then-current policies – Figure 3.2.

There have been two recent attempts to update these OECD 1996 projections of Roseveare et al. (1996). In Dang et al. (2001), the OECD's Economic Committee reported on the whole range of age-related programmes involving government spending, a far broader concept than merely pension spending.

In another recent study, Rother et al. (2003) consider the prospects for pension spending in the whole euro-zone, with particular attention to the largest four countries, Germany, France,

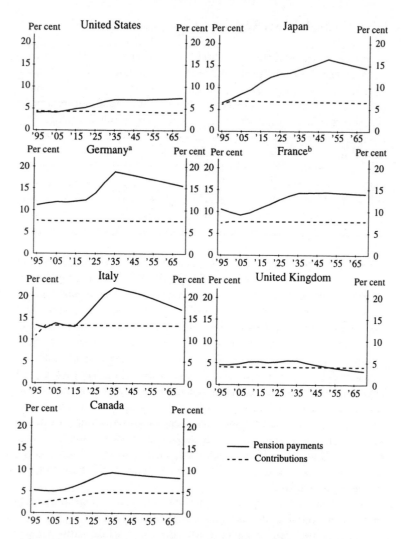

Notes:
a   Excluding statutory transfers from the federal government amounting to an average of 3.5% per year.
b   Excluding fictive contributions amounting to 1.7% of GDP per year.

Source: Roseveare et al (1996)

Figure 3.2: Pensions contributions and payments (% of GDP)

Table 3.4: Projected deficits 2050 (% of GDP)

	Roseveare et al. (1996)	Dang et al. (2001)	Rother et al. (2003)	Memo item Dang et al. incl. Other age-related
Germany	7.0	2,2	na	7.3[a]
France	6.0	(3.9)[b]	na	(9.0)[ab]
Italy	7.0	−0.2	na	4.9[a]
Spain	na	8.0	na	13.1[a]
EC 4	7.0	3.5	Baseline 4.8	8.6[ab]
			Realistic 5.9	
EC 9			Baseline 4.5	

Notes:

[a]   Assuming other age-related spending is the same as for the Netherlands.

[b]   Spending only.

EC 4:   Germany, France, Italy, Spain.

EC 9:   EC 4 + Belgium, Netherlands, Ireland, Austria, Finland.

Italy and Spain.

Both Dang et al. (2001) and Rother et al. (2003) (Table 3.4) deal with relevant pension revenues and total state pension spending, as well as taking account of recent reforms. The OECD study, as we have seen, additionally takes account of age-related spending. Both, as has become customary, leave out other revenues (basically all revenue other than National Insurance style contributions or taxes) and other state expenditures. Implicitly therefore they are assuming that other revenues and expenditures would (net) not significantly affect deficits over time, on the grounds that both sides can be relatively simply adjusted to the prevailing budgetary situation. Pensions and other age-related expenditure and associated contributions are by contrast assumed to be politically sensitive and difficult to adjust. As we will argue below, the problems of adjustment may be fundamental, affecting the whole gamut of taxes and spending, as well as the overall behaviour of the economy. Nevertheless it is plain that the pensions and age area of spending and the associated contributions burden on the young is indeed one of particular sensitivity.

The two recent studies differ in other ways. Dang et al. (2001) reflects the views of country officials and makes its calculations country by country. This leads it towards some rather surprising conclusions for three of the major EU countries. Thus Germany's 2050 deficit is projected at a mere 2.2 per cent of GDP even though its pension-related spending is projected to rise by 5 per cent of GDP. Italy is projected as being in balance by 2050 on the basis of recent reforms that supposedly commit the country to a system where benefits are based solely on contributions, indexed to prices and actuarially adjusted (downwards) to allow for increasing life expectancy; yet at this stage it is quite unclear whether these stated intentions are politically viable. France's 2050 spending is projected as rising by 3.9 per cent of GDP from 2000, but there is no revenue projection. Only Spain's 2050 deficit is projected at a substantial 8 per cent of GDP.

Thus, while the OECD 2001 study is an official document and contains an impressive amount of detail, its conclusions for this reason need to be treated cautiously. Roseveare et al. (1996) was not an official OECD study but a working paper, as is also Rother et al. (2003) at the World Bank. The judgements of officials are bound to be kinder to the member countries of the OECD than are those of independent economists. It is symptomatic of this official weakness that when it comes to other age-related spending the big four EU countries refused to report any results for the OECD 2001 study. Yet the smaller countries' results for this aspect make gloomy reading. The Netherlands for example projects an additional 5.2 per cent of GDP from this source. In the last column of Table 3.4 we show what the official projections for 2050 would look like for the big four EU countries if they too, as seems entirely likely, faced the Netherlands prospect. As a percentage of GDP, instead of the 3.5 per cent deficit in 2050 they face an 8.6 per cent deficit on pensions alone. Nevertheless adding in age-related spending appears to violate the general assumption of these studies that non-pensions spending and revenues would be reasonably adjustable. We are left with the relative optimism of the OECD 2001 official study on the pensions prospects themselves.

Yet this optimism is substantially undermined by the Rother et al. study. On 'baseline' assumptions they project that the big four EU countries' deficits will worsen by 4.8 per cent of GDP by 2050. On 'realistic' assumptions (especially in respect of the labour market, where they assume constant unemployment and participation, and thus a constant employment ratio as against the rising one of the baseline) it worsens by 5.9 per cent of GDP. The present value of future deficits is 47 per cent of GDP under the baseline, rising to 87 per cent under the realistic, scenario.

Rother et al. (2003) usefully also looks at more optimistic possibilities:

1. Increase of the retirement age by one year (from the assumed age of 63). This reduces the 2050 projected deficit by 0.3 per cent of GDP and the present value of deficits by 12 per cent of GDP.

2. Doubling of net immigration; this reduces the 2050 projected deficit by 1 per cent and the present value of deficits by 13 per cent (all of GDP).

3. A rise of 0.5 per cent per annum in productivity growth: the 2050 deficit falls by 0.8 per cent, the present value by 2 per cent.

4. A fall in real interest rates by 1 per cent (to 3 per cent per annum): this increases the present value of deficits by 18 per cent of GDP.

What these variants reveal is that there is scope for reforms to get rid of the problem. For example, just increasing the retirement age by 5 years (to 68) would make a very large impact on it.

However, the difficulty with this 'solution' is the lack of employment in the EU context. To implement later retirement one has to create equivalent jobs. Yet this presupposes a flexible labour market capable of this job creation.

Here one trips over the fundamental difficulty of solving euro-zone problems generally. Mostly these problems relate precisely to the inflexibility of the labour market and the general presence of obstructive regulation. These factors are there because of the interests of unions and other strong pressure groups – such as the Church and the social democratic party support groups – with active 'social agendas'. If one inspects the list of changes above, one sees that they all involve material incursions into these agendas. The retirement age increase requires job creation and therefore the permitting of large-scale entry into the labour market of older people. Net immigration requires the permitting of large-scale entry by immigrants. Productivity growth requires changes in working practices.

It is hard therefore to avoid a sense of the impossibility of genuine reform on the continent. Hence the concern from the UK's viewpoint in getting too closely involved in a potential fiscal disaster. In the end if we compare Roseveare et al. (1996) with Rother et al. (2003) we see that on the latter's realistic assumptions there is little difference in the projected 2050 deficits; the former projects them at 6–8 per cent of GDP, the latter at 5.6 per cent of GDP. Such pensions-related deficits loom uneasily over the EU fiscal horizon from the viewpoint of the UK.

It follows that unless unemployment is lowered and participation increased, the official projections will prove highly optimistic.

The problem for the UK can therefore be simply put. On the one hand, projections of overall state finances are for large deficits associated with state pensions provision. On the other there is no mechanism to prevent bail-out; on the contrary the draft constitution puts an explicit obligation on member countries to assist a country 'in difficulties'. The reality of the implied pooling of resources to deal with potential state deficits is mirrored in the virtual absence of differential risk-premia on government debt yields across different EU Member States in spite of apparently quite different fiscal outlooks (which has in the case of Italy recently led to the downgrading of Italian government debt to AA−). In other words, markets assume that bail-out will take place.

To give a crude illustration of what this could mean for the UK, assume that the state budget deficits of the big four continental EU countries each reached 6 per cent of GDP in 2030; this would imply a total deficit across them equal to some 24 per cent of UK GDP. Were the UK to be asked to share this according to its 20 per cent share of EU GDP, the annual cost to the UK would be around 5 per cent of its GDP by 2050.

Plainly such a massive cost cannot be considered at all likely since there would be pressures both to reduce such deficits and from the UK resistance to such sharing. Nevertheless, there is a risk of significant sums being eventually payable.

3.4   CONCLUSIONS

The problems discussed in this chapter are not new: for example, similar discussions can be found in Minford (1998 and 2002) and references were widely made to them in the course of the UK debate on joining the euro. It is probably true to say that increasing public awareness of them has caused the deterioration in UK public opinion polls of enthusiasm for membership of the EU. Nevertheless this has been against a background assumption that the UK's trading interests required membership. We have seen in the trade chapters of this book that this assumption is wrong and that the UK loses significantly from its EU trade relationships. When added to this loss, the problems in this chapter – economic volatility inside the euro, the loss of output from imposed harmonisation and the loss of income due to sharing in other countries' fiscal deficits – take on a more sinister shape.

APPENDIX A   OTHER STUDIES – GENERAL

There are not many quantitative studies of Britain's economic relationship with the EU (apart from estimates of particular aspects which we cite in the relevant sections below).

A predecessor of this volume by Brian Hindley and Martin Howe *Better Off Out? The Benefits or Costs of EU Membership* paved the way for a cost/benefit analysis but stopped short of doing one. A few months ago Ian Milne published a study for Civitas whose main findings we summarise in Table 3.A.1.

In 2000 the NIESR published an analysis based on a projection of the NIESR model of the UK economy.[1] On 'a worst case scenario' it concluded that there would be a net loss from leaving the EU of some 2–3 per cent of GDP. The basis for this lay in an assumed loss of foreign inward investment, and of the associated increase of productivity and the capital stock.

In its study the NIESR looked at none of the issues we have raised here: viz., protectionism of food and manufactures, the euro, the harmonisation agenda, and the bail-out problem arising from state deficits on pensions. Notice that in our work we have con-

---

[1]This study has been recently published as Pain and Young, 2004

Table 3.A.1: Range of estimates for current direct net cost (% of GDP)

	Lower end of the estimate	Most Likely	Upper end of the estimate
Regulation	1.0	2.0	3.0
CAP	1.2	1.5	1.7
EU Budget	0.5	0.5	0.5
Single Market	0.0	0.0	More than zero
Inward Investment	0.0	0.0	0.0
Total	2.7	4.0	5.2+

Source: Milne (2004)

sidered 'general equilibrium' effects, that is effects after allowing for full adjustment in the economy; we have noted 'partial equilibrium' estimates (that only allow for effects in a given sector, before adjustment by the whole economy) but have not used them in our final calculations. Thus the NIESR has not provided any alternative estimates to ours in these areas.

What the NIESR has done is first to identify as a key factor the amount of inward investment and secondly to assume that it must be associated with the size of our manufacturing sector. Both elements in their argument must be questioned. Inward investment is simply *one* source of investment, that is of capital stock provision. However what matters is the level of output per (fully employed labour force) person which is arithmetically equal to the capital stock per person times its productivity. Home investment using state-of-the-art technology is by definition equivalent to foreign investment using the same technology. If the UK were to leave the EU customs union and go to free trade, then manufacturing and its capital stock would contract while services and its capital stock would expand: this would as we have already seen raise UK output and welfare since the UK is a world leader and large-scale net exporter of services. The rise in the capital stock and associated technology might well be provided by UK-based firms; but matters would be none the worse for that, given that UK firms are generally of high efficiency. On the other hand it is also possible that some of the required capital stock (in some service sectors) would come from foreign firms, as they sought to gain a further share of rising UK production. We actually do not know which; and it does not matter which. In sum, there is simply no basis in theory or evidence for saying either that inward investment would decline (compared with the current flow, some of it in manufacturing) or that, if it did, there would be an effect in lowering productivity. The NIESR's assumptions in its 'scenario' were simply ad hoc assertions.

Our point can be put succinctly another way: that FDI flows reflect rather than cause comparative advantage and growth. The UK's growth depends, via a 'production function', on its stocks of capital and labour and on their technological efficiency. What our analysis finds is that the UK has a comparative advantage in services and hi-technology manufacturing industries; this advantage is determined by the UK's stocks of skilled and unskilled labour operating with technology available to UK producers. Capital then flows into these industries as dictated by these stocks of labour.

Where then does the technological efficiency come from? Plainly it comes from knowledge available around the world as transmitted to the UK – often via multi-national companies investing but also via licensing agreements (such as Macdonald's and Best Western hotels). In different industries the UK both transmits and receives this knowledge and in a free market knowledge will flow both ways. The key point is that we do not impede this flow to and from the UK that both raises our knowledge and that of others. It is the existence, not the directions, of this flow that forces our knowledge to be the same as that of other developed countries.

It is then plain that foreign direct investment in different industries is simply a symptom of this free market working – as one of the ways knowledge is being transferred. What the free market does is to make the UK enjoy the best levels of knowledge available in each industry. It is probable that in industries where we are 'backward' (such as manufacturing of certain types) FDI will be inward reflecting inward knowledge transfer; whereas in others where we are 'forward' (such as services of the City type) FDI may be mainly outward. Thus given the pattern of best-practice technology that with our labour stocks determine our comparative advantage, the flows of FDI may well change as we move from a protected-manufacturing economy to one of free trade which favours services.

Hence the causal process is as follows: the free flow of knowledge ensures that the UK's is the same as that of other developed countries. The shared knowledge determines the UK's efficiency and, with its labour stocks, comparative advantage. Home prices as set by protection then fix the sizes of industries and their home demands. Finally actual FDI flows reflect this industrial pattern, as well as the UK's overall capital needs compared with its savings. Thus actual FDI reflects and does not cause growth.

APPENDIX B   OTHER STUDIES: THE EFFECTS OF THE SINGLE MARKET – THE CECCHINI REPORT, COMPETITION AND SCALE ECONOMIES

Traditional arguments for the formation of a regional trading block are based on trade creation and trade diversion effects, which assume perfect competition and constant returns to scale. In the 1970s and 1980s another mechanism through which the member states of a customs union may benefit was put forward. It relies on the idea that production at a large scale reduces average costs per unit and hence, access to a larger market via regional integration would increase production, restructure the industry into a smaller number of plants and make surviving firms bigger and more efficient (Smith and Venables, 1988). The presence of scale economies would encourage firms to choose one location and the presence of transport costs would encourage them to locate in the country that has a relatively large market for their goods (Krugman, 1980). According to this argument any barriers between the member states that limit cross border trade would prevent scale economies from being achieved.

Empirical evidence on the existence of the scale effect in the EU context was first put forward in the 'Costs of a Non-Europe' study (The Cecchini Report, 1988). It suggested that competition linked to the Single Market and establishment of single currency would trigger a restructuring effect leading to economies of scale, greater efficiency and employment creation. The study predicted that the gains from the completion of the single market to be in the range of € 174–258 billion which at the time of the report represented around 4 to 7 per cent of EU GDP. Around two-thirds of the total was a gain due to scale economies and due to an increase in competition. Given the mixed evidence on the existence of increasing returns to scale in services industries the Cecchini Report disregarded such gains in these sectors.

Since the 1980s various studies have investigated the scale economies effect in the context of regional trading blocks. Cox and Harris (1984) and Roland-Holst et al. (1994) examined economic integration in North America, while Venables and Smith (1986) and Pratten (1988), among others examined the European case. Recent studies analysing multilateral liberalisation include Haaland and Tollefsen (1994) and Francois et al (1995). According to Pratten (1988) potential gains from increased scale economies appear to be important in European industries such as transport equipment, chemicals, machinery and instrument manufacturing. Gasiorek et al. (2002) calculate that membership of the EU increased UK GDP between 1973 and 1985 by 3 per cent, about two-thirds of which came from increased competition and scale economies. Based on the partial equilibrium methodology Emerson et al. (1988) estimate the direct costs of barriers to be 2.2 to 2.7 per cent of GDP and indirect cost (due to unutilised scale economies and lack of competition) to be another 2.1 to 3.7 per cent. Similar results have been found in more recent studies, which use a CGE framework (Burniaux and Waelbroeck, 1992 and Mercenier, 1993).

Empirical studies such as those noted above suffer from several deficiencies, notably the various ways in which scale economies are estimated (Peridy, 2004) and it is no surprise, therefore, that existing studies find conflicting results. Whereas Caballero and Lyons (1990, 1991, 1992) find evidence of external economies of scale in four EU countries, Basu and Fernald (1995) report little findings of externalities and strong evidence of internal economies being constant. Henriksen et al. (2001) suggest that external economies of scale arising from international intra-industry effects are less prevalent in European manufacturing than are internal economies of scale arising from increasing returns at the level of the national industry. Further most studies do not account for the fact that scale economies, if they exist, may alter the pattern of specialisation and the studies also do not take into account inter-country differences in scale economies. Peridy (2004) finds only a small degree of increasing return and the small-scale elasticities, which imply the positive effect of scale economies on exports of EU countries, are likely to be limited.

Apart from empirical issues the theoretical scenarios are numerous once we depart from perfect competition and the precise assumptions adopted in any imperfect competition modelling exercise bear heavily on the results. The gains depend on the type of product under consideration, the relative size of national market when compared to the union market, existing industry structure and product variety. Partial equilibrium simulation exercises by Smith and Venables (1988) for 10 industrial sectors using a variety of different assumptions result in a wide variation in quantitative results: for the same initial shock, welfare gains (including scale economies) are between 0.5 and 4 per cent. Larger gains often imply a large relocation of production among member countries.

It has also been suggested that ever-increasing mergers and acquisitions (M&A) within several European industries point to a restructuring as a result of potential scale economies. M&A however, could also be equally attributed to processes of globalisation and technology and industry level factors. Further, mergers leading to a monopoly position are traditionally viewed as uncompetitive by the European Commission and some are indeed blocked, resulting in squandered scale economies if any. More generally, if scale economies are significant it must be true that free trade with the world economy and not just with the member states would maximise gains from this effect.

In the particular case of the UK, the main thing emerging from the studies above, whether one considers the theory or the empirical results, is that there should have been an effect of greater competition on the UK within the single market. These studies do not support much of an effect of scale economies, largely because UK manufacturing during the period since EU entry has contracted sharply, especially in those areas of manufacturing where large-scale operation is prevalent; essentially UK manufacturing has become concentrated in areas known as 'niche manufacturing' for the most part.

In our study we assume no contribution from scale economies, rather in line with these studies. As far as competition is concerned we assume in our benchmark case that maximum gains from competition have been achieved under the status quo. Our study is concerned with how far free trade would create still greater benefits from the lower prices forced on the UK by international competition. Of course what we find is that whatever the Cecchini-style competitive process may have generated within the UK, world competition can deliver a lot more on top. As we have seen, what happens is that a new industrial structure consistent with comparative advantage creates large benefits for the UK economy; competition under free trade largely eliminates manufacturing in favour of traded services. In short therefore Cecchini effects are fully incorporated implicitly in the benchmark case of our study and make no difference to our estimates.

Part 2

BACKGROUND ANALYSIS OF TRADE

4 Agriculture

4.1 INTRODUCTION

While protection to trade in manufactured goods has fallen steadily
in recent years, restrictions on agricultural trade such as tariff barriers, production support and export subsidies have remained high
in many countries. As measured by world price effects, developed
economies
account for nearly 80 per cent of the worlds agricultural market
distortions. However, among developed countries support levels
vary widely. In general – and unsurprisingly – support is smallest
in countries that have efficient, export-oriented sectors (notably
Australia and New Zealand) and largest in those that are relatively inefficient and import substituting (Japan, Korea, the EU).
The EU accounts for 38 per cent of world price distortions, compared to Japan plus Korea (12 per cent), the United States (16 per
cent), and Canada (2 per cent) (Diao et al. 2001). The EU also
accounts for over 90 per cent of global export subsidy expenditures.

Among numerous distortions in international agricultural trade,
those imposed by the EU are the most disruptive, resulting in substantial welfare costs both for the EU itself and the world economy. Under the Common Agricultural Policy (CAP) the EU has
switched from being a large net importer of agricultural products
to a large exporter. This has resulted in production surpluses, artificially depressed and volatile world prices and high food costs
for domestic consumers. Low agricultural prices have also created
tensions between the industrial countries, who have found their
budgets for agricultural subsidies escalating.

This chapter analyses the issues surrounding the impact of the
EU's trade barriers in agriculture and explores the welfare costs of
agricultural protection. Section 4.2 considers the role of agriculture

in the developed economies. Section 4.3 reviews data on trade volumes and prices of agricultural goods. Tariff barriers on trade in agriculture are described in section 4.4. Section 4.5 focuses on the evolution and the current state of the Common Agricultural Policy (CAP) of the EU. Recent agricultural trade disputes between the US and the EU are reviewed in section 4.6. Section 4.7 outlines the main empirical findings concerning the welfare effects of trade liberalisation of other studies for the EU, NAFTA and the rest of the world.

4.2   THE ROLE OF AGRICULTURE IN THE ECONOMY

Agriculture's contribution to GDP in EU countries is quite low – below 4 per cent, with the exception of Greece, and is decreasing (Figure 4.1). During the 1990s it fell by over 20 per cent in the core eight countries of the EU (France, Germany, Italy, the Benelux countries, the United Kingdom and Ireland). In other developed countries, agriculture accounts for 1 per cent in Switzerland, and less than 2 per cent in the United States and Japan. As for employment, agriculture (and hunting, forestry and fishery activity) accounted for around 4 per cent of the employed civilian population of the EU 15 Member States in 2001, the highest being in Greece at 16 per cent. With the entry of countries like Poland into the EU, where farming still accounts for more than 27 per cent of the workforce, with more farmers than France and Germany combined, the share of agriculture in total employment in the EU will go up. Enlargement of the EU has also added as many as 100 million new consumers to the EU's domestic market.

As for the UK, agricultural output is estimated at £15.1 billion in 2001, which represents 0.7 per cent of GDP. Milk represents nearly 19 per cent of this total followed by cereals (13 per cent), beef (13 per cent) and poultry (8 per cent). The sector employs 550000 people (2.2 per cent of the total workforce) and accounts for about 70 per cent of the total land area of the UK. Nearly half of the holdings are small and probably part time.

Compared with the US, average farm size is significantly smaller in the EU (46.2 acres), about one-tenth the size of the average US

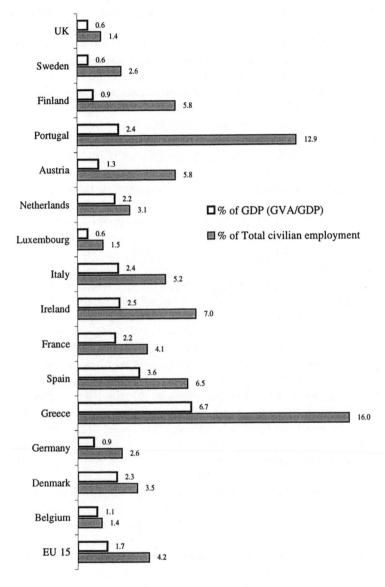

Source: European Commission (2003)

Figure 4.1: EU agriculture: basic statistics for 2001

farm (USDA, 2004). Within the EU, the largest holdings are in the UK (about 171 acres) and the smallest in Greece (11 acres). Both the EU and the US account for significant shares (20 per cent or more) of world production in several agricultural commodities. The US is one of the world's largest producers of corn, soybeans, beef and cotton, while the EU has a large share of world production in milk and pork.

4.3   TRADE VOLUMES AND DIRECTIONS

The relative importance of agricultural trade to total world trade has declined from 30 per cent of the value of merchandise trade in the 1950s to less than 10 per cent in the 1990s (Batavia et al., 2001).[1] Within agricultural trade, an increasing trend towards trade in processed goods has been detected since the early 1990s (WTO, 2004a.)

The EU is the world's biggest importer and second biggest exporter of agricultural products, the largest being the US. The EU is the largest agricultural importer from developing countries due to the numerous trade preferences granted to former colonies. Imports and exports of agricultural goods each account for approximately 6 per cent of total imports and exports in the EU respectively (Table 4.1). In 1999, EU exports of individual commodities accounted for a substantial portion of world trade: wine (41.5 per cent), milk powder (32 per cent), cheese (31.9 per cent), butter (20.5 per cent), wheat (15.1 per cent), and sugar (13.5 per cent). The EU's two largest agricultural import commodities are fruits and nuts, and coffee, tea and spices, together accounting for approximately one quarter of total agricultural imports.

As for the UK, the declining contribution of agriculture to the economy can be seen from the falling share of imports and exports of agricultural goods in total trade (Figure 4.2). Whereas the share of agricultural imports has fallen from 22 per cent in 1970 to 9 per cent in 2003, the exports share has fallen from 6.1 per cent to 5.7 per cent over the same period.

---

[1]However, as in most other sectors of world trade, the rate of growth of agricultural trade continues to outstrip growth in world agricultural production with the result that an increasing proportion of world agricultural production is now traded.

Table 4.1: Basic agricultural statistics for the EU, 2001

	Imports[a]	Exports[b]	Balance[c]	Prices[d]	Expenditure[e]
EU 15	6.0	6.1	−199	2.3	16.1
Belgium	6.7	5.7	−1078	2.4	16.8
Denmark	8.1	20.5	2750	2.3	17.4
Germany	4.8	2.9	−3283	2.4	15.8
Greece	5.4	21.8	686	3.7	21.4
Spain	8.2	10.4	−840	2.8	18.5
France	4.7	7.7	4930	1.8	17.6
Ireland	3.8	7.7	1891	4.0	17.2
Italy	6.4	5.1	−946	2.3	16.9
Luxembourg	1.2	1.2	−17	2.4	:
Netherlands	9.9	16.4	−2114	5.1	10.5
Austria	4.1	4.3	208	2.3	15.6
Portugal	11.8	8.6	−825	4.4	22.5
Finland	3.3	3.6	367	2.7	18.1
Sweden	4.1	3.1	183	2.7	16.7
UK	5.7	5.1	−3904	1.2	13.9
New member states	9.0	9.2	−2281	:	28.8[f]
USA	3.9	8.6	12083	2.8	:
Japan	10.1	0.7	−36532	−1.6	:

Notes:

a. Imports of food and Agri products to total imports (%)

b. Exports of food and Agri products to total exports (%)

c. Trade balance (€millions)

d. Trend of food prices (% change from previous year)

e. Expenditure on food, beverages and tobacco to total consumer expenditure of households (%, 2000)

f. For Member States intra + extra trade; for EU-15 extra trade includes total trade for individual countries and extra-EU trade at the EU-15 level

Source: European Commission (2003a)

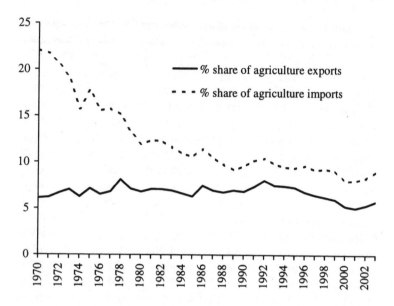

Source: ONS (2003)

Figure 4.2: UK imports and exports of agricultural goods, as a percentage of total

Although the US is the world's largest agricultural exporter, the value of US exports has fallen significantly since 1996 due to low world prices and the appreciation of the dollar. The US, however, continues to have one of the largest market shares in grains, oilseeds and poultry meat. On the imports side, beverages are the largest category of US agricultural imports and account for more than 15 per cent of the total.

Bilateral trade between the EU and the US in agriculture accounts for only a small share of total trade in goods between them. Since 1999 the US has been a net importer of agricultural goods from the EU with a decline in US exports of oilseeds, animal products and grains to the EU. Exports of corn by-products continue to dominate exports of the US, with Europe accounting for more than 78 per cent of US exports in that category. The EU main exports to the US on the other hand, are beverages (mostly wine and malt beverages) and cheese and other dairy products.

In the EU 15 countries, spending on food and tobacco accounts for about 16 per cent of consumer spending; in the 10 new countries, the average is 29 per cent (Table 4.1). In 1999 US consumers spent 13.6 per cent of household expenditure on food (BLS, 1999). The higher percentage of expenditure on food in the EU compared to the US is partly due to higher prices in the EU. Food is generally less expensive in the US than in the rich states of the EU (but more expensive than in relatively less wealthy countries of the EU). In purchasing power parity terms, a basket of bread and cereal that costs $100 in the US would cost $156 in Denmark and $147 in Finland (but $90 in the England and only $40 in the Czech Republic) (USDA, 2004). Similarly a quantity of meat costing $100 in the US would cost $210 in Denmark and $128 in the England (but only $73 in Poland and Hungary). It is also estimated that food prices in the England are over twice as high as those in New Zealand, a country with no subsidies or tariffs for agricultural production (Table 4.2). In 2001 the total cost of a basket of 15 food items including beef steak, lamb chops, olive oil and rice was £84.68 in the England, and (equivalent) £39.48 in New Zealand (Consumers' Association, 2001). Food prices also vary significantly among the EU Member States. However, on average the CAP is reckoned to add up to 20 per cent to food prices in the EU (*Guardian*, 26 Oct, 2002) and around €90 billion in higher food costs. Whereas the funding of the CAP is estimated to add £8 a week to the food bill of an average family of four (*Guardian*, 12 July, 2003), DEFRA (2003a) estimates that reforms of the CAP would lower the annual food bill of a family of four by around £65. Another study estimates that EU food prices are 44 per cent higher than they would be without the CAP, while US food prices are 11 per cent higher because of US farm supports (Rural Migration News, 2002).

4.4 TARIFF BARRIERS

There is little doubt that agricultural protection remains one of the major distortions in the world economy. While in recent years the average tariff on manufactured goods has fallen to about 5 per cent in developed countries, average tariffs on agricultural goods remain at 40 per cent. There is an even deeper problem of tariff peaks (that is, tariffs higher than three times the average) as high as 300 per cent and other prohibitive tariff rates on certain goods.

Table 4.2: Average price of a food basket

	England (£)	New Zealand (£)
Butter (500g)	1.73	0.66
Beef – filet mignon (1kg)	19.99	7.35
Beef – steak entrecôte (1kg)	9.61	5.21
Beef – minced (1kg)	3.46	2.64
Beef – stewing (1kg)	5.02	2.63
Beef – roast (1kg)	6.43	3.03
Olive oil (1 litre)	6.68	3.25
Lampchops (1kg)	9.22	3.32
Lamb – stewing (1kg)	7.58	2.71
Lamb – leg of (1kg)	6.62	2.73
Rice – white (1kg)	1.97	0.53
Margarine (500g)	1.06	0.65
Cheese, imported (500g)	4.20	3.95
Sugar, white (1kg)	0.60	0.40
Milk, pasteurised (1 litre)	0.51	0.42
Total cost	84.68	39.48

Source: Consumers' Association (2001)

Unlike manufacturing the level of agricultural protection has not fallen as a result of the Uruguay Round of trade talks. In fact many of these high tariffs came into practice as a result of the conversion of non-tariff barriers (often at levels above the 'tariff equivalent') during the Uruguay Round.[2]

As for the US, the average MFN tariff rate stood at 10.6 per cent for agri-food products in 2000. Along with tariffs, the US protected agriculture by providing direct support to farmers. The largest recipient of government outlays in the US is the agricultural sector, and these outlays nearly tripled between 1997 and 2000, exceeding the decline in the value of agricultural output. In

---

[2]However, in some cases the bound tariffs are above the levels actually in use, where a bound tariff is a commitment made at the WTO setting out the maximum tariff rate that a member will charge on a good. In these cases the distortion is potential rather than actual, but such tariffs should still be reduced so as to make market access more transparent.

2000, nearly US$30 billion was made available in direct payments to farmers. As a result, direct payments amount to over one half of net farm income. The Farm Security and Rural Investment Act of 2002 (the Farm Bill) provides subsidies as emergency payments in compensation for the decline in world commodity prices. This bill will increase average agricultural subsidies each year over the period 2002 to 2011 to $12.4 billion, compared to $4.3 billion in 1996. The Farm Bill appears to undermine 1996 reforms under the Federal Agricultural Improvement Act (the FAIR Act) that sought to improve efficiency and discourage overproduction by reducing price supports. Since most of the support under the Farm Bill is directed to programmes that are linked to prices, it would further reduce the sensitivity of US agriculture producers to market forces.

The EU's simple average tariff on agricultural goods is higher than the USA's at 16.1 per cent in 2002, down from 17.3 per cent in 1999 (WTO, 2002). The decline is not attributable to policy changes, but to different estimates resulting from the conversion to ad valorem equivalents (AVEs) of the non-ad valorem rates applied on 946 lines (45 per cent of agricultural product lines). In 2002 the average weighted tariff on agricultural products was, at 20 per cent, about five times higher than that on non-agricultural products (Table 4.3), with above average tariffs on products subject to the CAP. In general, tariffs are low on agricultural products not produced in the EU (for example, coffee, tea, spices), but are considerably higher on primary CAP products and products processed there. They average 30 per cent and range up to 233 per cent for dairy products, sugar refining and wine. Nearly 280 tariff lines carry rates with ad valorem equivalents exceeding 50 per cent. The highest-tariff items (above 120 per cent) are the meat of cattle, pigs and sheep, edible offal of animal origin, milk and cream, some cheeses, rice, wheat flour and bran, and manufactures of prepared animal feed (OECD, 2001a). The estimate does not include the 'snapback' tariffs imposed by the EU when using the special safeguard (SSG) regime of the WTO. An agricultural safeguard clause allows the imposition of supplementary tariffs in the event of import prices falling or import quantities surging relative to specified base-year levels (1986–88). Over the period 1995–98 the EU imposed price-based snapback tariffs 38 times and volume-based snapback tariffs 120 times.

Tariff peaks (triple the simple average) remain in evidence for

Table 4.3: International comparisons of government policies aimed
at protecting agriculture

Quad[b] economies	Tariff[a] on imports of			
	All goods and services from		Agricultural goods from	
	Quad	Non-quad	Quad	Non-quad
US	2	3	9	13
Canada	2	4	16	13
EU	3	4	19	20
Japan	7	7	57	44
Non-quad economies	Quad	Non-quad	Quad	Non-quad
Rest of Asia	6	6	24	21
Western hemisphere	8	11	18	14
Former Soviet bloc	9	8	21	16
Sub-Saharan Africa	11	12	22	23
North Africa and Middle East	12	13	51	46
India and China	14	16	43	26

Notes:

a.   Tariffs are a weighted average (by import value) of rates and include
an imputed value of subsidies spent on price support.

b.   In the language used by trade negotiators, the 'quad' is the premier
group of developed countries – US, Japan, Canada, the EU – which have
considerable power within the WTO, given their significant share of current
trade.

Source: IMF (2002a)

meat, dairy products, processed and unprocessed cereal products, processed fruits and vegetables. The range of applied tariffs, in terms of the minimum and maximum rates, is also wide (from 0 to 470.8 per cent). For a given overall tariff average, the greater the dispersion in tariff rates, the greater the likelihood that consumers' and producers' decisions are distorted by the tariff structure. Between 1993 and 1996 the dispersion of tariffs, as measured by the standard deviation, increased for primary agriculture and food products (OECD, 2001a).

Under the Uruguay Round Agreement on Agriculture, countries agreed to open agricultural markets by converting existing non-tariff barriers to tariff-rate quotas (TRQs). This system established a quota and a two-tier tariff regime for affected commodities. A lower tariff applies to imports within the quota while a higher tariff applies to imports exceeding the quota. The market access provisions under the Uruguay Round caused a proliferation of tariff-quotas in agricultural trade in most OECD countries including the EU.

Even though tariff barriers for agriculture are high, the agricultural sector relies heavily on domestic supports relative to assistance provided by border barriers. Domestic price supports and export subsidies compound the problem of trade distortion, costing taxpayers huge amounts while creating market distortions that spur demand for import protection. The Common Agricultural Policy of the EU is a prime example of such inefficiency.

4.5 THE COMMON AGRICULTURAL POLICY

The CAP was developed in the early 1960s largely around a price support mechanism which aimed to avoid food shortages by developing a stable internal food market on the basis of a high level of self-sufficiency. The main mechanisms of the CAP are guaranteed common prices and Common Market organisations (CMOs) for 18 product categories. For many commodities, support includes a minimum buying-in price, at which intervention agencies of the Member States purchase surplus production; charges are also levied on imported produce so that it enjoys no price advantage over that produced within the EU. The export of products is made possible by the payment of export refunds to enable EU exporters to sell on world markets at the going price. Market support arrangements are financed by the guarantee section of the European Agricultural Guidance and Guarantee Fund (the guidance section of which finances structural measures to promote rural development). Following the introduction of the CAP the average nominal rate of protection in western Europe increased from 30 per cent in the early 1950s to 40 per cent in the later 1950s, and 60 per cent in the late 1960s (Gulbrandsen and Lindbeck, 1973). In the UK, Ireland and Denmark, levels of agricultural protection were significantly lower before the introduction of the CAP (OECD, 2001a).

Overall, the level of support and protection to agriculture has decreased since the mid-1980s and there has been some shift towards less distorting policy measures. Nevertheless, the continued dominance of the most distorting forms of support means that farmers remain shielded from world market signals.

The current support levels impose a burden on consumers and taxpayers in the OECD countries. They also constrain agricultural growth and development opportunities in non-OECD countries. The OECD (2001a) estimates at $300 billion (1.3 per cent of GDP) the size of total transfers to the farm sector from taxpayers and consumers in the OECD. According to the OECD on a 'per farmer' basis, corrected for part-time farming, transfers to EU farmers averaged about $14,000 in 2000 and to US farmers about $20,000 (OECD, 2003a).

The latest estimate of the cost of the CAP in the EU15 stands at €92 billion (0.4 per cent of GDP) for 2001 (DEFRA, 2003b). This is made up of a cost to EU consumers of €53 billion, resulting from the difference between EU and world price levels, and to taxpayers of a further €39 billion. As the UK is a net importer of foodstuffs the impact in the UK is likely to be higher than the average. Firstly, for imports from outside the EU, the tariff and variable levy revenue which would normally accrue to the UK has to be handed over to the EU as part of the EU budget's own resources.[3] Secondly, for imports from the rest of the EU, the UK must pay the high EU price and thus suffers a terms of trade loss on its imports, compared to the alternative of importing them at world market prices. In addition, the UK also contributes to the EU

---

[3] Although since 2001 the Member States keep 25 per cent of total revenue, there is no net gain since it pays for administrative costs incurred during the collection of agricultural duties.

agricultural budget to pay for the export subsidies paid to the net exporting EU countries. Leach (2000) estimates the overall annual cost of the CAP to the British economy at 1 per cent of GDP (£9–10 billion annually). Similar estimates have been previously calculated by Minford (1996) and Hindley and Howe (2001).

There are various measures of protection used by the OECD and the EU. Total support estimate (TSE) is the annual monetary value of all gross transfers from taxpayers and consumers arising from policy measures that support agriculture, net of the associated budgetary receipts. The TSE amounted to $318 billion in 2002 and accounted for 1.3 per cent of the GDP in the EU (and 1.2 per cent in the OECD area), compared with 2.7 per cent in 1986–88 (and 2.3 per cent in the OECD area). Compared with the US, the EU spent more on support to farmers as a percentage of GDP (Table 4.4).

Table 4.4: US–EU farm total support estimate

	US	EU
Total support estimate (TSE)	$97.4 billion	$119.4 billion
TSE per capita	$342	$268
TSE as % of GDP	1.00%	1.30%

Source: OECD (2001a)

The level of support to producers, as captured by the producer support estimate (PSE), varies widely across countries and commodities. It is an indicator of the annual monetary value of gross transfers from consumers and taxpayers to agricultural producers, measured at the farm gate level, arising from policy measures which support agriculture, regardless of their nature, objectives or impacts on farm production or income (OECD, 2004c).[4] The

---

[4]An alternative to the PSE is the WTO's aggregate measure of support (AMS). AMS however, is a narrower concept than the PSE and covers only domestic policies considered to be trade distorting. The AMS excludes explicit trade policies covered by the PSE such as export subsidies and import restrictions. It also excludes certain types of budgetary payments. Moreover, the AMS is not a measure of the current support to agriculture because some of its components are calculated using historical (base period) prices instead

EU, Japan and the US collectively account for around four-fifths of all support, although as a percentage of the value of gross farm receipts, support is highest in Switzerland, Norway and Korea. Rice, sugar and milk are the most supported commodities, with transfers to producers exceeding 50 per cent of gross receipts for these products.

As Table 4.5 reflects, compared with the 1986–88 period,[5] 2000–02 was characterised by a lower overall level of support to producers, as a result of the Uruguay Round implementation. Whereas in the US the PSE was 18 per cent of farm receipts in 2002, it was 36 per cent in the EU. Prices received by OECD farmers in 2002 were on average 31 per cent above world prices (OECD, 2002a). While this is a significant reduction from the mid-1980s when producer prices were 57 per cent higher, farmers in many countries remain shielded from world market signals. Whereas prices received by farmers were 10 per cent higher in the US, farmers in the EU received 35 per cent higher prices. If we turn to the extent to which consumers paid for this support through higher prices (the consumer subsidy equivalent) rather than taxpayers through direct farmer subsidy, we find that the CSE varies from a small consumer subsidy of 4 per cent in the US to an implicit consumer tax of over 28 per cent in the EU in 2002 (Table 4.5).

In 2001 France received the largest amount of CAP funding, claiming 22.2 per cent of the total budget of €41.53 billion (EC, 2002a). The next biggest recipients were Spain (14.8), Germany (14.1), Italy (12.8). In 2000 the UK was a net contributor to the EU, accounting for 15.8 per cent of EU financing and only 10.6 per cent of EU spending (Table 4.6). France, Spain, Greece and Ireland are clearly strong beneficiaries. Germany is the main net contributor with a net contribution of €4.4 billion, accounting for 24.8 per cent of financing and only 14 per cent of spending. The CAP spending in Germany is much lower than countries such as France and Ireland. Yet Germany continues to support the CAP – a policy which is clearly not based upon simple national benefit.

The primary pressures on the CAP come from the EU's budget constraints, and the enlargement of the EU to include the first wave of Central and Eastern European Countries (CEEC). If the CAP is

---

of current prices as is done in the PSE calculations.

[5]During the Uruguay Round 1986–88 was the base period for negotiations related to reduction in market access and domestic support.

Table 4.5: Producer and consumer support estimates of support to agriculture (PSE, CSE)

Producer support estimates of support to agriculture (US$ billion)[a]

	EU		US		Canada		Japan	
1986–88	95.4	(40)	41.8	(25)	5.7	(34)	48.9	(61)
2000–02	92.3	(35)	46.9	(21)	4.3	(19)	47.8	(59)
2000	88.6	(34)	49.7	(22)	4.2	(19)	54.1	(60)
2001	83.7	(34)	51.7	(23)	4.0	(17)	45.4	(59)
2002p	100.7	(36)	39.6	(18)	4.6	(20)	43.9	(59)

Consumer support estimates of support to agriculture (US$ billion)[b]

	EU		US		Canada		Japan	
1986–88	−70.5	(−41)	−8.7	(−7)	−2.5	(−22)	−55	(−57)
2000–02	−45.2	(−26)	3.8	(2)	−2.1	(−14)	−59	(−51)
2000	−44.7	(−27)	4.7	(3)	−2.1	(−14)	−67	(−51)
2001	−41.3	(−24)	−0.15	(0)	−1.9	(−13)	−56	(−51)
2002p	−49.6	(−28)	6.8	(4)	−2.2	(−14)	−54	(−51)

Notes:
a. In brackets: % PSE which is the ratio of PSE to the value of total gross farm receipts measured by the value of total production at the farm gate prices.
b. In brackets: % CSE which is the ratio of CSE to the value of total gross farm receipts measured by the value of total production at the farm gate prices.
p Provisional estimate.
Most CSE figures are negative since it is an indicator of gross transfers from consumers due to support to agricultural producers. It is a measure of negative protection or costs to consumers.

Source: OECD (2003a)

Table 4.6: Member states' contributions to and benefits from the
EU, 2000

| | Share in budget contributions % of total budget | | Net budgetary positions | |
	Without UK rebate	With UK rebate	Billion €	% of GDP
Belgium	3.7	3.9	−0.4	−0.2
Denmark	1.9	2.0	0.2	0.2
Germany	23.4	24.3	−9.6	−0.5
Greece	1.6	1.7	4.4	3.6
Spain	7.3	7.8	5.1	0.8
France	15.8	16.9	−1.4	-0.2
Ireland	1.2	1.3	1.7	1.6
Italy	12.1	13.0	0.7	0.2
Luxembourg	0.2	0.2	−0.2	−0.3
Netherlands	6.2	6.5	−1.7	−0.4
Austria	2.3	2.4	−0.6	−0.3
Portugal	1.4	1.5	2.2	1.8
Finland	1.4	1.5	0.3	0.3
Sweden	2.6	2.7	−1.0	−0.5
UK	19.1	14.3	−3.8	−0.2

Source: Swinnen (2003)

to be fully implemented in the new Member States, it would substantially increase CAP expenditure. At the Copenhagen Summit in December 2002 it was decided that direct payments will gradually be phased in over a 10-year period. During this period farmers in the new Member States will receive payments at a reduced but gradually increasing rate compared to that received by farmers in the EU 15. Only the complete liberalisation of the CAP will reduce expenditure significantly. But given that any reform proposal must attract support from France and Germany, it is clear that only a partial liberalisation scenario seems to be a realistic option in the near future.

Efforts to Reform the CAP

The CAP's inefficiencies, combined with pressures from green issues and falling farm prices, have led to momentous efforts for reform. Reforms to curb overproduction were introduced in 1984, 1988, and, most radically, in 1992. These involved a market-oriented price strategy (the resulting drop in agricultural incomes being cushioned by specific income support); quantitative and qualitative control of production through quotas and compensatory payments; premiums for set-aside schemes (grants to farmers to take land out of production); and diversification of production to bring supply more in line with demand.

Of all the reforms of the CAP, the most important were the McSharry reforms of 1992. The core of the reforms was a nominal cut of 30 per cent in the cereal price, phased over three years, complemented by a smaller cut in the institutional prices for beef and butter. Farmers were compensated for these price cuts by payments per tonne, translated on the basis of regional yields to a per hectare payment. In reality, as noted by Ackrill (1999), it is estimated that over the four year period 1993/94 to 1996/97, EU farmers were overcompensated between €8.5 billion and €14.3 billion. This was due to the unexpectedly high market prices that were used to calculate compensation.

Johnson (1995) and Messerlin (2001) confirm that although the 1992 reforms represented a significant change in the structure of farm support in Europe, they did not reduce the level of support and thus failed to reduce the welfare cost of agricultural protection. Since the McSharry reforms, the EU has continued to pursue

a strategy of agricultural exports by a combination of export subsidies, internal price support and direct aid to producers to compensate for revenue losses. Despite production costs being considerably higher in the EU, it has maintained market share in many
agricultural commodities through the CAP's complex range of subsidies. Policies providing support prices, implemented through
trade barriers and/or other export support, or deficiency payments
that raise producer revenues to target levels, shield producer returns from world market signals. Other support, such as payments
linked to land or other inputs, also tend to increase short-run supply and investment, with long-term consequences in the form of
greater production potential.

The recent reforms of the CAP, called the Agenda 2000 reforms,
agreed in Berlin in March 1999 failed in several respects. Firstly,
according to an agreement reached between France and Germany,
there will be no change in the size of the CAP budget, which
at some €50 billion ($58 billion) a year will continue to take up
nearly half of all EU spending. Secondly, cereal prices, which the
commission had proposed should be cut by 5 per cent, will remain
unchanged. Thirdly, France has secured agreement that it can put
off applying the new terms of the CAP until 2007, even though
other countries can bring in the rules in 2005 if they wish (precisely
how this can be made compatible with the free movement of farm
products inside the European Single Market remains unclear).

In June 2003 the Council of Agriculture Ministers of the EU
reached another agreement on the reform of the CAP. The agreement is based on the EC's previous proposals set out in January
2003. The main elements of this package were decoupling [6], single
farm payments, modulation (a reduction in direct payments), rural
development measures and market reforms in dairy and cereal sectors. However, it has left the EU with massive overproduction as
measured by self-sufficiency rates. This is 115 per cent in wheat,
116 per cent in wine, 113 per cent in sugar, 104 per cent in beef
and veal and 107 per cent in pig meat. Nor does this help small
farmers: according to the Australian-based agricultural think tank
ABARE, large farms in Europe which constitute 17 per cent of the

---

[6]The key change in recent EU reform proposals is 'decoupling' or separating
payments from production. This means that farmers will still receive money at
a level based on past income, but it will be in the form of a one-off payment that
it is hoped will encourage them to farm for the market rather than subsidies.

farming community get 50 per cent of total subsidies while small farms (39 per cent of the farming community) get only 8 per cent of the total resources (De Boer, 2002). The main beneficiaries of farm support measures are the largest farmers and agri-businesses.

Export subsidies became an important policy instrument in the 1980s when domestic support policies generated excess supplies mainly in Europe and in North America. Even though between 1990 and 1999 export subsidies have fallen from 31 to 14 per cent of CAP expenditure, subsidies for a wide range of agricultural commodities and processed products have continued. Export prices of wheat, powdered milk and sugar are fixed at 34 per cent, 50 per cent and 75 per cent respectively of their production costs. Cheese, other milk products, beef, sugar and feed grains are most reliant on subsidies. Dairy products accounted for 30 per cent of total export subsidies in the 1995–1998 period. Beef accounted for 22 per cent, sugar 12 per cent, grains 13 per cent and incorporated products 11 per cent.

One of the most damaging features of the CAP is that the money is tied to production, with surpluses dumped on world markets via the payment of export subsidies.[7] The EU argues for the retention of export subsidies, and yet strongly argues the case for anti-dumping policies at the same time. Export subsidies for agriculture are, by definition, dumping, and the CAP is the world's largest dumping programme.

4.6 THE EU'S AGRICULTURAL TRADE DISPUTES WITH THE US

While both the EU and the US provide significant support to their agricultural sectors, there are key differences in their approaches and in the policy instruments they use.[8] For example, whereas

---

[7]The sufferers are mainly developing countries, many of whose economies depend heavily on agriculture. Not only will their exports to rich-country markets still be heavily obstructed; even their domestic markets will continue to be distorted by the dumping of EU surpluses. That is why the rest of the world insisted that the Doha Round of trade talks should aim to phase out all farm-export subsidies. For most countries, indeed, this is the biggest single objective of the round.

[8]For a detailed review of US and the EU farm policies, see Normile et al. (2004).

the EU remains much more reliant on price support mechanisms, the US is more dependent on income support measures. The two countries also differ in their reliance on tariffs and subsidies. These differences have given rise to numerous trade disputes between the EU and the US over the years.

In the 1980s nearly 90 per cent of all US actions against the EU (seven of eight) involved agriculture. In fact, three-fourths of all lawsuits by any country against the EU involved agricultural products (12 of 16). By contrast, only roughly 40 per cent of all lawsuits against the US covered agriculture (5 of 12), and mostly due to actions brought by the EU (three of five). The US was initially concerned with the shrinking market in Europe, as trade diversion took place, encouraged by the high trade barriers after the introduction of the CAP. Later the use of export subsidies in the EU, which tried to keep surpluses from depressing the internal market, became a cause for concern for the US. In the 1980s there were major differences between the EU and the US over what constituted a subsidy and over how to determine the magnitude of subsidies.

The US retaliated against the EU subsidies with its Export Enhancement Program (EEP) expressly targeted at those markets where the EU was increasing its share.

The 1990s once again witnessed a sharp intensification of trade disputes between the EU and the US. The main agricultural trade disputes between the US and the EU in the last decade have been: 1) the beef hormone dispute, 2) the Banana dispute, 3) bans as a result of bovine spongiform encephalopathy (BSE), 4) problems due to Foot and mouth disease, and 5) Genetically Modified Organisms (GMOs).

In 1989, the EU banned the use of six growth hormones used for cattle and prohibited the imports of beef containing such hormones. The ban led to a GATT lawsuit, and later to a WTO dispute settlement case filed in 1996 by the US and other beef-exporting nations. The ruling was in the US's favour. In view of the non-compliance by the EU with the WTO ruling, in 1999 the Dispute Settlement Body authorised the US to impose retaliatory tariffs on imports from the EU of $117 million per year. This measure is still active.

In 1993, following the implementation of the Single Market, the EU imposed an EU-wide system of import quotas for bananas.

The new system led to two GATT lawsuits, and later to two WTO dispute settlement cases filed in 1995 and 1996 by the US and several Latin American countries. This dispute was also settled in favour of the US. In 1999 the US imposed retaliatory tariffs on imports from the EU of $191 million per year. This measure was deactivated in 2001, but $116 million in punitive duties remains in effect due to the beef dispute. This, in turn, led the EU to threaten retaliation against US exports that the WTO found in violation of an export subsidy agreement. In addition, the EU has filed numerous WTO dispute resolution petitions alleging that a variety of US trade laws violate international obligations in some technical fashion.

More recently some of the most contentious EU-US agricultural trade issues have been in the area of sanitary and phytosanitary standards (SPS) and other more technical trade issues. These include the dispute over the import of hormone-treated beef into Europe, the potential ban by Europe of imports of beef by-products ('specified risk materials') that may harbour vectors of BSE, or mad cow disease and the regulation of the use and labelling of genetically modified organisms (GMOs). It is estimated that the EU will be isolated from the downward pressure on world prices brought about by the global productivity boost as a result of GM crops (Meijl and Tongeren, 2002). In addition the CAP isolates the EU from productivity increases in GMO-adopting regions through flexible import tariffs.

4.7 WELFARE COSTS

In recent years agricultural trade liberalisation has been one of the most contentious issues in world talks. Both the US and the EU are in the process of making significant changes to their agricultural policies. Welfare gains to the EU and the US as well as to the world economy from such reforms have been estimated by numerous studies, mostly using computational general equilibrium (CGE) models, especially the global trade analysis project (GTAP) model. In this section we discuss some of the recent studies in brief.

Global Welfare Gains

Table 4.7 summarises the global welfare gains due to the liberalisation of worldwide barriers to agricultural trade. It is estimated that complete elimination of agricultural support would raise global welfare in the region of typically 0.4 per cent (IMF, 2000b) and 0.7 per cent of world GDP (World Bank, 2002). Whereas Elbehri and Leetmaa (2002) estimate that removal of all export subsidies, domestic support and tariff barriers to agricultural trade would increase global welfare by 0.2 per cent of GDP, Hertel et al. (2000) calculate an annual gain of 0.5 per cent of world GDP from the complete elimination of world support to agriculture in all forms including tariffs and export as well as production subsidies. The largest gain in terms of percentage of GDP from agricultural liberalisation is estimated by Stoeckel (2002) at 2.2 per cent.

Table 4.7: Welfare gains due to reduction in worldwide barriers in agricultural trade

Studies in 2000s	% Reduction in global barriers	World gain (% of world GDP)	EU gain (% of EU GDP)
Hertel et al. (2000)	40	0.2	–
	100	0.5	–
Diao et al. (2001)	100	0.2	–
IMF (2000b)	100	0.4	0.41
CIE (2002a)	50	0.3	0.12
	100	0.5	–
Elbehri and Leetmaa (2002)	100	0.2	0.13
Stoeckel (2002)	100	2.2	–
IMF (2002b)	50	–	0.29
	50 subsidies in QUAD	–	0.24
Brown et al. (2002)	33	0.03	0.02*

Note: *EU and EFTA

The above estimates from different studies are difficult to compare. Even when the same CGE model (the GTAP) is used, different liberalisation scenarios are applied and policies are modelled in different ways. Nevertheless, it is clear that the potential gains from agricultural trade reform are large.

Gains to the EU

Studies which estimate gains to the EU from agricultural reforms have used both the CGE and partial equilibrium framework. Table 4.8 summarises the welfare cost of the CAP to the EU as calculated by studies in the 1980s and 1990s. Estimates range from 0.1 per cent of GDP (Harrison et al., 1995) to 2.7 per cent (Burniaux and Waelbroeck, 1985). The relatively large gains are generally associated with CGE models. The estimates from the studies vary significantly which reflects the differences in model structures, liberalisation scenarios and level of aggregation, among other things.

Tyers and Anderson (1992) estimate that the benefits to producers from EU protection amount to about 25 per cent of gross farm income. Similarly, it is calculated that approximately $142 billion was transferred from consumers via high domestic prices to the agricultural sectors in the EU in 1991 (OECD, 1992). In addition to the studies discussed above, which estimate welfare gains of agricultural liberalisation to the EU using world CGE models, there are several studies which focus on specific CAP policies and reform agenda to calculate the cost of such protection to the EU.

Results of recent empirical studies which focus on welfare gains from the reforms of the CAP are summarised in Table 4.9. Using a CGE model Elbehri and Leetmaa (2002) estimate a welfare gain of 0.13 per cent of GDP to the EU from agricultural reforms the world over (including the EU), largely from improved allocative efficiency, as opposed to terms of trade gains. The US welfare gain of $US7.2 billion (0.1 per cent of GDP) on the other hand, is mostly from improved terms of trade. Using the GTAP model the IMF (2002b) calculates that the EU would experience a significant (near 0.25 per cent of GDP) increase in welfare because of the distortions removed in the EU economy.

Borrell and Hubbart (2000) estimate the total welfare cost of the CAP to the EU at 0.9 per cent of GDP. The study suggests that the CAP has made the non-grain sector eight times larger than

Table 4.8: Estimates of welfare costs of the CAP to the EU (studies between 1980 and 2000)

Studies in 1980s and 1990s	Model Structure*	% of GDP
Morris (1980)	PE	0.5
Harvey and Thomson (1981)	PE	0.5
Buckwell et al. (1982)	PE	0.5
Tyers (1985)	PE	1.1
Roberts (1985)	PE	0.3
Spencer (1985)	GE	0.9
Burniaux and Waelbroeck (1985)	GE	2.7
Tyers and Anderson (1987)	PE	0.3
Stoeckel and Breckling (1989)	GE	1.5
EC (1994)	PE	0.22
Harrison et al. (1995)	GE	0.1
Hubbard (1995a)	GE	0.8
Hubbard (1995b)	GE	0.14–1.3
Folmer et al. (1995)	GE	0.3
Blake et al. (1998)	with Cournot Oligopoly reforms (GE)	0.42
Weyerbrock (1998)	GE	0.1–0.2
Blake et al. (1999)	GE	0.12–0.18

Note: * PE – Partial equilibrum model, GE – General equilibrium model.

Source: Philippidis and Hubbard (2001)

Table 4.9: Estimates of welfare costs of the CAP to the EU (studies in 2000s)

Studies in 2000s	% Reduction in Barriers	% of EU GDP	% of UK GDP
Borrell and Hubbard (2000)	100	0.9	–
EC (2002a)	100 in support price for cereals, meat, milk and eggs (partial equilibrium)	0.1	–
Philippidis and Hubbard (2001)	CAP abolition in 2005	0.2	0.5
	Domestic support, export subsidies and 30 reduction in tariffs	0.2	0.3
Gohin and Meyers (2002)	Phasing out of export subsidies	0.02	–
Dimaranan et al. (2003)	50 in market price support (wheat)	0.001	–
DEFRA (2003b)	Reforms under Agenda 2000	0.05	0.05
Frandsen et al. (2003)	Decoupling payments	0.1	0.2
	Domestic support	0.1	0.3

it would otherwise be and has enlarged milk products and grain sectors by more than 50 per cent. It confirms that without the CAP the EU would greatly increase its agricultural imports and decrease imports of other products because non-agriculture sectors would expand. The scrapping of the CAP would increase US and Canadian exports of dairy products by over 70 per cent and crop exports between 25–46 per cent. These results may underestimate the welfare cost because they do not take into account dynamic gains from higher capital accumulation and the productivity boost that would occur as a result of open competitive markets. The results from Stoeckel and Breckling (1989) suggest that omitting these factors could underestimate the costs by at least 20 per cent.

Gersfelt et al. (2002) assess the impact of liberalising domestic support in the EU at the individual Member State level in the EU and in non-member regions. In the first scenario, removal of domestic support in the EU results in an increase in EU GDP of 0.1 per cent. At the EU Member State level real GDP increases by between 0.1 per cent and 0.7 per cent, of which a major part is explained by the significant changes in the inter-regional transfers between the individual EU member countries. In particular, Germany gains from a lower contribution to the common financing of the CAP, and the UK gain of 0.3 per cent of GDP is due to significant budgetary savings and an efficiency gain.

Frandsen et al. (2003) examine the economy-wide effects of full decoupling (a uniform land payment) measured against a baseline of 1997–2013. Using the GTAP general equilibrium model the study estimates that the EU would gain welfare benefits of 0.06 per cent of GDP in 2013, with the UK gaining approximately 0.04 per cent of GDP as a result of the move towards decoupling payments. The overwhelming majority of the welfare gains would be achieved through a more efficient allocation of resources. In addition to eliminating all direct support as illustrated in the previous case, if all export subsidies (which mainly affect the export of other grains, dairy products, processed rice and sugar) are eliminated, and this is supplemented by a 30 per cent reduction in the import tariff equivalents, real GDP in the EU would increase by 0.2 per cent and the efficiency gain is 50 per cent higher in this scenario as compared with scenario 1. At the Member State level real GDP increases by 0.1–0.8 per cent. Real GDP increases the most in Greece (0.8 per cent), Portugal (0.5 per cent) and Ireland (0.5 per cent). For the UK the efficiency gain amounts to €4 billion (0.2 per cent of GDP).

In recent years, empirical studies have focused their attention on measuring the cost of protection in specific commodity markets. It is estimated by the European Union (2000) that full implementation of a reduction in support prices for cereals, beef and dairy products under Agenda 2000 CAP reforms would result in an increase in consumer welfare of €8.8 billion in 2005/06 and €10.5 billion in 2006/07 (0.1 per cent of GDP).

The CIE (2002b) estimates the effect of reducing protection levels in the sugar market. The results suggest that halving of the intervention price by 2012 would lower the EU producer prices for refined sugar to the world market price – a fall of 50 per cent, and would increase EU consumption by 10 per cent and decrease production by 64 per cent. This would increase EU net imports from −3.7 million tonnes to 9.3 million tonnes a year. Complete removal of the export subsidy on sugar would raise the world price by about 2 per cent in 2012. It would reduce the average EU producer price by around 10 per cent and would decrease EU exports from 6.4 to 3.6 million tonnes.

Messerlin (2001) estimates the cost of protecting the five farm sectors (cereals, milk, meat, sugar, bananas) in the EU at roughly a third of the value added for these five sectors. If the study is extended to the whole of the agriculture sector assuming the same level of protection as enjoyed by these five sectors, the costs of EC protection would represent roughly 12 per cent of EU total farm value added. The study also estimates that the average price for agricultural goods would decline by 14–17 per cent and only around 5 per cent of total jobs in agriculture would be lost if protection were altogether removed. Colman et al (2002) showed that the milk quota removal and the price reduction to world levels planned under the Agenda2002 reforms would bring gains of broadly €0.7 billion (0.04 per cent of GDP) to farmers in the EU. The study also estimates that the marketing chain would benefit by about the same magnitude.

In a series of studies, DEFRA analyses the impact on the UK and the EU of the CAP reforms (DEFRA, 2003b). It estimates that the proposed CAP reforms (under the European Commission's mid-term review published on 22 January 2003) would deliver substantial benefits for consumers in the form of lower relative food prices; the economic benefit of the price reductions would be worth broadly £1 billion a year in the UK, when the reforms were fully implemented in 2008. Benefits to consumers would exceed the combined cost of the reform to taxpayers and producers, resulting in a significant benefit to the UK economy, worth broadly £500–£900 million a year once fully implemented. The net benefit to the EU economy would be in the region of £5.7 billion (0.1 per cent of GDP). The reforms would encourage productivity growth and restructuring (dynamic gain), which would generate extra economic benefits of about €0.4 billion in the UK (0.03 per cent of GDP)and €2.2 billion in the EU (0.03 per cent of GDP). In the dairy sector alone the net welfare gain would be £60 million in the UK and € 870 million (0.01 per cent of GDP) in the EU.

As the above evidence suggests, the benefits of agricultural trade liberalisation and reforms of the CAP are well established. Beyond the direct observable cost, agricultural support policies pursued in the EU have caused distortions in the allocation of resources. Higher domestic prices have given incentives to retain more resources – land, labour and capital – in agriculture than would have been the case if farmers had faced world market prices. Additional benefits of the reforms would come from the dynamic long-term effects from increased savings and investment and from increased productivity when resources are allocated efficiently.

Logically, it should be in the EU's self-interest to reform agricultural protection as quickly as possible. However, agricultural trade reforms in the EU have been slow. There has been resistance to liberalisation by those who would stand to lose and the sector is viewed as being fundamentally different from other sectors because of environmental protection and food security.

4.8   CONCLUSION

This chapter has reviewed barriers to agricultural trade and gains from reforming such barriers, particularly in the EU. It is well known that the CAP is beset with many problems. EU consumers are forced to pay a high price for their food, not only because they have to pay large sums of money in taxation, most of which is spent on farm subsidies, but also because competition from foreign imports is hampered by various trade barriers. Attempts have been made to alleviate some of the barriers, but with little effect. France has led the anti-reform campaign along with Spain and Ireland, and given their political influence within the EU it is unlikely that fundamental CAP reforms will take place in the near future.

5 Manufacturing

5.1 INTRODUCTION

During the last half century the importance of manufacturing industry in most European Union Member States has greatly diminished in terms of both production and employment. However, protection remains high and widespread especially in sectors such as textiles and consumer products. This chapter analyses the issues surrounding the impact of the EU's trade barriers in industrial products.

Section 5.2 discusses the significance of manufacturing for output and employment in the EU and the US. Section 5.3 reviews the pattern and direction of trade in manufacturing goods. The level and evolution of barriers to trade in goods in recent years are discussed in section 5.4. Section 5.5 presents estimates of trade barriers which take into account both tariff and non-tariff barriers. Section 5.6 outlines the main empirical findings concerning the welfare effects of trade liberalisation.

5.2 ROLE OF MANUFACTURING IN THE ECONOMY

Over the last three decades the share of manufacturing production in GDP has continuously declined in the US and the EU Member States, with the exception of Luxembourg and Spain (Figure 5.1).[1]

---

[1] Although the relative decline in manufacturing's share of output is real, its extent may have been overstated. Some sectors that used be classified as manufacturing are now classified as services. For example, if software design is outsourced it is classified as a service. If it is done in-house, it is classified

UK manufacturing output as a proportion of GDP fell from 26 per cent in 1980 to 17 per cent at present. In the same period it declined from 21 to 14 per cent in the US and from 31 to 22 per cent in Germany.

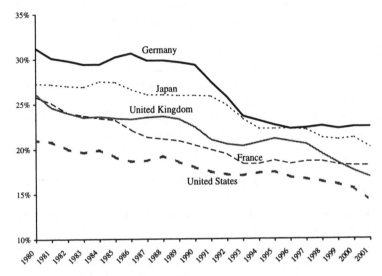

Source: UNCTAD (2003)

Figure 5.1: Manufacturing value added as per cent of total value added

In the EU the largest decline was recorded in the steel, petroleum and textile fibre sectors. Technology-driven industries grew at the fastest rate between 1985 and 1998, followed by marketing-driven industries, with pronounced growth in the media, publishing, printing and sports goods industries. In the UK over the last decade, the chemical (including pharmaceutical), electrical and optical sectors – which include IT and communications – have all grown faster than the economy as a whole. Certain industries, such as basic steel, shipbuilding, textiles and clothing, suffered from their competitive advantage moving to less developed countries and experienced a decline in manufacturing capacity and employment. In the US leading industries include motor vehicles, aerospace, telecommunications, chemicals, electronics and comput-

---

as part of the manufacturing sector.

ers.

As the share of manufacturing in total output has tended to decline across all the leading economies, the proportion of workers employed in the manufacturing sector has also fallen. During the last three years (2000–2002) around 400,000 manufacturing jobs were lost in the UK, accounting for a 10 per cent reduction in the sector's workforce (TUC, 2002). Manufacturing jobs now account for 14 per cent of total jobs compared to 17 per cent three years ago. Manufacturing has some of the lowest skilled sectors in the economy; almost 40 per cent of workers in the clothing sub-sector do not possess any educational qualifications. However, this low average hides some of the highest skilled sub-sectors, such as computers.

5.3   TRADE IN MANUFACTURING

Measured by the volume of merchandise trade, the world economy has become increasingly integrated in the years since the Second World War. The volume of world merchandise trade is today 18 times what it was in 1950, a period during which the value of world output increased by a factor of six (OECD, 2001b). Associated with this trend there has been a substantial rise in import penetration across all OECD countries, particularly in manufacturing goods: whereas in the largest four European countries manufacturing imports as a percentage of GDP moved from an average of 8.4 per cent in 1970 to 16 per cent in 1999, they rose from 2.7 per cent to 9.7 per cent during the same period in the US.

The EU continues to be the world's largest exporter of merchandise trade (20 per cent of world exports in 1998) and is the second largest importer (19 per cent of the total). The US is the EU's largest trading partner with shares of 21.3 per cent and 22 per cent in 1998 in imports and exports respectively. Among the Member States, Germany is the largest trading nation, followed by the UK and France. Among the manufacturing sectors, exports of telecommunications and office equipment overtook those of automotive products in the 1990s, growing from a little less than 9 per cent of total exports to 15 per cent, while automotive sector exports remained relatively constant at just over 9 per cent. Exports of garments and textiles slowed in the 1990s, with textiles in

Table 5.1: Merchandise export expansion by region and level of technology, 1980–2000 (average annual percentage change)

	Primary products	Resource based man.	Low-tech man.	Medium-tech man.	High-tech man.
North America	2.2	5.1	8.4	7.0	9.1
Latin American	5.1	5.1	11.8	14.8	21.0
Western Europe	3.5	4.2	4.8	5.5	9.3
EU 15	2.9	4.1	4.6	5.5	9.4
Developed countries	3.2	4.5	5.1	5.9	9.5
Developing countries	2.4	6.3	10.4	13.7	19.8
World	3.2	5.2	6.7	6.8	11.3

Source: Bacchetta and Bora (2003)

particular growing at a slower rate than total merchandise exports.

During the 1980s and 1990s, the EU has lagged behind North America in the of growth of low and medium technology manufacturing exports (Table 5.1). Within the EU exports of high-technology goods as a proportion of total goods exports have been higher in the UK than in France and Germany. This partly reflects the UK's strength, vis-à-vis other European countries, in pharmaceuticals and aerospace. Although there is some concern about a possible shift of pharmaceutical R&D to the US, the factors that have supported the growth of this industry in the UK – a favourable regulatory regime, a high level of public support for scientific research and the strength of British universities in life sciences – seem likely to persist. On the aerospace side UK production is dominated by two large companies, Rolls-Royce and BaeSystems.

The IT hardware sector, including computers and communication equipment, is also a strong performer; exports of these products, as a proportion of total exports of manufactures, is higher in the UK than in Germany or France. Most of these exports derive from foreign-owned companies, which are also large importers.

These companies may be using the UK as a relatively cheap production base in the EU.

As for the sectoral composition of imports, between 1980 and 2000 high-tech imports grew at a faster rate than low- and medium-tech imports in the EU. In the US, however, the growth rate of imports of low-tech goods was the highest, mainly due to a significant increase in imports of textiles, toys and similar labour-intensive goods from Asia, particularly China (Table 5.2).

Table 5.2: Merchandise import expansion by region and level of technology, 1980–2000, (average annual percentage change)

	Primary products	Resource based man.	Low-tech man.	Medium-tech man.	High-tech man.
North America	3.0	6.5	102.0	9.1	13.7
Latin American	10.5	12.4	16.0	13.3	17.7
Western Europe	1.0	3.6	5.3	6.4	9.6
EU 15	0.8	3.5	5.2	6.3	9.6
Developed countries	1.6	4.3	7.0	7.3	11.1
Developing countries	6.7	7.9	10.1	9.0	15.6
World	2.7	5.1	7.7	7.9	12.3

Source:　　Bacchetta and Bora (2003)

As for the US, merchandise trade amounted to $1.87 trillion in 2001, with exports of $730 billion and imports of $1142 billion. Of the $177 billion increase in goods exports since 1994, capital goods accounted for 48 per cent of the increase, industrial materials and supplies accounted for 19 per cent and consumer goods accounted for 14 per cent. In 2002 manufacturing exports accounted for 88 per cent of total goods exports. High technology exports, a part of manufacturing exports, accounted for 26 per cent (Table 5.3).

Since 1980 the US has experienced an important shift in its exports away from traditional European markets toward Asia and Mexico. During 2000–01 the top five US merchandise trade part-

Table 5.3: US goods exports

Exports Total (BOP basis)	1999	2000	2001	2002p	01–02p	94–02p
	Billions of dollars				% change	
Agriculture	48.2	52.0	55.2	54.3	−1.6	17.3
Manufacturing	611.8	689.5	640.2	604.0	−5.7	40.1
High Technology	200.3	227.4	199.6	177.9	−10.9	47.3

Note: p – Provisional estimate.
Source: USTR (2003)

ners (in terms of total trade) were Canada, China, the EU, Japan and Mexico (Table 5.4). Over 85 per cent of US trade with NAFTA countries is in manufactured goods. This sector grew over 66 per cent between 1993 and 1998. In contrast, US manufacturers' export growth to the rest of the world from 1993 to 1998 was less than 47 per cent. In 2002 Canada was the largest US export market, accounting for 23 per cent of exports, followed by the EU, accounting for 21 per cent of aggregate US exports.

Since 1994, US imports of consumer goods have more than doubled, while imports of autos and auto parts, industrial supplies and materials, and capital goods have increased 72 per cent, 62 per cent, and 52 per cent respectively. Both general manufacturing and high-tech imports have risen substantially since 1994 (Table 5.5). Increasing import categories included foods, feed and beverages (up 10 per cent), consumer goods (up 9 per cent), and autos and auto parts (up 11 per cent). Imports from the EU have increased 86 per cent since 1994 and accounted for 19 per cent of total US imports in 2002 (Table 5.6). Imports from its NAFTA partners declined 1 per cent in 2002, but were up 127 per cent on 1993, the year prior to the implementation of NAFTA. NAFTA imports accounted for 30 per cent of aggregate US goods imports in 2002, up from 27 per cent in 1994.

Manufacturing intra-industry trade has risen in most OECD countries including the US and the EU since the 1980s. In the US it rose from 64 per cent of total manufacturing trade in 1988–91 to 69 per cent between 1996–2000. In several countries, like Austria, France and the UK, manufacturing intra-industry trade

Table 5.4: US goods exports to selected countries/regions

Exports to	1999	2000	2001	2002p	94–02p
		Billions of dollars			% change
Canada	166.6	178.9	163.4	159.7	39.6
European Union	151.8	165.1	158.8	143.5	33.1
Japan	57.5	64.9	57.5	51.2	−4.4
Mexico	86.9	111.3	101.3	97.2	91.1
China	13.1	16.2	19.2	22.2	138.6
Pacific Rim (except Japan and China)	103.2	121.5	104.8	104.7	23.1
Latin America (except Mexico)	55.2	59.3	58.2	51.3	23.1

Note: p – Provisional estimate.
Source: USTR (2003)

Table 5.5: Total US imports (BOP basis)

Imports to	1999	2000	2001	2002p	94-02p
		Billions of US$			% change
Agriculture	36.7	39.2	39.5	41.6	60.2
Manufacturing	882.7	1013.5	950.7	963.3	72.9
High technology	181.2	222.1	195.2	193.6	97.3

Note: p – Provisional estimate.
Source: USTR (2003)

Table 5.6: US goods imports from selected countries/regions

Imports to	1999	2000	2001	2002p	94–02p
		Billions of US$			% change
Canada	198.7	230.8	216.3	208.5	62.4
EU	195.2	220	220.1	222.1	85.9
Japan	130.9	146.5	126.5	119.0	−0.2
Mexico	109.7	135.9	131.3	134.1	171
China	81.8	100	102.3	122.4	215.5
Pacific Rim (except Japan and China)	147.1	171.5	147.3	145.2	40.7
Latin America (except Mexico)	58.5	73.3	67.4	68.4	77.8

Note: p – Provisional estimate.
Source: USTR (2003)

has been in the 70–75 per cent range for over a decade (Turner and Richardson 2003).

5.4 BARRIERS TO TRADE IN GOODS

Tariffs: European Union

After the successive tariff cuts during the various GATT rounds, average MFN tariffs on manufactures are rather low, with the US and the EU both among the low-tariff regions (Table 5.7). The average EU tariff on non-agricultural products was 4.1 per cent in 2001, down from 4.5 per cent in 1999; the decline is explained by lower tariffs on certain paper and paperboard, chemical, textile, iron and steel products, and toys.

Despite this, tariff protection in some sectors remains high and, in some cases such as chemicals, maximum tariffs increased after 1995. Many developed countries including the EU continue to levy higher tariffs on consumer goods than on capital goods. For example, tariffs on consumer goods are more than five times higher than

Table 5.7: Imports and tariff peaks, 1999

	US	EU 15	Japan	Canada
Number of tariff peak products				
All products	311	317	233	732
Agricultural products	48	290	178	85
Industrial Products	263	27	55	647
Tariff peak products as percentage of all tariff lines	6.1	6.2	4.6	14.3
Average tariff rates (unweighted)				
Tariff peak products	20.8	40.3	27.8	30.5
All products	5.0	7.4	4.3	8.3
Maximum tariff rate (%)	121.0	251.9	170.5	342.7
Imports of tariff peak products (in billions of US$)	42.1	27.1	15.8	8.7
Imports of tariff peak products (as per cent of all imports)	4.6	3.4	4.9	4.6

Notes: Applied tariff rates; Excludes all intra-EU trade in world totals.

Source: Hoekman et al. (2002).

on capital goods (DTI, 2004) and tariff peaks occur in footwear and automotive industries. The sectors with higher rates than the average include video recording instruments, certain type of radio cassette-players, radio-broadcast receivers, reception apparatus for colour television and video monitors. In the transport equipment sector, the EU imposes higher than average tariffs on bicycles and motor vehicles including buses, cars, and trucks as well as on motor vehicle chassis. Tariff protection for passenger cars remains at 10 per cent and is substantially higher than the USA (2.5 per cent) and Japan (0 per cent). Vehicles with large engine capacity and used for passenger transport face a tariff of 16 per cent while the majority of transport vehicles face a tariff of 22 per cent. In addition, all such motor vehicles are subject to special taxes, VAT or registration fees at the Member State level. High tariffs also apply to 40 lines in electrical equipment (all at 14 per cent), 20 in vehicles (of which 10 are at 22 per cent) and 5 in organic chemicals and alcoholic solutions (WTO, 2002).

Textiles

The EU has long maintained restrictions on imports of textile and clothing products from a number of developing countries and transition economies. Tariffs well above the average apply to textiles and clothing products with articles of apparel and clothing having average tariff rates above 12 per cent. In fact, out of 402 lines with tariff rates in excess of 12 per cent, 337 are in textiles and clothing.

Trade in textiles and clothing products continued to be subject to a special regime under the multilateral trade rules until 1 January 2005. Until that time a significant share of world trade in textiles and clothing was distorted by the complex set of quantitative restrictions inherited from the Multi-Fibre Agreement (MFA). To date, the EU has lifted restrictions on 20 per cent of products restricted in 1990, leaving the elimination of the remaining 80 per cent of restricted imports 'back-loaded' for the final stage at the end of 2004. The EU has also delayed removing restrictive quotas from textiles and clothing exports from developing countries. The Uruguay Round commitments are less dramatic than has been often said because EU tariff reductions have been concentrated on already low tariffs. It is estimated that in 1997 EU consumers paid roughly ECU 25 billion (1.8 per cent of GDP) more than the world price for textile and clothing products due to quotas, tariffs and indirect effects (Francois and Glismann, 2000).

Tariffs: United States

In July 2002 the US announced a proposal to eliminate all tariffs on consumer and industrial goods worldwide by 2015. Prior to this, in 1997 tariffs were eliminated on all semiconductors, computers, computer peripherals and computer parts, electronic calculators, telecommunication equipment, electronic components (capacitors, resistors, printed circuits), semiconductor testing and manufacturing equipment and certain consumer electronic items.

Despite the substantial reduction and elimination of tariffs agreed in the Uruguay Round by the US, a number of significant duties and tariff peaks remain in various sectors including food products, textiles, footwear, leather goods, jewellery and certain transport equipment such as trucks, railway cars and bicycles. There are products of importance for EU trade which continue to face high tariffs. These include hotel and restaurant ware, on which the duty rates currently are 30 per cent if made of porcelain or china and 31.5 per cent for others, and certain drinking glasses and other glassware on which the duty rates currently are 33.2 per cent and 38 per cent respectively. In the textile and leather sector for certain woollen fabrics and articles of apparel duty rates in 2002 reached 27.6 per cent plus a specific rate of 9.7 cents/kg in certain fabrics and 32.5 per cent for some apparel and several footwear products for which the current duty rates are 48 per cent, or 37.5 per cent plus a specific rate of 90 cents/pair. The US jewellery sector is protected by an average tariff of 6 per cent with the highest tariff after the Uruguay Round being 13.5 per cent. The corresponding EU rates stand between 2.5 per cent and 3 per cent. Furthermore, the US maintains significant import duties on certain semi-finished products made of precious metals. The high raw material cost in this sector means that even modest tariff barriers reduce significantly the access to the US jewellery market. A customs duty of 25 per cent was placed on vehicles for the transport of goods with a weight greater than 5 tonnes but less than 20 tonnes.

In October 2001 the USITC ruled that steel imports during January 1996 and June 2001 had injured domestic industry and in March 2002 the US imposed safeguard tariffs. Duties ranging from 8–30 per cent were imposed in the first year and the rates were scheduled to fall to 7–24 per cent and 6–18 per cent respectively, in the subsequent two years. A broad range of products were exempted as were all imports from Canada, Mexico and many developing countries. According to the Consuming Industries Trade Action Coalition (CITAC) those steel tariffs imposed in 2002 were largely responsible for the loss of nearly 200,000 American jobs (BBC, 5 Feb, 2003). The effect of protection has been to raise the price of steel and some steel consuming companies have switched to suppliers outside the US.

In sum, although average tariff rates have fallen in recent years, tariff peaks and tariffs dispersion remain significant in the EU and the US.

Tariff Escalation

Tariff escalation occurs when relatively high rates of tariff are levied on processed commodities compared to those on unprocessed commodities or raw materials. This results in higher 'effective' tariffs expressed as a fraction of value added after deducting intermediate inputs from product value. For example, suppose a country chooses not to impose a tariff on the import of raw leather, but a positive tariff on the import of leather manufactures such as shoes, garments or accessories. The domestic leather manufactures enjoy a higher rate of protection than the nominal tariff would suggest. Table 5.8 shows the incidence of tariff levels in Quad countries (Canada, the EU, Japan and the US) by technology-based product categories. The highest tariff dispersion in the EU is found in automotive and textiles, followed by electronic products. These are also the industries with the highest maximum rate in the EU.

The structure of tariffs in terms of stage of processing continues to show evidence of tariff escalation for the EU, notably for food, beverage and tobacco products, as well as textile products. Whereas raw textile materials show the average rate of 1 per cent, semi-processed items have an average rate of 8.2 per cent while fully processed items show an average tariff of 10 per cent and clothing 11.6 per cent. Further, Messerlin (2001) notes that there has been a continuous reshuffling of the tariff schedule since 1995. This makes possible tariff increases on new products, especially when the EU is having difficulties in following a fast transition to the latest technological progress. For example: before 1983, CD players were considered as 'record players' with a 9 per cent tariff. In 1984, they were granted a specific tariff line in the EU schedule with a tariff increase to 16.5 per cent.

The EU applies preferential rates, providing for elimination or partial elimination of tariffs to the countries with whom the EU has entered into preferential or free-trade agreements. The normal tariff rates are applied to most countries including Australia, Canada, the US, Japan, New Zealand, and since May 1998 to Hong Kong, Singapore and the republic of Korea. As a result the import share of EU trade under the normal tariff schedule increased from 35 per cent in 1990 to 39 per cent in 1999.

Table 5.8: MFN tariff peaks in manufactures, by technology-based product groups, 2000

Product group		Canada	EU	Japan	United States
Low technology textile/fashion cluster	Standard deviation	7.67	3.60	6.61	7.44
	Domestic peaks*	0.75	0.00	0.08	0.87
	International peaks*	0.40	0.02	0.09	0.15
	Maximum rate	22.50	17.00	37.5	48.00
Low technology manufactures, n.e.s	Standard deviation	3.6	2.14	1.85	4.03
	Domestic peaks*	0.66	0	0	0.67
	International peaks*	0.01	0	0	0.02
	Maximum rate	18	12	17	38
Medium technology, automotive products	Standard deviation	3.12	5.85	0	5.25
	Domestic peaks*	n.a.	0	0	0.56
	International peaks*	n.a.	0.16	0	0.04
	Maximum rate	13	22	0	25
Medium technology, process industries	Standard deviation	5.27	3.41	3.7	4.58
	Domestic peaks*	0.59	0	0	0.74
	International peaks*	0.12	0	0	0.07
	Maximum rate	20.5	12	27.2	23.1
Medium technology, engineering Industries	Standard deviation	3.77	2.03	1.17	2.14
	Domestic peaks*	0.37	0	·0	0.38
	International peaks*	0.01	0	0	0
	Maximum rate	25	14	8.4	14
High-tech electronic/ electrical products	Standard deviation	2.87	3.37	0.42	2.22
	Domestic peaks*	0.36	0	0	0.48
	International peaks*	0	0	0	0
	Maximum rate	9.5	14	3.3	15
High technology n.e.s.	Standard deviation	2.35	1.75	0.28	2.2
	Domestic peaks*	0.27	0	0	0.38
	International peaks*	0	0	0	0
	Maximum rate	11	7.7	3.9	16

Note: * – As a share of total number of lines

Source: UNCTAD (2003)

Non-tariff Barriers (NTBs): European Union

As tariffs are lowered other impediments to trade become more apparent. The use of NTBs is difficult to monitor because these instruments are generally less transparent than tariffs. Most indicators focus on the incidence or frequency of use of NTBs (Table 5.9) and do not capture the restrictiveness of such measures. In general, however, the EU and the US seem to have a more restrictive NTB regime than the other countries.

Table 5.9: Frequency of core NTBs of selected countries

	1993	1996
Australia	0.7	0.7
Mexico	2.0	14.1
Canada	8.3	7.3
US	23.0	16.7
EU	22.1	13.0
Japan	11.4	9.9

Note: The frequency ratio is the proportion of national tariff lines that are affected by a particular non-tariff barrier (NTB) or by a specified group of NTBs, irrespective of whether the products affected are actually imported.

Source: WTO (2001)

Quotas

The EU continues to impose quotas on imports from China of footwear, tableware and kitchenware (ceramic, porcelain and china), as well as surveillance on certain products. Upon the accession of China to the WTO, the EU made the commitment progressively to liberalise these quotas, removing them by 2005. Products from China that are subject to surveillance include glassware, toys, footwear and bicycles. The EU also maintains quotas on certain steel products imported from Kazakhstan, the Russian Federation and the Ukraine, and maintains surveillance on imports of certain steel products from these origins.

Anti-dumping duties

As tariffs and quotas on agricultural products and textile and apparel products are phased out, anti-dumping actions are emerging as the major form of trade restriction. The 1947 GATT agreement defines dumping as the practice whereby 'the products of one country are introduced into the commerce of another country at less than normal value of the products'. It permitted dumping duties only if such actions caused 'material injury' to domestic industry. However, in the EU anti-dumping law the conditions under which the duties are allowed are not laid out clearly and the EC has considerable discretion in the choice of measures it can take (Tharakan, 1991). Further, the EU, like other countries, often tinkers with the rules to broaden the scope and availability of AD protection (Hindley and Messerlin 1996). Anti-dumping measures by the EU have become an important device of protectionism, thereby reducing consumer welfare and distorting the working of free markets. As Blonigen and Prusa (2001) note "antidumping is a trade policy where the institutional process surrounding the investigation and determinations has significant impacts beyond the antidumping duty we observe, and where the filing decision, the legal determination, and the protective impact are all endogenous with firms' decisions in the market, leading to a wealth of potential strategic actions and distorted market outcomes."

During the period 1990–1999 quotas and AD duties tended to be concentrated in the same sectors. The decline in quotas during this period has often been compensated for by expanding products under AD measures, in particular consumer electronics, textiles as well as fisheries and mining. The few sectors where NTBs have not been replaced by AD duties are cars and other transport equipment, which rely on lack of competition at the distribution level, subsidies, tied contract and public procurement as well as on some not-too-specific informal agreements that succeeded the formal ones when quota arrangements were lifted in 2000. The AD duty levels are significant. In the EU they are typically of the order of 25 per cent; the percentage for the US is slightly higher at about 30–35 per cent. Individual measures often exceed this percentage with AD duties of more than 100 per cent (Table 5.10). This suggests that anti-dumping measures are likely to have had a major impact upon trade. The average duty is considerably higher than the level of tariff protection with the exception of agricultural goods and products such as tobacco and alcoholic drinks.

Table 5.10: Duty level of AD orders imposed by the European Union

Product	Against	Duty level
Television camera systems	Japan	200%
Woven polyolefin sacks	China	124%

Source: Neufeld (2001)

As of 1 January 2002, the EU had in place definitive anti-dumping measures (duties and/or undertakings) on 175 product categories, down from 192 in 1999. Tables 5.11 and 5.12 report AD initiations and final measures taken by the EU, Canada, the US and Mexico between 1995 and 2002. The EU is the second most frequent user of these measures, behind the US. Although some 40 per cent of the anti-dumping investigations initiated by the EU are terminated without measures being taken they are still protective in effect, because of the threat that they might be imposed. This threat induces foreign producers and their importers to raise prices, as in a cartel, to avoid AD duty. Also, needless to say, the amount of duty collected may be very small because of the duty's effect in preventing and discouraging trade.

Over the years certain broad patterns have emerged in terms of the countries being targeted by the EU. For periods during the early 1980s the countries of central and eastern Europe were generally the most frequently targeted. During the mid to late 1980s these were to a large extent replaced by Asian countries, initially Japan and then, in turn, South Korea, Thailand, Indonesia, Malaysia and so on. At present, it is India and China which are facing the largest number of complaints. Indeed, over the six year period 1993–1998, China has been the major target of EU anti-dumping cases with 26, followed by India (22), Korea (17) and Thailand (14). At the end of 2001 China was the most affected, with 34 cases, followed by Chinese Taipei, and Thailand, with 13 cases each. Since 2000 the EU has launched anti-

Table 5.11: AD sectoral distribution of initiations by reporting member – 01/01/95 to 31/12/02

Reporting member	VI	VII	XI	XV	XVI	Others	Total
EU	45	17	32	92	38	37	267
Mexico	10	4	5	20	4	8	59
US	26	20	3	190	14	7	292
Canada	4	0	0	73	2	15	107

Note:

VI   Products of the chemical or allied industries

VII   Plastics and articles thereof, Rubber and articles thereof

XI   Textiles and textile articles

XV   Base metals and articles of base metal

XVI   Machinery and mechanical appliances, electrical equipment, parts thereof, sound recorders and reproducers, television image and sound recorders and reproducers, and parts and accessories of such articles.

Source: WTO (2003)

Table 5.12: AD sectoral distribution of measures by reporting member – 01/01/95 to 31/12/02

Reporting member	VI	VII	XI	XV	XVI	Others	Total
Canada	1	0	0	48	1	7	67
EU	31	13	15	65	21	17	164
Mexico	9	4	2	28	1	4	55
US	20	6	2	131	7	6	192

Note: Categories as for Table 5.11

Source: WTO (2003)

dumping proceedings against electronic firms (CDs) from Taiwan and India as well as against Chinese colour television firms such as Xoceco, Changhong, TCL, HiSense, Skyworth, Panda, Furi and Konka. When anti-dumping tariffs are applied, they are significant (Table 5.13 and Table 5.14).

As for sectoral distribution, four industries accounted for 80 per cent of all cases initiated by the EU between 1995 and 2003: base metal, textiles, chemical, and electrical and non-electrical machinery (Table 5.15). Further, around 70 per cent of all initiations resulted in the imposition of anti-dumping duties. The number of initiations of new investigations in 1999 rose three-fold to 66 and included items such as compact disc boxes and colour-television picture tubes. The EU also had 16 definitive countervailing measures in place, up from six in 1999, with products from India the most frequently affected. Safeguard action was taken in March 2002 on 15 steel products in response to the US safeguard action on steel imports. Supplementary duties are to be triggered if volumes rise above 2001 levels to prevent diversion of trade from the US market onto the EU market. The Commission also proposed the Council agree additional duties of between 8 per cent and 100 per cent on imported products from the US as 're-balancing' measures, given the failure of the two parties to agree compensation for the Article XIX measure on steel imposed by the US. The EU continues to make frequent use of the special safeguard mechanism under the WTO Agreement on Agriculture to impose 'snap-back' tariffs (whereby tariffs are raised in response to a surge in imports).

AD duties impose significant costs on the economy. Domestic and foreign firms alter their pricing behaviour to influence the outcome of potential AD investigations (Blonigen and Prusa, 2003) typically raising prices in order to avoid an AD duty. This effectively transfers AD revenue to the foreign firm via a cartel-style benefit. Analysing a case where four Japanese exporters were alleged to be selling a chemical product in the EU at a price below the competitive market price (dumping), Lloyd et al. (1998) find that the unwarranted imposition of an AD measure increased the cost to consumers by 35 per cent of the import bill. EU producers initiated a case against four Japanese exporters on 24 June 1981 and an AD measure was imposed on 18 June 1982. While the product is a minor one – polypropylene film (PPF), a bulk thermoplastic polymer used in packaging and as a structural material

Table 5.13: EU Anti-dumping tariffs on Taiwanese companies

Company	Tariff (%)
Ritek, Prodisc, Auvistar, Unidisk	18.8
Acer Media, Digital Storage, Gigastorage, Lead Data Megamedia, Po Hsin Multimedia	20.1
Princo	29.9
All others	39.5

Source: DigiTimes (2001)

Table 5.14: EU Anti-dumping duties against Japanese consumer electronics and office machinery imports

	Investigation started	Definitive measures	Duty levels (%)	Date of repeal
Typewriters	1984	1986	17–35	16.06.1993
Copiers	1985	1987	7–20	04.10.1997
CD players	1987	1989	8–32	24.08.1993
Computer printers	1987	1988	5–47	17.11.1993
Videorecorders	1987	1989	13	16.02.1994
Halogen lamps	1989	1991	36–47	20.01.1996
Audiocassettes	1989	1991	2–26	04.05.1996

Source: Belderbos (2003)

Table 5.15: Anti-Dumping sectoral distribution of initiations and measures, 1995–2003

| | Anti-dumping sectoral distribution of initiations | | | | | | | | |
	(1)	(2)	(3)	(4)	(5)	(6)	(7)	(8)	Total
EU	45	20	9	34	92	39	12	23	274
US	43	20	2	6	200	17	2	39	329

| | Anti-dumping sectoral distribution of measures | | | | | | | | |
	(1)	(2)	(3)	(4)	(5)	(6)	(7)	(8)	Total
EU	35	13	7	17	71	26	3	15	187
US	24	9	1	2	134	7	2	26	205

Notes:

(1) Products of the chemical or allied industries

(2) Plastics and articles thereof; rubber and articles thereof

(3) Wood and articles of wood

(4) Textiles and textile articles

(5) Base metals and articles of base metal

(6) Machinery, mechanical appliances; electrical equipment

(7) Miscellaneous manufactured articles

(8) Others

Source: WTO (2004b)

(a substitute for wood, paper, metals and plastic) – and the absolute amounts are low, the implications are that EU anti-dumping measures can impose a high cost to consumers.

There are further non-tariff measures which the EU imposes on certain sectors. The most burdensome regime of all concerns the pharmaceutical sector. It remains among the few with price controls in the EU resulting in wide differences between prices among Member States. Foreign pharmaceutical companies encounter consistent market access problems throughout the EU due to the price, volume and access controls placed on medicines by national governments and Member States's public health authorities. As a result, since controlled prices vary greatly from one Member State to another, intermediaries engage in parallel trade (profiting at pharmaceutical companies' expense by buying drugs in countries where the price is lower and selling them in Member States where the price is set at a higher level). It is estimated that parallel trade within the EU increased in the 1990s – from approximately 1 per cent to 1.4 per cent of the total market value between 1990 and 1997 (European Communities, 1997). In the Netherlands the share of parallel trade rose from 5 per cent in 1990 to 14 per cent in 1997, and for certain products in some Member States the market penetration rate of parallel trade is as high as 50 per cent (European Communities, 1997). Another impediment stems from the EU policy of testing each batch of pharmaceuticals imported from the US for quality at the point of entry. The testing obligation is costly and time-consuming, delays market access and increases market costs. It places US-based pharmaceutical manufacturers at a competitive disadvantage. Each EU Member State still maintains widely differing standards, testing and certification procedures for some pharmaceutical products.

State Aid

State aid is another way, though not always visible, of protecting domestic industries. Although state aid to manufacturing relative to value added fell in the majority of Member States between 1995 and 2000, EU-wide aid granted to manufacturing in 2000 still amounted to a significant € 24 billion or 1.6 per cent of value added in this sector. During the period of 1997–99 grants were the leading form of state aid to manufacturing (61 per cent), followed by tax exemptions (22 per cent). Among the Member States, over 90 per cent of state aid is provided in grant form in Greece, Luxembourg, Spain and the United Kingdom, while less than one-third is provided in this form in France and Ireland. As a share of value added Greece had the highest level of manufacturing sector assistance (4.3 per cent) between 1997–99, followed by Italy (2.7 per cent), Denmark (2.6 per cent) and Germany (2.4 per cent). The lowest proportion of state aid at 0.6 per cent of value added during the same period was in the UK (Figure 5.2). In February 2002, the Commission issued a new framework for regional aid to large investment projects to apply to all sectors for the period 2004–09, and to the motor vehicle and synthetic fibre industries as of 2003.

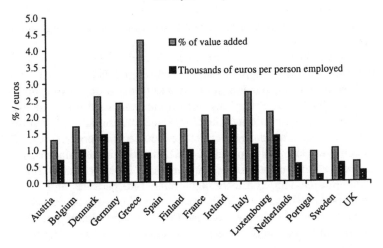

Figure 5.2: State aid to the manufacturing sector – annual averages 1997–99 in constant prices (1998)

Source: EC (2001)

As a result, the Community framework on state aid to the motor vehicle industry granted as regional assistance was extended until 31 December 2002, with a transitional mechanism in place for 2003.

Aid to shipbuilding was to be discontinued but its prolongation has been proposed on a 'defensive' basis. Aid to the coal mining industry will continue until 2010. Although most EU mines cannot compete with imported coal, the industry that remains in four Member States has long been assisted on social and regional grounds. In 2000, the Commission authorised €6.8 billion in state aid to coal under the current framework, mainly to cover operating losses, averaging €192 per tonne, or €76,405 for each of the 89,000 workers employed in the industry.

Non-tariff Barriers: United States

Quantitative import restrictions in the US are imposed mainly under the Agreement on Textiles and Clothing. Quotas apply to over half of clothing imports and 32 per cent of textile imports. Over 1000 quotas are applied to 45 countries, including 37 WTO members. These measures are combined with relatively high MFN tariffs.

Tax breaks are another form of NTB used by the US. The WTO last year gave the EU permission to impose tariffs, ruling that the US offers generous but illegal tax breaks to big American exporters such as Boeing Co. The Commission initiated a safeguard investigation on 21 steel products on 27 March 2002, and took provisional action on the same date on 15 steel products in response to the US safeguard action on imports of steel, effective on 20 March 2002; a dispute settlement proceeding was also initiated on 13 March 2002. Supplementary duties of between 14.9 per cent and 26 per cent are to be triggered by volumes rising above levels of trade set at 2001 levels (the average reached for 1999–2001 plus 10 per cent), to prevent diversion of third-party trade from the US market onto the EU market.

The US along with the EU continues to be the major user of anti-dumping actions. Lindsey and Ikenson (2003) show how healthy competition is termed 'unfair' and punished with high antidumping duties in the US. According to them the US antidumping law, as it currently stands, has nothing to do with maintaining a 'level playing field' and for years US companies have used the antidumping law to see off competition from foreign firms that give consumers a lower price. The US continues to make active use of AD and countervailing (CV) measures, mainly in the steel sector. Assistance to non-agricultural sectors, notably fisheries, lumber and timber, aeronautics and shipbuilding, is provided mainly in the form of tax incentives.

To sum up the evidence on NTBs, both the EU and the US make use of non-tariff barriers in manufacturing. However, compared to the EU the US imposes relatively fewer non-tariff controls on manufactured imports (OECD, 1997a). The protected sectors now occupy relatively insignificant roles in both production and employment in the EU as well as in the US as these economies have graduated to higher value added sectors in high-tech manufacturing and services. However, trade in manufacturing continues to be stifled by a combination of import quotas and anti-dumping duties.

5.5 QUANTIFYING 'OVERALL' BARRIERS TO TRADE IN MANUFACTURING PRODUCTS

As we have just seen, the considerable reduction of tariffs in recent years has rendered other forms of protection more important including quotas, voluntary export restraints (VERs), anti-dumping duties, subsidies and biased government procurement.

How does the EU raise prices above world prices using such non-tariff barriers?

Manufacturing is a declining industry in the West: it is uncompetitive for obvious reasons, because we have emerging markets like China that undercut it so massively. What is left is in specialised, high-technology and niche areas. In our economy we have largely let market forces take effect, with generally favourable results for employment and growth; as a result we have let manufacturing go where it was essentially uneconomic. That has not happened to the same extent on the continent. As a result we find there a great deal of protectionist pressure. The EU is accordingly a customs union: for raising tariffs externally on manufactured imports, so that prices are kept up inside the European Union for manufactures. The evidence of this systematic raising of prices above world levels is widespread and striking – as Tables 5.17–5.19 of this chapter clearly show. In addition to tariffs, now generally quite small, the European Union protects manufacturing through quotas in certain areas like textiles, but mainly through anti-dumping measures and equivalent measures. Anti-dumping operates both through explicit duties and through the threat of levying them, which often results in importers raising their prices instead. The latter action is more costly to us because not only do our consumers pay higher prices, the excess revenues resulting do not go to EU governments including the UK but rather to foreign non-EU producers.

Measures with an equivalent effect to anti-dumping threats are formal and informal agreements within industries to restrict external trade – for example, the agreement between EU and Japanese producers over cars which limited Japanese imports in return for permission to the Japanese to invest in the EU. This agreement has formally expired; but there has been no effective action to bring prices down to world levels since it expired. It would seem that in industry after industry the EU authorities have allowed or encouraged effective cartels to flourish; any foreign producer wishing to break into the market is either persuaded to do so at existing EU prices or else is discouraged from entering at all. EU competition authorities make great play with investigations of 'domestic competition' to establish that prices are no higher than other EU prices; but they make no effort to ensure that prices come down to world levels through effective international competition. The result of this neglect is to be seen in the high margins by which EU prices exceed world prices.

Why does the EU not ensure that full competition prevails in the EU market? The reason is likely to be job losses, given the high levels of unemployment already prevailing in the EU. The EU Commission is already unpopular with member governments and their client industries for preventing public subsidy of favoured sectors and firms. Imagine how this unpopularity would grow were the Commission to force down prices to world levels, thus reducing employment and output in EU industries. Consumers in these countries should applaud; but their voices are not powerful at the EU level because of the EU's 'democratic deficit'. It is only governments by and large that wield power at the EU level and they are most beholden to their industries' representatives. It is no doubt for this reason that the EU Competition authorities devote their time to attacking foreign firms' 'monopoly' actions in the EU market – the most notable recent example being Microsoft whose products have greatly benefited EU consumers.

The EU domestic market in manufactures has thus become one in which there are no prizes for undercutting the prevailing cartel level of prices. A foreign producer breaking into this market with lower prices to gain a substantial share would face retaliation from existing suppliers; this would frustrate its plans in spite of its no doubt substantial marketing costs. The cost meanwhile to the much-larger dominant cartel would be simply a loss of revenue equal to the incursor's price advantage times its attempted volume of sales. It is well-known that such tactics pay a cartel and are likely to lead to a settlement in which the incursor either goes away or else agrees to limit its share and raise its prices to the cartel level.

For international competition to prevail it would be necessary for the EU Competition Office to protect foreign producers in their efforts to enter the home market; they should penalise any retaliation by home producers and break up home cartels. Of such actions however there is no sign.

Measuring 'overall' barriers to trade which take into account all NTBs such as discussed above is not straight forward. Messerlin (2001) estimates 'overall' protection taking into account all the key trade barriers – the study estimates and then combines the ad valorem tariff equivalents of the NTBs (for the manufacturing sector, for example, these include essentially import quotas and voluntary export restraints together with tariffs). His results suggest that the level of protection for industrial goods in the EU economy was roughly 10 to 11 per cent from 1990 to 1995 and continued to be at around 8 per cent in 1999, almost two times higher than the conventional estimate. Further, the most heavily protected sectors such as textiles and apparel and consumer electronics exhibit almost constant rates of protection between 1990 and 1997, and a limited decline from 1997 to 1999. Most of this protection will remain unchanged at least until 2005, when the dismantling of the quota regime in textiles and clothing is to take place. The rate of overall protection was over 10 per cent for one-fourth of the industrial sector, over 20 per cent for almost one-sixth, and more than 30 per cent for the clothing sector. AD duties contribute 13 per cent to the rate of overall protection where they occur. Labour-weighted rates of overall protection are higher than corresponding simple averages, suggesting that the EU overall protection is concentrated in labour-intensive sectors where unions are powerful.

Price Gaps as a Measure of Protection

With so many barriers to trade it seems that the only way to account for all of them is to exploit the information on prices of the similar goods in different countries. Free trade should eliminate (quality-adjusted) price disparities in traded goods apart from a margin for transportation, distribution and marketing.

Before we review the evidence on price disparities within the EU and the US, it should be noted that there has been a rising trend in the seizures of counterfeit goods in the EU (Table 5.16) which could be attributed among other reasons, to relatively high prices in the EU of original brand goods. In 1999, fraud amounted to €377 million (2.7 per cent of total import duty revenue collected); cigarettes and dairy produce were the two leading products. With respect to counterfeit and pirated goods, the customs administra-

Table 5.16: Seizures of counterfeit and pirated goods in EU Member States, 1999–2000 (Number of cases)

	EU	D	E	F	I	P	UK
1999	4694	2173	159	252	129	5	866
2000	6253	3185	144	435	174	15	1179

Note: D: Germany; E: Spain; F: France; I: Italy; P: Portugal; UK: United Kingdom

Source: WTO (2002)

tions recorded an increase of one-third in seizures from 1999 to 2000, under legislation implementing the TRIPS Agreement at the border. About half of the 6253 cases concerned clothing and accessories, followed by books and audio/video material (16 per cent). The trend continued in 2001 with a further increase of 27 per cent in the number of cases.

Evidence on international price differences between the EU and the US is provided by three recent surveys: 1) the Arthur Andersen survey (1999) for electrical goods, 2) ACNielsen (2000) survey for food products, and 3) the Bradford and Lawrence study (2004) for food and manufacturing products.

The Arthur Andersen study confirms that electrical goods prices are higher in the EU compared with the US: between 21 per cent and 80 per cent in 1998. There are two clear findings (Table 5.17). First, the US is significantly cheaper than the EU, notably for brown goods. Second, the UK is in about the middle of the pack of European countries.

ACNielsen on behalf of the UK government (ACNielsen, 2000) undertook a study to compare prices of a large number of goods in the UK, US, France and Germany. The comparisons were based on the price spread rather than the average price. The study originally collected 21,023 prices for 106 items in four countries. For their final report, Nielsen was forced to drop 10,374 price observations for lack of comparability and lack of availability of goods. Almost all consumer durables such as fridges, washing machines,

Table 5.17: Percentage deviation from the US price

	PCs[a]	Brown Goods[b]	White Goods[c]	Small Domestic Appliances[d]
US Price (£)	647	799	854	103
UK	24.0	66.3	11.2	55.3
Belgium	69.6	102.3	36.4	23.3
Sweden	38.9	118.8	47.3	14.6
France	27.0	74.1	18.9	68.0
Germany	8.2	77.0	32.9	37.9
Italy	38.9	65.8	−0.4	9.7
Spain	−3.2	64.6	0.1	5.8
European Average	29.1	81.3	21.0	30.7

Notes:

[a] PCs: notebooks and desktops,

[b] Brown goods: Audio home systems, cameras, camcorders, TVs and VCRs,

[c] White goods: refrigerators, dishwashers and washing machines,

[d] Small domestic appliances: Irons, toasters, vacuum cleaners.

Source: The Arthur Andersen study reported in Haskel and Wolf (2002)

cameras and camcorders were discarded since they were 'genuinely non-comparable' (ACNielson, 2000). A large number of items were also excluded, citing high within-country price variations. For 45 out of their remaining 56 goods the study found an overlap between the spread of prices in two countries. Hence, it was concluded that there were no significant differences between countries for the bulk of the products. Eleven goods showed significant price difference among countries, eight of which were significantly more expensive in the UK and three were significantly cheaper in the UK (Table 5.18). The survey concluded that the results do not provide much support for the 'rip-off Britain' hypothesis. The results indicate that the difference between the UK and the rest of the EU are minor relative to the difference between the EU and the US.

Table 5.18: ACNielsen survey: price comparison

	UK	Germany	France	US
More expensive in the UK				
Top 10 CDs	12.91	8.88	11.06	9.18
Sega Dreamcast	200.12	160.77	163.00	132.26
Coca-cola, 21	1.31	0.85	0.82	0.80
Ground coffee	1.95	1.26	1.37	1.31
Non-branded lager	0.92	0.36	0.36	0.49
Dog food (800g equiv)	0.79	0.64	0.64	0.62
Shampoo, 250 ml equiv	2.18	1.35	1.56	1.13
Toilet paper	1.82	1.01	0.81	0.88
Less expensive in the UK				
Kellogg's Cornflakes 500g equiv	1.09	1.4	1.38	1.63
Chocolate chip cookies 200g equiv	0.62	0.99	0.72	0.84
Long-sleeved men's shirts	14.87	22.86	21.63	23.02

Source: ACNielsen (2000)

The most comprehensive and detailed study of price comparison between the US and Europe is by Bradford and Lawrence (2004) who analyse price data for food and industrial products. Effort is made to ensure comparability and to eliminate the effects of distribution margins. Results (Table 5.19) show that in 1999 consumer prices were relatively low in the US (Canada had the lowest). European consumer prices were lowest in Italy and highest in the UK. The absolute price differential between European countries averaged 17.5 per cent.

Based on imputed producer prices, which is a better way to measure the effect of trade barriers (it excludes distribution costs), again it is the US which had the lowest prices. European countries had significantly higher producer prices in 1993 with Italy having prices 85 per cent above the lowest in the sample and the UK with 72 per cent.

The information on price disparities within different markets

Table 5.19: Prices relative to the lowest price in the sample

| | 1990 | 1993 | 1999 | 1990 | 1993 | 1999 |
	Consumer prices			Producer prices		
Belgium	1.41	1.57	1.45	1.66	1.82	1.7
Germany	1.48	1.67	1.38	1.61	1.75	1.48
Italy	1.44	1.71	1.24	1.57	1.85	1.34
Netherlands	1.36	1.64	1.38	1.62	1.80	1.65
UK	1.38	1.54	1.61	1.60	1.72	1.78
US	1.16	1.13	1.21	1.19	1.16	1.24

Note: Data are expenditure weighted average ratios of goods prices to the lowest price in the sample.

Source: Bradford and Lawrence (2004)

Table 5.20: Fragmentation indices

	1990	1996	1999
Belgium	1.42	1.65	1.42
Germany	1.39	1.60	1.29
Italy	1.38	1.36	1.21
Netherlands	1.42	1.58	1.41
UK	1.41	1.41	1.50
US	1.16	1.14	1.15

Note: Data are expenditure-weighted average ratios of imputed producer prices to the landed prices of goods from the country with the lowest level of price in the sample.

Source: Bradford and Lawrence (2004)

presented above needs to be converted into an estimate of trade
protection if it is to be used to measure welfare costs of trade barriers. Bradford (2003) uses OECD price data on 124 traded goods
for eight countries – the US, the UK, Canada, Australia, Germany,
Japan, Belgium and the Netherlands – to arrive at an estimate of
price gap (adjusted for distribution and transport costs) as a measure of the extent of protection. The results are aggregated into 28
sectors – agriculture/fishery/forestry and 27 manufactured products. Bradford and Lawrence (2004) extend the work of Bradford
(2003) to add Italy to the original eight countries and calculate
implied tariff levels for 1996 and 1999 in addition to the 1993 estimates in the earlier paper. Input-output tables are used to eliminate distribution margins from final goods prices and thereby provide estimates of border and ex-factory prices. The results of protection measures confirm that the US consistently has the lowest
level of protection between 1990 and 1999 (1.15 in 1999), suggesting that price competition in the US is greater than in European
countries. Excepting Italy, the indices for European countries were
high in 1999: Germany 1.29, the Netherlands 1.41; Belgium 1.42;
and the UK 1.50 (Table 5.20). In the present study we have used a
modified version (trade weighted averages) of the protection rates
from Bradford (2003) to calculate welfare gains to the EU and the
UK from liberalisation (Table 5.21).

Table 5.21: Protection estimates: ratio of domestic to world price (1993)

ISIC2 Code		US	Australia	Canada	Japan
1000	Agri, fisheries and Forestry	1.16	1.07	1.11	1.58
3110/ 3120	Processed Food	1.09	1.09	1.19	2.10
3130	Beverages	1.06	1.45	1.54	1.54
3140	Tobacco	1.06	1.47	1.96	1.00
3210	Textiles	1.05	1.11	1.16	1.48
3220	Apparel	1.16	1.26	1.18	1.38
3230	Leather and Products	1.14	2.94	1.24	1.33
3240	Footwear	1.11	1.66	1.42	2.29
3320	Furniture and fixtures	1.02	1.30	1.56	2.71
3410	Paper and Products	1.05	1.44	1.06	1.80
3420	Printing and publishing	1.01	1.12	1.21	1.19
3522	Drugs and Medicines	3.11	1.00	2.68	1.22
3529	Chemical Products	1.04	1.09	1.06	1.56
3540	Petroleum and Coal Products	1.01	2.13	1.32	3.36
3550	Rubber Products	1.03	1.22	1.02	2.02
3610	Pottery, China etc	1.07	1.73	1.15	2.38
3900	Other Manufacturing, Nec	1.17	1.43	1.33	1.98
3810	Metal Products	1.02	1.01	1.23	1.00
3825	Office and Computing Machinery	1.18	1.34	1.30	1.56
3829	Machinery and Equipment, nec	1.03	1.18	1.20	1.23
3832	Radio, TV, and Communication Equipment	1.07	1.54	1.32	2.11
3839	Electrical Apparatus, nec	1.00	1.28	1.11	1.20
3841	Shipbuilding and repairing	1.02	1.37	1.09	1.24
3842	Railroad Equipment	1.11	1.22	1.20	1.00
3843	Motor vehicles	1.06	1.23	1.25	1.00
3844	Motorcycles and Bicycles	1.00	1.19	1.08	1.02
3845	Aircraft	1.06	1.52	1.11	1.32
3849	Transport Equipment, nec	1.07	1.13	1.08	1.08
3850	Professional Goods	1.03	1.24	1.21	2.35

Source: Bradford, 2003

Table 5.21: Protection estimates: ratio of domestic to world price (1993) continued

ISIC2 Code		Belgium	Netherlands	Germany	UK
1000	Agri, fisheries and Forestry	1.16	1.53	1.08	1.65
3110/ 3120	Processed Food	1.37	1.45	1.30	1.20
3130	Beverages	1.44	1.77	1.33	1.69
3140	Tobacco	1.95	3.53	1.39	2.22
3210	Textiles	1.22	1.10	1.14	1.24
3220	Apparel	1.57	1.46	1.28	1.07
3230	Leather and Products	1.78	1.44	1.66	1.17
3240	Footwear	1.82	1.33	2.24	1.03
3320	Furniture and fixtures	1.96	1.39	1.47	2.17
3410	Paper and Products	1.66	1.61	1.97	1.78
3420	Printing and publishing	1.31	1.02	1.34	1.03
3522	Drugs and Medicines	1.69	2.64	3.35	1.85
3529	Chemical Products	1.14	1.11	1.08	1.06
3540	Petroleum and Coal Products	3.38	2.85	4.34	4.07
3550	Rubber Products	1.68	1.71	1.66	1.57
3610	Pottery, China etc	1.01	1.51	1.02	1.08
3900	Other Manufacturing, Nec	1.62	1.77	1.84	1.60
3810	Metal Products	1.51	1.45	2.10	1.67
3825	Office and Computing Machinery	1.68	1.33	1.52	1.39
3829	Machinery and Equipment, nec	1.56	1.30	1.43	1.24
3832	Radio, TV, and Communication Equipment	1.94	1.71	1.56	1.32
3839	Electrical Apparatus, nec	1.27	1.35	1.55	1.54
3841	Shipbuilding and repairing	1.31	1.40	1.51	1.50
3842	Railroad Equipment	1.35	1.32	1.65	1.68
3843	Motor vehicles	1.76	1.60	1.39	2.00
3844	Motorcycles and Bicycles	1.20	1.28	1.46	1.45
3845	Aircraft	2.03	1.89	2.07	1.92
3849	Transport Equipment, nec	1.57	1.38	1.37	1.59
3850	Professional Goods	1.81	1.86	1.64	1.42

Source: Bradford, 2003

5.6 COST OF TRADE PROTECTION

There have been a number of attempts to estimate in quantitative terms the potential gains from trade liberalisation. However, in recent years there have been only a few studies which concentrate on the manufacturing sector, some of which we review here. This is not surprising since the liberalisation of trade in industrial goods, especially reduction in tariff protection, is well advanced compared with agriculture and services in the developed countries.

Hufbauer et al. (2002) estimate the potential benefits to the world economy from attaining the degree of competition and market integration that currently exists within the US (Table 5.22). The study uses partial equilibrium analysis to assess the benefits from narrowing the worldwide price dispersion to the range now observed in the US. The potential benefits of price convergence for selected regional groups are larger for the ASEAN free trade area and the Southern Cone Common Market than for the NAFTA and the EU.

Table 5.22: Potential Benefits at Regional Level (% of GDP) of attaining US level of competition and market integration

	Market exchange rates	EIU PPP rates
EU 11	0.75	0.59
NAFTA	0.13	0.14
AFTA	4.54	6.05
Mercosur	7.11	1.73

Source: Hufbauer et al. (2002)

Using a CGE model, Gallaway et al. (1999) estimate the net cost of hundreds of AD/CV orders at around 0.06 per cent of GDP in 1993 for the US. This figure is substantially higher than if AD duties were just standard tariffs. They found that if one only estimates the effect of the AD duties that are observed in 1993, the net welfare loss to the US is $209 million annually. However, when one takes into account the previous recalculations that had occurred through administrative reviews, the welfare loss for the

US is of a larger magnitude, with a range of 0.03 to 0.06 per cent of GDP annually. Of this loss, changes in rent transfers account for roughly half of the impact, with the remaining portion attributable to efficiency gains and relative price effects.

Using a trade gravity model Wall (1999) estimates the total effect of US protection on US merchandise imports, and ROW protection on US merchandise exports for 1996. A gravity model relates trade to the size ('gravity') of economies as well as their distance from each other (reflecting transport costs). US protection decreased its merchandise imports from non-NAFTA countries by 15.4 per cent or about 1.7 per cent of US GDP. Including trade with Mexico and Canada, US protection decreased its imports by 10.4 per cent, whereas ROW protection decreased US exports by 17 per cent. As for welfare costs Wall (1999) estimates that on average, a $1 decrease in imports due to import protection translates into a $2 decrease in consumer surplus. Also, of each $1 that consumers lose, $0.49 is transferred to producers, and $0.11 is deadweight loss (that is, loss of welfare). Applying these numbers to the estimates above, import protection in 1996 cost US consumers $223 billion or 3.3 per cent of GDP. Of this, $109 billion was transferred to producers, and $24 billion (0.3 per cent of GDP) was welfare loss. The remainder consists of tariff revenue and quota rents. Using the Hufbauer and Elliott (1994) estimate of an average decrease of 9 per cent in the world prices of protected goods, the terms of trade gain to the US from its tariffs was $1.5 billion, making the net welfare cost of protection to the US 1.43 per cent of GDP in 1996.

As for the gains from EU integration, Gasiorek et al. (2002) use a CGE model incorporating imperfect competition and increasing returns to scale to study the accession of the UK to the EC. The results suggest that the gains from European integration are rather small – in the order of 1 per cent of GDP. Significant costs are however, imposed by the protection measures imposed by the EU on the rest of the world. Messerlin (2001) estimates that costs of protection (including NTBs) for European consumers in agriculture and industrial goods amounted to €93 billion or 2.2 per cent of GDP in 1990. The costs are reduced to €71–74 billion if the effects of only tariffs are taken into account. Messerlin (2001) notes that these estimates are larger than the costs of tariff protection for the US estimated by Hufbauer and Elliott (1994) at €55 billion (at the 1990 exchange rate) or 1.25 per cent of US GDP. In the manufacturing sector, costs of protection represents almost one-fifth of the value added of these sectors (Messerlin, 2001).

In a recent study Bradford and Lawrence (2004) calculate the effects of eliminating these barriers using the CGE model of Harrison et al (1995) for three scenarios:

1. Unilateral removal of barriers in each of the countries considered against all other countries worldwide.

2. Multilateral removal of barriers by all 8 countries at once.

3. A preferential trade agreement between the eight countries, with barriers on the Rest of the world.

Table 5.23: Gains from removal of protection (% of GDP)

	Unilateral liberalisation	Multilateral liberalisation*	FTA*
Germany	1.28	2.26	1.96
Italy	1.97	3.46	4.61
Netherlands	3.84	7.71	9.38
UK	3.21	4.29	2.79
US	0.40	1.02	1.35

Note: *Other countries included here are Australia, Canada and Japan.

Source: Bradford and Lawrence (2004)

As Table 5.23 shows, the relatively low trade barriers in the US and its low ratio of trade to GDP result in relatively small gains to the US (0.4 per cent of GDP from unilateral opening and 1 per cent from multilateral opening). At the other end, the Netherlands gains 3.8 per cent and 7.7 per cent of GDP from unilateral and multilateral liberalisation respectively. The UK benefits 3.2 per cent and 4.3 per cent of GDP from the UK and multilateral opening respectively. The simulations confirm that substantial benefits will accrue to European Union countries from trade competition.

5.7 CONCLUSION

Contrary to widely-held belief trade protection remains high in certain manufacturing industries in the EU, notably labour-intensive products and consumer goods. With a decline in tariffs over the past few decades, their place has been taken by import quotas, anti-dumping penalties, state aid and other non-tariff barriers. Time and again, economic studies have shown that import restraints result in high costs to consumers and reduce economic welfare. It is clear that the potential gains from eliminating remaining trade barriers in manufacturing are considerable and the EU needs to undertake trade reforms for its own benefit.

6 Services

6.1 INTRODUCTION

Developed economies around the world have become increasingly service oriented, the EU being no exception. Services account for more than two-thirds of employment and GDP in the EU. In most other industrial countries services now typically account for around 70 per cent of output. Services also play an important intermediary role that is not easily reflected in statistics. Well functioning financial, transportation and distribution systems are critical for the smooth running of the economy.

The role of services in production is, however, not reflected in its share of world trade. Services account for no more than one-fifth of total cross-border trade, though this does not include the substantial volume of trade done through the other modes of supply – in particular through commercial establishments in the export market. All services are in principle internationally tradable. The non-tradability of a significant number of services has been mainly due to two reasons. First, the very nature of services and technical constraints make it difficult to disconnect production from consumption and to supply customers at a distance. In recent years, however, technological advances have enabled consumption of certain services (for example, online banking) without having to be physically present. Second, the low volume of trade in services has been policy induced; there have traditionally been significant barriers to service trade in many countries.

Within the EU core services such as telecommunications, air transport and to a lesser extent financial services have long been shielded from both internal and external competition. In recent years, the 1985 Single Market Programme in Services and the 1990s extensions to it such as the 1997 Single Market Action Plan (SMP) have sought to liberalise intra-EU services trade. Liberalisation of services is also taking place outside the EU with the evolution of the General Agreement on Trade in Services (GATS). In spite of these measures, the expansion of services activities across national borders in Europe continues to be hampered by a wide range of barriers.

Section 6.2 of this chapter considers the structural shift from a manufacturing to a services economy in developed countries. It discusses the significance of services for output and employment in the EU and other industrial nations. Section 6.3 reviews the statistics on trade in services. It particularly focuses on the vital role of foreign direct investment in international trade in services. Sections 6.4 and 6.6 review and quantify barriers to trade in services. The main empirical findings concerning the welfare effects of services liberalisation are outlined in section 6.7. It considers the implications of further liberalisation and how it might impact on the EU economy.

6.2   THE ROLE OF THE SERVICE SECTOR

Since the 1980s the importance of the services sector for production and employment in most developed countries has increased substantially (Table 6.1). In all countries, the services sector accounts for more than 60 per cent of output. The shift towards the services economy is most pronounced in the US and the UK with services accounting for over three-quarters of employment and total value added.

Services, which are less capital intensive than manufacturing and benefit more from increased demand as incomes rise, hold the key to more jobs in developed economies. Many traditional services such as distribution, construction, education, health and social services are particularly labour intensive. At the same time, knowledge-intensive services are increasingly important for overall job creation, both because they are growing rapidly and because they play a role in the upgrading of workers' skills. At present, regulatory barriers, taxes and minimum wages impede the development of these types of services in a number of countries, particularly in continental European countries.

Job creation in services is exceeding overall job growth in the

Table 6.1: Share of services in total value added at current prices and employment (%)

Country	Share of total value added			Share of total employment		
	1989	1994	1999	1989	1994	1999
Austria	62.2	65.0	64.9	52.7	56.0	59.2
Belgium	63.9	68.6	70.8	70.4	72.0	74.2
Denmark	68.2	71.2	71.9	69.2	71.4	73.0
Finland	57.9	62.8	63.3	60.5	64.7	65.6
France	65.9	69.5	72.0	64.8	68.7	70.6
Germany	60.7	64.4	67.7	59.2	63.6	67.5
Greece	–	66.8	68.5	–	55.9	57.6
Ireland	55.4	55.3	60.3	–	61.5	63.2
Italy	61.5	65.3	67.3	60.1	62.7	64.9
Luxembourg	–	73.4	78.4	–	69.9	73.6
The Netherlands	63.8	67.2	70.4	67.9	70.5	72.9
Portugal	–	63.6	65.4	–	57.3	58.1
Spain	–	64.4	65.7	–	63.0	62.6
Sweden	–	67.5	68.8	–	73.2	73.1
United Kingdom	61.8	66.8	70.3	68.7	73.3	75.3
United States	71.1	73.5	75.4	73.1	75.2	76.3
Canada	62.9	65.7	64.7	70.6	74.0	74.1
Mexico	62.9	67.2	66.3	52.4	54.3	53.9

Source: OECD (2002b)

OECD area. By 1997, about 64 per cent of OECD civilian workers
(which includes government workers, but excludes armed forces
personnel) were engaged in activities related to services; in nine
countries, the share exceeded 70 per cent. The overall level is up
from about 55 per cent in 1980. The share is expected to rise over
time as fast-growing knowledge-based services expand. While the
largest proportion of persons engaged in service activities in 1997
were employed in community, social and personal services (45 per
cent), implicit growth between 1980 and 1997 was strongest in the
finance, insurance, real estate and business service sector (4 per
cent per year), which increased its overall share by 4 percentage
points, to about 15 per cent. Growth in community, social and
personal services was also relatively strong (2.4 per cent), followed
by distribution (1.9 per cent) and transport and communication
(1.3 per cent). According to the OECD (2002c) some 20 million
jobs (net) were created during 1993–99 in the US, close to 90 per
cent of which were in service-related areas (including public utilities
and government). Since 1980 the service sector in the UK has
generated a net increase of over 3.75 million jobs (DTI, 2000), more
than offsetting a continued sharp contraction in manufacturing jobs
and taking the economy back to full employment.

Table 6.2 provides a summary of earnings differentials across
services sectors relative to manufacturing. Average earnings in the
service sector are higher or around the same as in the manufacturing sectors in most OECD countries (based on data for countries
with complete coverage). The main exceptions are the US and
Australia. Whereas earnings for full-time workers are substantially higher in the service sector in Australia, relative earnings for
American workers in services industries are substantially lower.

6.3   TRADE IN SERVICES

The intangibility of services makes trade in services difficult to define. Although some services may be defined through their physical
presence, for example, transport or hotel services, others such as
education are conceptually more abstract. The need in many services for proximity between the consumer and the producer implies
that one of them must move to make an international transaction
possible. Since the conventional definition of trade – where a prod-

Table 6.2: Ratio of average earnings in each sector to average earnings in manufacturing

	Total	Producer services	Service sector Distributive services	Personal services	Social services
UK*	n.a.	1.15	0.85	n.a.	n.a.
Australia	1.32	1.42	1.12	0.94	1.43
Canada	0.98	1.04	0.89	0.71	1.17
France	1.02	1.22	0.95	0.73	1.03
Netherlands	0.99	1.02	0.90	0.84	1.11
United States	0.91	1.11	0.83	0.61	1.00

Notes:
* Based on partial coverage of sectors
Data: 1999 Netherlands and US, 1998 for others

Source: OECD (2001c)

uct crosses the frontier and is registered at the border – would miss out on such transactions in services, it is now customary to define trade in services – following the General Agreement of Trade in Services (GATS) – by four modes of supply:

1. Cross-border supply from the territory of one country into that of another (for example, airlines).

2. Consumption abroad, in which the service is supplied in the territory of one country to the consumer of another (for example, tourism).

3. Supply though commercial presence in which the service supplier is legally established in the export market (for example, retail banking).

4. Supply through the movement of natural persons, meaning the temporary presence of individuals without legal personality to supply services in a country's market (for example, migrant workers).

Measurement of trade in services is inherently more difficult than measurement of trade in goods and as a result statistics on international trade in services are incomplete. No country has ever published comprehensive data of services trade covering all four modes. However, it is known that cross-border supply (mode 1) and commercial presence (mode 3) are the economically most important modes. The main source of data to capture a part of service trade is through the balance of payments statistics. These record cross-border trade, consumption abroad and to some extent trade through movement of natural persons (even then the BOP-based data cannot be clearly broken down into modes 1, 2 and 4, and nor do they provide a complete picture of mode 4). However, they do not capture services trade under mode 3, the trade of services though commercial presence. This is because a subsidiary that establishes commercial presence is a resident of the country in which it is set up: accordingly its sales to the local population are transactions between residents and so escape BOP recording. At the same time, such sales are considered trade in services under the GATS definition.[1] The only data that are readily available on mode 3 trade are those published by the US Department of Commerce on sales of foreign affiliates in the US and the sales of US affiliates abroad. It is known that a large amount of trade in services takes place via this mode and the available evidence suggests that commercial presence has been the most dynamic model of service supply in recent years. US statistics show that indirect exports of services between Europe and the US via foreign subsidiaries are twice as high as the level of cross-border trade in services between the two regions. Sales of services in Europe by US-owned affiliates were $233.6 billion in 2001, while cross-border exports of services were $104.9 billion in the same year (BEA, 2004). Correspondingly, within the EU FDI in services has grown much faster than trade in services (Figure 6.1).

The growing importance of FDI in services trade has been confirmed by other studies. The World Bank estimates the total value of world exports of services amounted to US$3.5 trillion

---

[1] A statistical domain known as Foreign Affiliates Trade in Services (FATS) is being developed by the UN Statistical Commission to measure international trade in services via mode 3. It would measure sales of services by affiliates established in foreign countries to local persons and so correspond to the GATS notion of service trade through commercial presence.

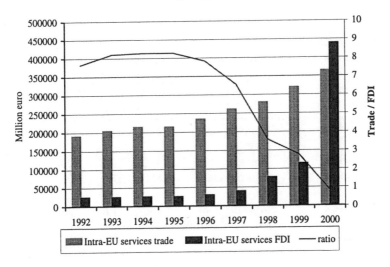

Source: EC (2002b)

Figure 6.1: Comparative evolution of intra-EU trade and FDI in services, 1992–2000

in 2001 (Table 6.3). Twenty-eight per cent of services trade was via mode 1 and 14 per cent via mode 2, with mode 3 (commercial presence such as through FDI) accounting for the lion's share with 56 per cent (Figure 6.2). According to Karsenty (2000), in 1997 cross-border supply and commercial presence each accounted for approximately 40 per cent of total world services trade (Table 6.3).

It is clear, therefore, that FDI is an important aspect of international trade in services. For many service industries, a subsidiary abroad is indispensable if a market is to be developed. Banks, insurance companies and retailers rely on direct contact with their customers. Important contributions to services FDI are being made in retailing, banking, business services and telecommunications, and, to a limited extent, in hotels and restaurants. A major reason for the expansion of international investment in services is that there is relatively more liberalisation and deregulation of investment rules than there is deregulation of barriers to cross-border trade in services.

Table 6.3: World trade in services by modes of supply (billion US$)

	Category	1997	% in total	2001	% in total
Mode 1	Commercial services	890	41.0	1000	28.2
Mode 2	Travel	430	19.8	500	14.1
Mode 3	Commercial presence	820	37.8	2000	56.3
Mode 4	Movement of natural persons	30	1.3	50	1.4
Total		2170	100	3550	100

Sources: Karsenty (2000), World Bank (2003)

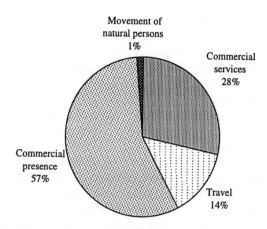

Source: Table 6.3

Figure 6.2: Value of world trade in services by mode (%) in 2001

Conventionally trade in services, which is measured excluding trade via FDI, is dominated by developed countries. OECD countries account for approximately 80 per cent of world service exports. Further intra-OECD exports account for some 80 per cent of total OECD exports (Table 6.4). The EU is the largest importer of services (39 per cent) followed by NAFTA (17 per cent). Intra-EU trade largely accounts for this dominant position of the EU in the OECD compared to other OECD regions. The US is the world's largest exporter of commercial services. US commercial services exports in 2000 were $279 billion – more than double their level 10 years ago. In addition, sales of services by US-owned affiliates overseas were $338 billion in 1999.

The quality of statistics for total trade in services is variable between pairs of countries and discrepancies persist: for example, US service exports to the EU in 2000 as recorded by US statistics were $93 billion while EU imports of services from the US were $109 billion, as recorded by EU statistics. Japan's service exports to the EU were $11.6 billion while EU imports from Japan were $9.4 billion. US exports to Japan were $35 billion while Japan's imports from the US were reported as $38 billion. The figures must be interpreted with this in mind.

UK Trade in Services

In 2001 the UK accounted for almost 8 per cent of global exports and 6 per cent of the world's imports, making it the fourth largest importer of services after the USA, Germany and Japan (ONS, 2003). The overall value of UK exports more than doubled between 1991 and 2001, from just over £32 billion to just under £78 billion. In the same period the surplus has increased from £4.1 billion in 1991 to £11.3 billion in 2001.

In 2001 the UK had a surplus with all continents except Europe (Figure 6.3) and in all service categories except travel and transport, communications and government services. The deficit with the EU is driven by a combined travel and transportation deficit of £13 billion, which is partly offset by significant surpluses for financial and other business services. The UK's deficit with Spain and Greece continued to grow, due to the rise in the number of UK visitors to these countries. However, the deficit with France decreased from £2.6 billion to £2.2 billion. The UK recorded a

Table 6.4: Estimated patterns of world and OECD trade in services, % of total world exports, 2000

Exporting region	World	Destination regions						
		OECD				America	A&O	Europe
		Total	NAFTA	EU	Other Europe			
World	100.0	75.8	21.4	39.9	4.2	27.0	24.7	45.3
OECD	77.5	61.7	16.5	34.0	4.2	20.8	14.4	40.2
NAFTA	22.5	15.9	4.9	6.9	0.6	7.8	6.2	8.0
EU	41.4	36.2	8.2	22.6	3.3	9.1	4.3	26.8
Other Europe	5.8	4.4	0.8	3.3	0.2	0.9	0.5	3.9
America	26.3	19.4	7.0	7.8	0.6	10.9	6.9	7.8
Australasia and Oceania (A&O)	22.9	12.4	4.8	3.8	0.1	5.4	12.5	4.1

Source: IMF (2002b)

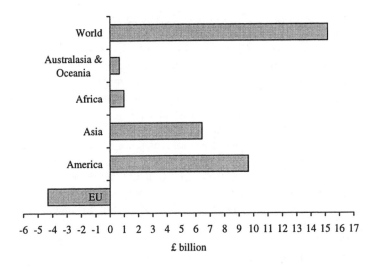

Source: ONS (2003)

Figure 6.3: UK trade balance in services, 2002

surplus of £4.8 billion with the USA in 2001 – the largest surplus for any country

The UK's single largest trading partner for both exports and imports of services, accounting for over 22 per cent of total exports and 19 per cent of total imports in 2001, is the US. The UK recorded a surplus of £4.8 billion with the US in 2001, driven mainly by insurance, financial and other business services. In comparison, the next most important export markets, Germany and France, together account for only 15 per cent of total trade in service exports.

6.4 BARRIERS TO SERVICE TRADE

Throughout the post-war period, trade in services was largely unaffected by the process of liberalisation taking place in merchandise trade. Even in industrialised countries that have relatively liberal merchandise trade regimes, barriers to trade in services and movements of natural persons remain restrictive, partly due to a possibility of market failures in some industries, but mainly as a result of the domestic influence of special interest groups sheltered from foreign competitive pressures. Traditionally service markets such as transport and telecommunications have been reserved for the monopoly supplier or made subject to strict regulations and border control. Unlike trade in goods, governments usually apply restrictions on the sale of services of foreign origin inside their territories rather than at their borders.

Because of the nature of trade in services, measures restricting trade in services differ in important ways from those in goods. Firstly, border taxes equivalent to tariffs are difficult to impose on services imports because they are often not delivered across borders. Secondly, services trade can be greatly affected by numerous internal policies that discriminate against foreign producers. These include measures that directly provide a cost advantage to domestic producers, such as subsidies, measures that impose a cost or create a competitive disadvantage for foreign producers (for example, internal direct or indirect tax instruments) and other measures which wholly or partially block market access to foreign suppliers. Finally, because of the simultaneous nature of production and consumption of many services, restrictive measures that affect the movement of factors (labour or capital) must also be considered as part of the impediments to trade in services.

Hoekman and Braga (1997) identify the following types of barriers to services trade: (i) quotas, local content, and prohibitions; (ii) price-based instruments; (iii) standards, licensing, and procurement; and (iv) discriminatory access to distribution networks.

Quantitative restrictions (QR) affect all four modes of services trade. On cross-border trade, they are most evident in the transport sectors. Foreign providers are either completely shut out of certain segments, such as cabotage (domestic flights within the boundaries of one country by an air carrier of another country), or only given limited access. In many countries, there are prohibitions directed against foreign providers of services such as domestic transportation, basic telecommunications, and legal, insurance, education, surveying, and investment advising services. On consumption abroad, quotas are sometimes implemented through foreign exchange restrictions whereby the ability of citizens to consume foreign services, such as tourism and education, is curtailed. On commercial presence, quotas are imposed on the number of foreign suppliers in the domestic market or via restrictions on foreign equity ownership in individual enterprises. Finally, quotas are most stringent on the movement of service-providing personnel and affect trade not only in professional services, but also in a variety of labour-intensive services such as construction.

Price-based barriers may take the form of visa fees, discriminatory airline landing fees, and port taxes. Tariffs can be significant barriers to trade in goods that embody services (for example, films, television programmes, computer software) or goods that are used in producing services (for example, computers, telecommunications equipment, advertising material). Further, many service sectors are subject to government sanctioned or monitored price controls; examples include air transportation, financial services, and telecommunications. Government subsidies are commonly used in service sectors such as construction, communications, and road and rail transport.

Licensing requirements are imposed on foreign providers of professional and business services which can discourage or prohibit foreign participation in the provision of services. Environmental standards may also affect service providers, particularly in transportation and tourism. Government procurement policies are often designed to favour domestic over foreign providers of services by means of preference margins and outright prohibitions. Lastly, in many countries the foreign providers have discriminatory or limited access to distribution channels and communications systems.

Services Barriers within the EU and Progress in Deregulation

In spite of the Single Market Programme, the EU is highly fragmented by national service barriers. We now proceed to detail these by sectors.

Financial services

Adopted in June 1999 in Cologne, the Financial Services Action Plan (FSAP) aims to develop a single, integrated EU capital market by 2005. It aims to create a single wholesale financial market to allow companies to raise capital on an EU-wide basis, including improvements in the EU's financial reporting structure; to complete a single EU retail market, ensuring consumer choice while maintaining consumer confidence and protection; and to underpin all this through state-of-the-art prudential rules and supervision.

According to a study by Notaro (2002) a single market for securities in the EU and improved market access could result in an
increase in EU-wide GDP of 1.1 per cent in 2002 prices over a
decade. Total employment could increase by 0.5 per cent. Reforms
since 1992 have led to a fall in credit card fees and to a narrowing of the range of price divergence by about 30 per cent. And in
securities, common rules against insider trading and a European
passport for investment firms offering their services to investors in
other Member States were adopted.

Significant work remains to be completed, especially on the key
capital market directives. Further, the need to develop and admin-
ister the regulations successfully in each EU Member State will take
an enormous effort. This was recognized in the Gyllenhammar
Report (2002), which notes that 'Particularly for retail financial
services, national borders still constitute a considerable de facto
barrier. Even in the Euro age it is extremely rare for private individuals to compare domestic offers of, for example, life insurance
or mortgages with offers from suppliers in other countries of the
single currency area.'

Professional services
In the area of professional services, there are significant variations
in EU Member State requirements for foreign lawyers and accountants intending to practice in the EU. While many of these are not
explicit barriers, disparities among EU Member State requirements
complicate access to the European market for foreign lawyers and
accountants.

Legal services, and accounting and auditing services
Among other things, there are nationality requirements, bans on
majority holdings, a requirement to pass local professional exami-
nations and companies must have a registered office in one of the
EU member states.

Energy services
The Barcelona European Council in Spring 2002 agreed that all
non-household consumers should have freedom of choice of gas and
electricity supplier by 2004 (that is, 60 per cent of the market is to

be opened up). Energy ministers recently also reached a political agreement that will lead to full market opening by July 2007, that is, for household users as well. It should be noted that electricity customers in the UK pay around 19 per cent less than in Italy and 11 per cent less than in France (Electricity Association, 2003).

Postal services

The prevalence of postal monopolies in many EU countries restricts market access and subjects their competitors to unequal conditions of competition. In 2001, the European Commission ruled against Deutsche Post (DP) in two complaints brought by competitors. The first decision, in March, found DP to have abused its dominant market position by granting fidelity rebates and engaging in predatory pricing in the business parcel services market. In July 2001, the Commission ruled again against DP, confirming that the company had blocked the delivery of mailings from within the EU. In October 2001, EU Member States agreed to open additional postal services to competition beginning in 2003 including all outgoing cross-border mail.

Air transport

Some of the most striking changes in the EU services sector have occurred in air transport. In the past, the industry was tightly regulated on the basis of bilateral agreements between Member States. But three successive packages of liberalising measures – adopted during the 1990s – have resulted in equal rights of access to all the Community's markets for all European-owned airlines.

These reforms have led to more competition. The number of routes linking Member States has risen by 46 per cent since 1992 – giving passengers a wider choice of destinations and carriers. The number of routes where more than two carriers are competing rose from 61 in 1992 to 100 in 2001. On such routes, business, economy and promotional fares were around 10 per cent, 17 per cent and 24 per cent lower (EC, 2002c).

Short-haul pricing by established airlines is now influenced by the need to compete with low-cost carriers such as Ryanair. In recent years Ryanair has opened 45 scheduled routes across 11 countries, offering fares that are at times less than 50 per cent of the lowest fares offered by the incumbent airlines. With this kind of competition, established carriers had to restructure their fare strategies. For example, British Airways has lifted many of the restrictions on its cheaper fares, such as the requirement to spend a Saturday night at the destination.

Telecommunications

Since the late 1980s, there has been a general trend towards increased competition and openness in European telecommunications. Liberalisation and harmonisation, however, have been uneven across the EU. In most markets significant problems remain with the provisioning and pricing of unbundled local loops, line sharing, co-location and the provision of leased lines. The presence of government ownership in some EU Member States' incumbent telecommunications operators also has the potential to raise problems for new entrants. Enforcement of existing legislation by national regulatory authorities appears hampered by unnecessarily lengthy and cumbersome procedures in France, Italy, Austria and Portugal. The European Commission also found that incumbents in Germany, Greece, Spain, Italy, Ireland, Austria, Finland and Sweden have slowed the arrival of competition by systematically appealing against their national regulators' decisions despite the fact that in most cases the appeals have not been successful.

According to the EC (2003b), the long distance prices charged by incumbent operators have dropped 11 per cent since 2000, principally as a result of increased competition. The market share held by incumbents has fallen 10 per cent for local calls, 20 per cent for long distance calls and 30 per cent for international calls since liberalisation began in 1998. In twelve euro member states consumers can now choose between more than five operators for long distance and international calls. Prices charged by the old national monopolies for national calls have been reduced in nominal terms by around 50 per cent on average since liberalisation, and those for international calls by around 40 per cent. New operators in many Member States offer even lower prices, even for local calls: new entrant tariffs for national calls are up to 56 per cent lower and for international calls up to 65 per cent lower in some countries. As a result, the cost of a basket of national calls – including fixed charges and subscriptions – has fallen for both business and residential users since 1996. Business users pay, on average, 30 per cent less for the same service, while residential users pay 16 per cent less. The average level of internet penetration in EU households was around 40 per cent in June 2002 – up from 18 per cent in March 2000. Furthermore, high-speed internet access is progressively gaining ground, and in October 2002 there were around 11 million retail broadband customers in the EU. In spite of these positive results, incumbent operators remain dominant in many EU national markets.

Problems with the EU's Liberalisation Approach

The approach to the liberalisation of services markets in the EU seems against the spirit of competition. The thrust of the approach has been to negotiate common regulative standards for services. The focus has thus been placed on regulatory convergence between the Member States rather than on competition. The motive behind the choice of regulatory convergence has essentially been political since each Member State could then hope to insert parts of its own regulations into the common EU regulations (Messerlin, 2001).

In addition, the sectoral approach to liberalisation implies that many services, such as tourism and medical services, have as yet been left untouched. Even within the sectors where the Single Market Programme in Services (SMPS) has been implemented many restrictive measures have survived and substantial state aid or subsidies to service firms continue. For example, in air transport, preferential access to airport slots has restricted competition on existing routes as well as developments of new ones. Moreover the Member States and incumbent firms have adopted protectionist measures against new entrants, often relying on ambiguities in the EU directives (Amatori, 1999). As a result, protection of EU services is unlikely to have declined substantially since the beginning of liberalisation of services trade.

In December 2000 the EU announced a two-stage strategy for removing the remaining barriers to trade in services. In the first stage, during 2001 the EU undertook, for the first time since 1962, a review of existing directives as well as regulatory and administrative practices in member countries creating barriers to intra-EU trade in services. Based on the analysis completed in the year 2001, three types of initiatives were planned for 2002 – removal of barriers by direct application of treaty principles, actions of a non-legislative nature and actions that make use of targeted harmonisation to remove barriers. In spite of these measures, the

SMPS will remain incomplete in the near future. The EU still has to adopt some legislative proposals affecting trade in services from the 1985 white paper, particularly in the fields of company law, corporate taxation, and in VAT. There is an even greater delay in the translation of internal market rules relating to services into national laws. In a recent survey by the EU, half of the companies providing business services regarded the absence of transparency in national regulations as one of the main barriers restricting EU trade. The recent Commission report on the state of the internal market for services (2002b) has provided a comprehensive inventory of remaining barriers to cross-border activity in services sectors.

Thus, in sum, the progress of the SMPS is well short of the objective set out in the SMPS that the provision of services between Member States should be as easy as within a Member State.

Meanwhile, the worldwide liberalisation in services activities via the GATS has been a slow process. Although the GATS established a structure and framework of rules for global trade liberalisation in services, little actual liberalisation was achieved, with many countries' commitments often representing the status quo or in some cases less than the status quo.

Unless current obstacles to cross-border activities are removed, European firms and consumers will not be able to benefit from the competitiveness advantages offered by new technologies and the knowledge-based economy as concluded by Ark et al. (2003) who investigated the reasons for the significant difference in the economic performance of the US and EU economies. The difference in performance of the services sectors using information and communications technologies (ICT) is one of the main reasons behind the increasing competitiveness gap between the US and EU economies.

Figure 6.4 shows productivity growth in sectors that produce ICT technologies, sectors that use ICT technologies and non-ICT related sectors. The US ICT-producing manufacturing sector outperformed its European competitor whereas the European ICT-producing services sector outperformed its American counterpart. These sectors account for a very small share of their respective economies though, and therefore, they have a limited influence on the different overall performance of the US and EU economies. In contrast, ICT-using services sectors contribute to a large portion

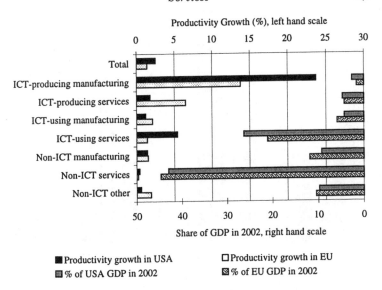

Figure 6.4: Productivity growth by sector and sectoral share of GDP in the US and the EU in 1995–2000

Notes:
EU includes Austria, Denmark, Finland, France, Germany, Ireland, Italy, Netherlands, Spain, Sweden and the United Kingdom, which represents over 90% of EU GDP.
Productivity is defined as value added per person employed.

Source: Ark et al. (2003)

of both the European and US economies, and the large difference in the productivity performance of these sectors in the US and Europe explains to a large extent the difference in the overall economic performance of the American and European economies.

Figure 6.5 shows that ICT-using services subsectors exhibit very different labour productivity growth rates. Securities, wholesale and retail distribution experienced remarkable growth rates in the US in the second half of the past decade while productivity growth was much more modest in Europe in those sectors.

Insufficient integration in services sectors may have been one of the reasons (besides others such as labour market rigidities or planning regulations) delaying the diffusion of ICT and therefore preventing European firms from benefiting from the large productivity increases experienced by their US competitors in recent years.

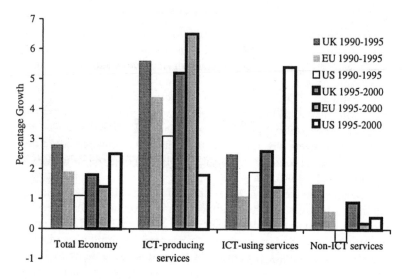

Source: Ark et al (2003)

Figure 6.5: Labour productivity growth in ICT/non-ICT service sectors 1990–1995 and 1995–2000

This failure also holds back progress in other sectors using services, notably manufacturing.

6.5   RECENT EU PROPOSALS FOR THE INTERNAL MARKET IN SERVICES

In a departure from the previous attempts at liberalisation of EU service sectors as outlined in the forgoing section, the European Commission has launched a new proposal to reduce regulation-based impediments to intra-EU trade in services in recent months. In March 2004, the European Commission proposed a directive which aims to boost the EU's internal market in services by reducing impediments to trade and investment within the member states. The proposal aims to reduce differences in regulation across the EU by applying the country of origin principle, by enforcing the single point of contact, and by the elimination of discriminatory elements against service providers from other member states.

The directive does not cover extra-EU trade. Changes in extra-EU barriers would take place as per the GATS negotiations. The proposal amounts to a creation of an area similar to a free trade zone, which would reduce and harmonise service trade barriers between the members without a common external barrier with respect to non members. The proposed EU directive concentrates on construction, distribution and business services, and excludes finance and insurance, and transport. The directive is likely to cover over 60 per cent of the UK service sector, which is equivalent to 43 per cent of the UK economy, or around 400 billion of gross value added in 2002 (DTI, 2004).

The idea behind the latest proposal is that it is the heterogeneity in regulation rather than its level that adversely affects service trade between the member states. Once having incurred fixed costs of complying with regulations in one country, a common regulatory structure would allow firms to reap economies of scale by expanding their market access to other EU member states without any incremental cost.

The main proposals in the directive include:

- The establishment of EU subsidiaries in any member state to be facilitated by introducing a single point of contact in one country. A single point of contact will be the place where a firm can fulfil all their EU-wide administrative and regulatory obligations.

- The application of the country of origin principle, making a service provider subject only to the requirements of the country in which it is established.

- Aim to eliminate unnecessary and discriminatory regulation such as nationality and residence restrictions.

- Mutual assistance between national authorities with a view to effective supervision of service activities.

- Removal of specified prohibited requirements.

- A 'horizontal' approach to liberalisation which implies the same principles as applied to a large part of the EU service sector.

In addition, member States must also assess requirements imposed on access to, and exercise of, service activities and report to the commission on the results, specifying which requirements Member States plan to retain and their justifications for doing so. The proposed rules in the Directive are intended to complement other European Community law that covers services. The proposal differs from traditional free trade zones in one significant manner. Current proposals do not abolish all barriers to service trade between the member states, but aim to equalise the level of barriers across the board. In practice, it is likely that the EU-wide regulative barriers would be somewhere between the most liberal (currently the UK) and the most restrictive regimes currently in place with each member state continuing with its own extra-EU trade barriers against the rest of the world. The effect is therefore like a tariff cut on trade between EU members while maintaining existing country tariffs unchanged on external trade; the internal tariff would be standardised somewhere between the highest and the lowest external tariffs of the member countries.

The following diagrams (Figures 6.6–6.8) attempt to illustrate how such type of deregulation can benefit EU consumers while reducing EU production (presumably against producer lobbying) compared to the existing situation. Figure 6.6 shows the present situation in which the UK is subject to world prices while other EU countries have protective regimes. Under the deregulation proposal (Figure 6.7) prices are driven down in these EU countries – part of the mechanism being entry by UK firms into EU markets at the new price $P_W (1 + t_{EU})$. It shows two EU countries, A (like the UK, with no external barriers) and B (with high external barriers, like rest of EU countries). The original situation is shown by the thick lines. In A the price is low and there are net exports. In B trade is balanced and the price is high. After the proposed deregulation the internal EU tariff in B is lowered, allowing A firms to export to B at the price $P_W (1 + t_{EU})$. Presumably A firms would divert their output to the B economy to undercut firms supplying at $P_W (1 + t_B)$; B firms' output would be cut back and A firms would supply imports equal to the difference between B's demand and those B-firms' supplies. Notice however that A firms would in the end enjoy no difference in prices, as world prices would continue to prevail in A. Hence there would be no change in A's welfare; its net exports, supply and demand would be the same. The only change would be that now it would divert enough output to B to satisfy its import demand and drive its prices down; this diversion of supply would be made up as necessary by extra imports. Therefore the only effect would be on prices in B; these would be lowered and B citizens' welfare would be increased. Notice that the directive in effect amounts to a lowering of the external tariff to the same level as the new within-EU tariff; this is because competition within the EU will force prices in the protected EU countries down to the internally-protected level.

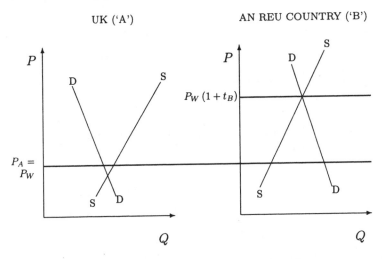

Figure 6.6: Services: the current situation

Other EU countries' interests in avoiding a customs union in services and instead proposing deregulation can be further illustrated by the following diagram. Figure 6.8 shows how under a customs union with the same rate t_{EU} EU consumers obtain the same price but now they also pay a transfer to UK firms (previously they paid this to their own governments who used this revenue to reduce other taxes). It is obvious that they are better off with deregulation than with a customs union. The UK might prefer a customs union but why should the rest of EU provide one?

The only possible qualification to the recent deregulation proposal lies in the 'harmonisation' of regulations proposed. The diagram assumes that this is mere standardisation of unnecessarily different and complex regulative regimes, as perhaps is intended

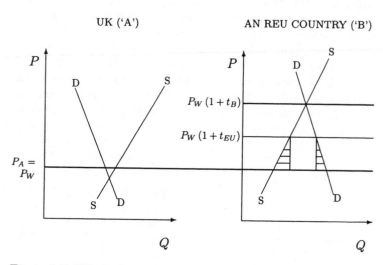

Figure 6.7: EU single market partial deregulation without common external barrier

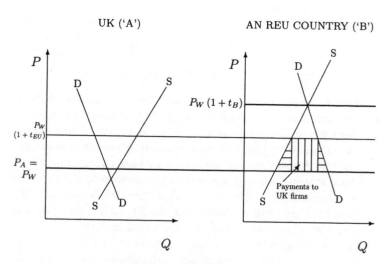

Figure 6.8: EU customs union

by the Commission. Were the harmonisation however to force on a reluctant (liberal-regime) A a rise in regulation that is intended to raise A's costs to reduce its competitive threat to B, then A would be damaged, in much the same way as is modelled in Chapter 3 under the heading of 'harmonisation'. In the diagram it could be seen as an enforced rise in A-firms' costs, shifting the A supply curve leftwards. Under this assumption the proposed directive would actually reduce A's welfare. It is hard at this stage to know how big a threat this is; given the difficulties of regulating services in this way against the wishes of a liberal-regime country like the UK, we will tentatively assume it away.

If so, then overall, as a result of this directive EU-wide competition would increase and result in a decline in prices in EU countries of the B-type, that is, the great majority (with the UK a general exception). Kox et al. (2004) estimates that after the implementation of this proposal bilateral trade in commercial services between member states is likely to increase by 15–30 per cent (1–3 per cent of total intra-EU trade including trade in goods) and FDI in commercial services may increase by 20 per cent to 35 per cent.

How does the proposed directive affect extra-EU firms? It may appear that foreign firms can first enter a member state with the lowest external barrier (the UK) and then gain access to the rest of the EU. However, the directive makes clear that the internal market rules will not apply to the operators from third countries who in future wish to establish in a member state (first establishment in the EU). As far as we can gather, a foreign firm established in the UK would still be subject to individual member country international rules if it wants to export to the rest of the EU.

Extra-EU firms may be able to get around this problem via two routes. First, by establishing themselves in one of the member states (the least protected) before this directive is implemented. If they are already in operation in 2010, apparently they may be considered as a 'local' firm.

Second, foreign firms which enter the EU after 2010 may take on a local partner with a majority-stake making it an 'EU-owned' firm in a legal sense.

How far they will do this depends plainly on how credible the EU liberalising proposals are; at this stage their credibility is weak, as we explain further below. What the diagram shows however is that outside firms can be drawn into the EU's least protected A-type economies in as profuse a manner as needed to replace A-firms diverting their output to B-markets. Only in the unlikely case that the total output in A is exhausted by exports to B countries would any limit on outsiders bite; even then it appears that there are enough ways in which outsiders can masquerade as A firms via joint ventures to get around even that limit. In sum, the Commission's proposal is for more competition within the EU service economy, fuelled by supplies from the least restricted A-type countries, with those supplies in turn being replaced in A-markets by supplies from outside entrants. As such the proposal is beneficial to B-type countries in the EU while not affecting A-type countries; however the benefits in B-type countries are achieved at the expense of incumbent suppliers.

This last feature should make one wary of the prospects for the proposal's acceptance. Since it is intended to become effective only from 2010 onwards, the losing parties have substantial time to create political pressure to alter the directive. European trade unions have already criticised the directive on the basis that it comprises a direct threat to the European social model. The unions claim that the quality of public services will diminish due to the removal of many regulations. The unions have also targeted the country of origin principle, which according to them creates a legal incentive for companies to move to countries with the most relaxed legislation on social, fiscal and environmental issues and the creation of 'letterbox companies' offering services at low prices. The directive itself consists also of measures to protect the interests of buyers and users of services such as the system of providing assistance to consumers and the harmonisation of consumer protection. Inevitably these issues would lead to new regulations and regulatory bodies to protect consumers against the non-national firms. Lastly, this latest proposal does not include services such as financial/telecommunication and energy in which the UK traditionally has comparative advantage (although some form of deregulation in these services is on-going).

Even if the directive is implemented it will not affect important aspects of regulations in the service sector. Although the explicit barriers to trade and investment are likely to be lowered, other barriers to competition such as administrative burdens for start ups, the restriction of participation in public tendering, the restriction on the number of firms in some service sectors will at best only be moderately affected. The regulations related to subsidies and state control will hardly be affected since they are exempt from the proposed directive. These regulations form a substantial form of regulatory burden in the service sectors. For example, out of 183 regulatory indicators considered in the Netherlands Bureau for Economic Policy Analysis study (2004), 61 were identified as barriers to competition and 45 were related to state control. By leaving out these important aspects of regulatory barriers the proposed directive (if successfully implemented) will only partially improve the competitive environment and not create a fully functioning single market in services.

In conclusion, given the problems discussed above and the past dismal record of the EU on such initiatives, we should not expect much benefit from this proposal for the rest of the EU and in any case there would be none at all for the UK; on the other hand we may worry that the initiative may perversely lead only to a rise in obstructive regulation in the name of harmonisation.

6.6 QUANTIFYING THE BARRIERS TO TRADE IN SERVICES

Quantification of barriers to services trade poses formidable challenges and only a few systematic attempts to do so have been undertaken. Much like the measurement of non-tariff barriers (NTBs) for trade in goods, it is hard to come up with a simple measure that is comparable across modes of trade, sectors and countries. Naturally, the analysis of estimates of services barriers suggests that they vary on the basis of the data sources and estimation techniques employed.

Roughly three types of estimates have been used in the empirical analysis:

1. Frequency measures first calculated by Hoekman (1995).

2. Quantity-based tariff equivalents estimated by Francois and Hoekman (1999).

3. Price-based tariff equivalents estimated by Francois and Hoek-

Table 6.5: Ad valorem tariff equivalent for the EU and the US (%)

	Construc- tion	Wholesale and retail trade	Transport, storage and communi- cation	Business and financial services	Social and personal services
EU	10.0	10.0	182.0	27.2	23.6
USA	5.0	4.6	111.4	21.7	31.4

Source: Hoekman (1995)

man (1999), Kalirajan et al. (2001), Warren (2000) among others.

The frequency ratio method involves calculating frequency of occurrence of NTBs across countries and sectors. Typically, to develop these indices, the actual restrictions on trade and investment in a service industry are compiled. These restrictions are then assigned scores and grouped into categories, each of which is assigned a numeric weight. Finally, the indices are computed using these scores and weights. Among these indicators of protection the most widely used measure of protection on service sector liberalisation was constructed by Hoekman (1995) (Table 6.5). He classifies GATS commitments by a country into three categories and assigns a numerical score to each category:

- If no restrictions are applied for a given mode of supply in a given sector, a value of 1 is assigned.

- If no policies are bound for a given mode of supply in a given sector, a value of 0 is assigned.

- If restrictions are listed for a given mode of supply in a given sector, a value of 0.5 is assigned.

Using these factors, Hoekman calculated sectoral coverage indicators and then assigned a value to each country and sector using a benchmark multiplied by the calculated frequency ratio. He does so by first constructing a list of benchmark guesstimates of tariff equivalents for the most protectionist country. Then the tariff equivalent of a given country is obtained by multiplying this guesstimate by (1 minus sectoral coverage indicator). Thus, if the most restrictive country had restrictions equivalent to a 50 per cent tariff, then a country with a 0.9 restrictiveness index, as in the preceding example, would have a tariff equivalent of 45 per cent (that is 0.9×50).

Hardin and Holmes (1997) improve on Hoekman's methodology by using FDI restrictions and by incorporating information on the economic impact of different types of barriers. They constructed an index of FDI restrictions by calculating weights to reflect the relative restrictiveness of different barriers.

Various more elaborate frequency indexes and openness indicators have been constructed for specific service sectors. Such estimates are calculated among others, by the Pacific Economic Cooperation Council (1995), by Mattoo (1999), McGuire (1998), and McGuire and Schuele (2000) for financial services, by the OECD (1997b) for accounting services, by Warren (2000) for telecommunications, by McGuire et al. (2000) for maritime services, and by the OECD and the Australian Productivity Commission in a series of studies for various services sectors.

Recent research from the OECD (2000) allows an assessment of the level of protection in services across the OECD countries (Table 6.6). They measure the extent to which entry barriers and other regulations have affected energy and most marketable services over the past two decades. By 1998 the UK was the least restrictive area and Switzerland was the most. This relative level of liberalisation is reflected in the employment performance of the developed economies. Whereas these reforms have been estimated to have added 2.5 per cent to the employment rate in the UK and New Zealand, the low level of reforms in Greece, Italy and Spain have added only 0.5 to 1 per cent to their employment over the period 1982–98 (OECD 2001d). Additional industry-wide analysis of the regulatory and market environment in OECD countries shows considerable divergence among various EU members (Table 6.A.1), which confirms that the single market in services is not yet working. In 1998 among the EU Member States Britain had the most liberalised services sector in five out of seven sectors under consideration.

Table 6.6: Progress of regulatory reforms in OECD countries (scale 0–6 from least to most restrictive)

	1978	1988	1998
UK	4.3	3.5	1.0
REU	5.4	5.1	3.4
US	4.0	2.5	1.4
Australia	4.5	4.2	1.6
Canada	4.2	2.8	2.4
Japan	5.2	3.9	2.9
Switzerland	4.5	4.5	3.9

Note: Simple averages of indicators for seven industries – gas, electricity, post, telecoms, air transport, railways and road freight. Depending on the industry the following dimensions have been included: barriers to entry, public ownership, market structure, vertical integration, price controls. For the rest of the EU (REU), simple averages of individual EU countries.

Source: Nicoletti and Scarpetta (2001)

The fact that Britain's services sector is more open than the rest of the EU is also confirmed by Nguyen-Hong (2000) and McGuire and Schuele (2000) (Table 6.7). Both these studies calculate an index by identifying existing policies affecting entry and operations post-entry, assigning each a weight based on interviews with the private sector, and summing across weights to obtain an overall index. The domestic index measures the restrictions affecting domestic service providers and the foreign index quantifies the restrictions facing foreign service providers in seeking to provide services in the local market. The domestic and foreign restrictiveness index scores range from 0 to 1. According to these surveys the services sector in Britain is less restrictive in all services under review compared to the average for the rest of the EU Member States (Table 6.A.2). Given the fact that Britain is the world's biggest services exporter after the US, she has a vital economic interest in seeing services markets liberalised around the world. Colecchia (2001) calculates indices for trade barriers in accountancy services for four countries – the UK, France, Australia and the US. The restrictiveness index values in these four countries are 0.5, 0.7, 1.15

Table 6.7: Global welfare gains from services liberalisation

	Total gain $ bn (%GDP)	Services $ bn (%GDP)	Goods $ bn (%GDP)
Brown et al. (2001) projected gains of 33% removal of barriers	613 (2.5)	390 (1.6)	222 (0.9)
Brown et al. (2001) projected gains of removal of all barriers	1857 (7.6)	1169 (4.8)	689 (2.8)
Dee and Hanslow (2000) projected gains of complete removal of post-Uruguay Round trade barriers	270 (1.0)	133 (0.5)	133 (0.5)

Note: The figures in bracket are % of world real income.

and 1.55 respectively. These numbers suggest that, among the four countries, the UK is the most open while the US is the most restrictive for accountancy services.

The use of frequency indicators to measure service sector openness is, however, imperfect for several reasons. First, the method does not take account of the importance of certain service activities in international trade, as it assumes that all indicators are of equal value. Second, it does not take into account the relative importance of differing modes of supply, again due to data limitations. Third, frequency measures do not provide any information on the economic impact that barriers have on prices, production and consumption and the consequences of eliminating these barriers.

The second type of trade restrictiveness measure is quantity-based. This is derived using econometric models, typically the gravity model. In these models trade between the two countries is explained by their size and the distance between them (along with cultural factors). The size of barriers is measured either by the difference between the actual and predicted trade or by using dummy variables. Such studies include Francois and Hoekman (1999) for various services and Warren (2000) for telecommunications. Francois and Hoekman (1999) have fitted a gravity model to bilateral service trade for the US and its major trading partners (Table 6.8).

The differences between the actual and predicted imports were normalised relative to the free trade benchmark for Hong Kong and Singapore. Combining this with an assumed elasticity of demand of four yields the estimated tariff-equivalents. The results indicate that barriers to business and financial services are about the same magnitude as for trade in goods. Higher barriers were estimated for construction.

Table 6.8: Estimated tariff-equivalents in trade services gravity model-based regression method (%)

	Business/Financial Services	Construction
North America	8.2	9.8
Western Europe	8.5	18.3

Notes: North America values involve assigning Canada/Mexico numbers to the US

Source: Francois and Hoekman (1999)

Price-based measures derive estimates of barriers to trade from differences in domestic and foreign prices. The percentage difference between the domestic and foreign price is comparable to a tariff provided price differences are due to government-imposed barriers. Francois and Hoekman (1999) propose a method for calculating a price-based measure based on gross operating margin, defined as (total sales revenue minus total average costs) divided by total average cost. These margins provide an indication of the relative profitability of different industries, hence, the relative magnitude of barriers to entry that may exist. Hoekman (2000) suggests two methods to gauge the sizes of trade barriers through the use of these margins (Table 6.A.3). The first method is to use the differences between the average margins of a benchmark country with relatively free trade and the margins of the other countries in the sample. The second method employs the difference between manufacturing and service margins, with the margins in manufacturing serving as the benchmark.

Other studies which have calculated tariff-equivalents for the services sector using price data include Kalirajan et al. (2001) and Warren and Findlay (2000)for banking services, Kang (2001) for maritime transport, Kalirajan (2000) for food distribution, and Nguyen-Hong (2000) for engineering services (Table 6.A.4). These studies estimate an equation where the domestic price for the industry is modelled as a function of variables that affect the price, one of which is the trade restrictiveness index. The estimated coefficients and trade restrictiveness index are used to calculate the sizes of price differences for individual economies.

Messerlin (2001) estimates relative price variability by examining prices of the same product in two economies. He estimates tariff-equivalents for telecommunications, passenger air transport and film for EU services at 45 per cent, 71 per cent and 77 per cent respectively. In telecommunications the costs of protection are estimated on the basis of the difference between average British-Finnish-Swedish prices and EC prices. The former group is taken to consist of a competitive benchmark market. For passenger air transport the differential between a fully flexible fare for a domestic flight within the UK (the least distorted market) and an international fare (intra- or extra-EU) for an equivalent flight is taken as a measure of protection. For films, an estimate of tariff-equivalence is calculated by summing up the seat tax[2] (11 per cent) and the tariff-equivalent of subsidies (66 per cent).

The above overview of current work on measuring barriers to trade in services suggests that the quality of estimates of barriers has been improving in recent years, both in terms of the range of the barriers included and of the measurement techniques employed. However, it is difficult to determine if these estimates are realistic as a number of limitations remain related to data availability and the weight-assignment for different restrictions. The wide range of the estimated service trade barriers is reflected in the differing welfare effects from services liberalisation to which we now turn.

---

[2]The seat tax is a non-discriminatory excise tax imposed on both foreign and French films. An indirect tax of roughly 11 per cent is levied on every seat sold in French cinemas, independent of the nationality of the film shown. It is also one of the sources of subsidies which are granted to French film producers and cinema owners. As a result, in practice the seat tax is considered discriminatory.

6.7   GAINS FROM LIBERALISATION

Relatively little work has been completed on the potential gains from alternative liberalisation scenarios in services. The difficulties arise from poor data on international service transactions and the lack of a comprehensive measure of restrictions on trade in services. Modelling of trade in services also requires a modelling structure that can incorporate the various modes through which services are supplied and account for the movement of factors of production (OECD, 2000). As with goods trade, models used to analyse services liberalisation are either partial equilibrium or general equilibrium (CGE) in nature. They are calibrated with either the Global Trade Analysis Project model (GTAP) or the Michigan Model of World Production and Trade (MMPT). Parameter values are usually chosen from existing estimates; for example, most studies use the parameter values for service trade barriers from Hoekman (1995). Studies based on the GTAP models include Hertel et al. (2000), the Department of Foreign Affairs and Trade, Australian (DFAT, 1999), Dee and Hanslow (2001) and Verikios and Zhang (2004). Applications of the Michigan model are Brown et al. (1996), Chadha (2001), Chadha et al. (2000), and Brown and Stern (2000). OECD (2001d, 2003b), Dihel (2002) and Brown et al. (2002) provide an overview of current work on measuring and modelling gains from service trade liberalisation using CGE modelling.

Global Welfare Gains of Services Liberalisation

The estimates of benefits from services liberalisation vary for individual countries from under 1 per cent to over 50 per cent of total GDP – depending on the initial levels of protection and the assumed reduction in barriers. The studies indicate as one would expect that economies with high initial service trade barriers tend to gain most (in terms of percentage gains to GDP). As these estimated barriers are higher for developing countries than for developed countries, it suggests potentially large benefits for developing countries from liberalisation of barriers to trade in services.

Hertel et al. (2000) suggest that, while 40 per cent liberalisations in agriculture and manufacturing will each raise global welfare by about \$70 billion per annum (0.24 per cent of world GDP), a similar liberalisation in services could contribute over $300 billion (1 per cent of world GDP). Dee and Hanslow (1999) and Brown and Stern (1999) were the first CGE studies which explicitly allowed for FDI in services. Dee and Hanslow (1999) allow not only for entry through FDI, but also distinguish between entry and operating restrictions. The results indicate that the EU and the US would actually lose $6 billion (0.1 per cent of GDP), largely because of their loss of rents in the provision of FDI.

Verikios and Zhang (2004) find that complete liberalisation of telecommunications and financial services would increase world output by 0.2 per cent or $47 billion. According to a study by Brown et al. (2001), world income would increase (in base year of 1995) by 2.5 per cent if all services – not just telecommunications and financial – were liberalised by 33 per cent and by 7.6 per cent if all barriers were removed (Table 6.7).

A 1999 study published by the European Commission, quoted in Thum (2002), comes to similar conclusions, finding that trade liberalisation – a 20 per cent to 50 per cent global cut in applied protection in agriculture, industrial products and services, plus trade facilitation agreement – would increase annual global welfare by nearly $220 billion to $400 billion (1 to 1.5 per cent of GDP). In the first instance, the study looked at across-the-board cuts in trade protection across all agricultural, industrial, and services sectors by all countries. Two scenarios were considered – a 20 per cent cut and a 50 per cent global cut in protection. Each of these scenarios was combined with a WTO agreement on trade facilitation, which it is assumed leads to a modest reduction (conservatively estimated at 1 per cent) in the transactions costs associated with international trade. Their estimates indicate that the potential welfare gain for the EU would be between $US46 billion and $92 billion which represents a 21 per cent share of the global welfare gains and between 0.75 to 1 per cent of EU GDP.

OECD (1997c) looked at the effects of a plausible medium-term programme of regulatory reform in eight countries using estimates of efficiency gains in services industries. It reports long-run potential output gains ranging from 3 to 6 per cent in some European countries and Japan to 1 per cent in the US, reflecting the initial state of regulation in different countries.

Not much work has been undertaken to evaluate the effects of liberalisation of service trade via mode 4 – temporary movement of natural persons (TMNP). Although TMNP currently accounts for only 1.4 per cent of the value of services trade (Karsenty, 2000) (this low figure arises from the very high barriers to TMNP), this mode of service delivery possibly offers the greatest potential returns to liberalisation. Based on the global applied general equilibrium model of south–north temporary movement of labour, Winters (2002) suggests that an increase in developed countries' quotas on the inward movements of both skilled and unskilled temporary workers equivalent to 3 per cent of their workforces would generate an estimated increase in world welfare of over $US150 billion per annum (0.75 per cent of world GDP). These gains are shared between developing and developed countries and owe more to unskilled than to skilled labour mobility.

Welfare Gains to the EU

Here we present a brief summary of studies which model the EU as a separate economy (see Table 6.9). Most of these studies conclude, as expected, that the EU will benefit from liberalisation in trade in services:

1. Brown et al. (1996) simulate the impact of a 25 per cent multilateral reduction using Hoekman's (1995) tariff equivalents of service barriers. The estimated welfare gains for the EU are US$29 billion (0.4 per cent of GDP) based on assumptions regarding market structure and product differentiation.

2. Robinson et al. (2002) evaluate the impact of service and non-service sector trade liberalisation on the world economy. The EU stands to gain between 0.2 per cent to 4.7 per cent of GDP depending on the underlying assumptions and reform scenarios.

3. In Chadha (2001) who estimates the impact of a reduction in protection to services trade using Hoekman's (1995) tariff equivalents, the estimated welfare gain for the EU is US$66 billion or around 1 per cent of GDP for a 25 per cent reduction in services trade barriers.

4. Chadha et al. (2000) estimate the gain to the EU and EFTA economies from a 33 per cent reduction in services protection to be US$210 billion.

5. Verikios and Zhang (2004) simulate the impact of elimination of barriers to trade in communication and financial services. The study finds that a complete liberalisation of trade in telecommunication leads to a gain of around $US3.5 billion or 0.05 per cent of GDP to the EU. The reform of the financial services industry results in similar gains to the EU.

6. Brown and Stern (2000) simulate the impact of removal of service barriers under different scenarios for international capital markets. According to the results, changes to the EU's welfare range from a welfare decline of US$83 billion (1 per cent of GDP) to a gain of US$292 billion (3.6 per cent of GDP). Welfare effects are strongly associated with whether or not a country attracts or loses capital.

7. Brown et al. (2001) study the impact of a reduction in tariffs on agricultural and industrial products and services barriers by 33 per cent (and 100 per cent) in a new WTO trade round. The EU and the EFTA stand to gain US$169 billion (and US$507 billion) or 2.8 per cent (and 8 per cent) of GDP.

Due to the use of different databases and base years as well as different assumptions about liberalisation policies the estimates from different studies are not strictly comparable. However, the results indicate that the welfare gains from liberalisation of trade in services would be substantial for EU member countries as well as for the global economy.

Given the high share of services in GDP, it is not surprising that the EU stands to make large gains by liberalising services. The prediction of potentially large welfare gains for the EU derives mainly from its current high level of protection. Liberalisation of the services sector will provide the incentive for resources to move out of relatively highly protected sectors and into sectors in which the EU has a comparative advantage or which benefit from scale economies. With further liberalisation, the EU services sector would be in a relatively stronger position to expand and take advantage of improved access to foreign markets.

From the above discussion it is clear that estimates of economic impact on the EU vary widely. At one extreme, Dee and Hanslow (1999, 2001) predict that the EU is likely to lose rather than gain from trade liberalisation in services. At the other extreme, Brown

Table 6.9: Brief summary of CGE studies that model the EU as a separate economy

	Base year	Regions/ sectors	Barriers estimates	Model
Brown et al. (1996)	1990	8/29	Hoekman (1995)	Michigan
DFAT (1999)	1995	45/50	Modification of Hoekman (1995)	GTAP framework
Chadha et al. (2000)	1995	20/16	Hoekman (1995)	Michigan (with implementation of Uruguay Round in 2005)
Hertel et al. (2000)	1995	19/22	Francois & Hoekman (1999) Hoekman (1995)	Modified GTAP (with implementation of Uruguay Round in 2005)
Dee and Hanslow (2001)		18/3	Kalirajan et al. (2000), Warren (2000)	FTAP model with capital mobility and FDI
Chadha (2001)	1995	7/25	Hoekman (1995)	Michigan
Robinson et al. (2002)	1995	10/11	Brown et al (1996), Hoekman (1995)	Standard static CGE
Verikios and Zhang (2004)		19/8	Kalirajan et al. (2001) Warren (2000)	FTAP model with capital mobility and FDI

Table 6.9 Brief summary of CGE studies that model the EU as a separate economy continued

Policy Simulations	Welfare gains to Europe, billion US$ (% of GDP)
25% multilateral liberalisation in services	29 (0.4) (0.1 terms of trade change)
50% liberalisation in services	73.4 (1)
33% reduction in bilateral import tariff in services 33% reduction in bilateral import tariff in goods and services	210 (2.5) EU and EFTA 253 (3) EU and EFTA
40% cut in agriculture and service protection 50% liberalisation in goods and services & transport	−4.7
Multilateral services liberalisation	−6 (−0.8)
Multilateral goods & services liberalisation	0.2 (0.1)
25% multilateral liberalisation in services 25% multilateral liberalisation in goods and services	66 (0.9) 79 (1.1)
50% liberalisation in services 50% liberalisation in goods and services	(−1.2) (−1.7)
In post Uruguay Round environment, elimination of barriers to trade in communication Elimination of barriers to trade in financial services	3.5 (0.5) 3.4 (0.5)

Table 6.10: Estimated welfare effects of liberalising selected services in the EU

	Ad valorem tariff-equi.	Induced increase in imports (€bn.)	Consumer surplus gain (€bn.)		Net welfare gain (€bn.)
			A	B	B
Films (France)	76.8	0.3	0.6	0.4	0.3
Air Transport	71.0	2.3	9.0	8.8	7.0
Telecom	45.2	5.7	5.9	4.0	2.8

Notes:

A   Based on Francois-Hall (1997) model

B   Based on Hufbauer-Elliott (1994) model.

Source: Messerlin (2001)

et al. (2001) show that the EU is expected to gain as much as 2.5 per cent of GDP. The magnitude of welfare effects is strongly dependent on the accuracy of the estimates of services barriers and on the various modelling assumptions. The estimates of different services barriers vary on the basis of the data sources and estimation techniques employed. The studies which use Hoekman's estimates for the initial interventions generally report large welfare gains from services trade liberalisation. By contrast, studies which employ the estimates determined on the basis of price or quantity impact measures tend to generate lower, though still sizeable, welfare gains. Even though the quality of estimates of barriers has been improving both in terms and the range of barriers addressed, it is difficult to determine if these estimates are realistic as a number of limitations remain, related mainly to data availability and the nature of the barriers.

Messerlin (2001) uses partial equilibrium analysis to assess the cost to EU consumers from protection in three service sectors (films, passenger air transport and telecommunications) and estimates the cost of protection as 16 per cent of their value added (Table 6.10). Dobson and Jacquet (1998) evaluate the impact of the Financial Services Agreement (FSA) at the WTO in December 1997. The present value of total benefits from financial services reform by 2010 would be, with an assumed discount rate of 12 per cent, $US1 trillion. The EU would benefit in the region of 0.7 per cent of GDP. Empirical studies of efficiency differences among banks in Europe and the US indicate the following: banks could reduce their costs and increase profits by between 20 and 50 per cent by increasing productive efficiency; thrifts and credit unions could achieve 20 per cent efficiency gains by improving managerial efficiency and by using the same sophisticated technology as is used by best-practice institutions; national bank regulatory agencies could make efficiency gains of a similar magnitude by achieving greater economies of scale in clearing and payments services; and insurers (where comparable data are scarce) are estimated to be between 45 and 90 per cent efficient (Berger et al. 1993). In telecommunications it is estimated that the liberalisation would cut the cost of international calls by more than 80 per cent and the Institute of International Economics calculated that it could cut telecom bills by up to $1 trillion, equivalent to 4 per cent of world GDP (Artis and Nixson, 2001). Ian Taylor, the former UK science and technology minister has been quoted as saying 'the [telecom] market is already worth $600 billion annually and growing at 10 per cent a year. Some analysts predicted an extra £20 billion worth of telecom business for the UK alone over the next 10 to 15 years' (Williams and Cane, 1997).

6.8 CONCLUSION

Measuring trade in services and quantifying worldwide barriers to it is a difficult task. Naturally, calculating gains from liberalisation of services trade is a complicated matter. However, given that the UK is among the world's top services exporters and importers, she stands to gain from services liberalisation around the world, in particular from the formation of a EU single market in services. It is however, unlikely that the EU can successfully liberalise its services barriers – internal as well as barriers to trade with rest of the world – in the near future.

APPENDIX A   MEASURES OF RESTRICTIONS ON TRADE IN SERVICES

Table 6.A.1: Regulatory and market environment in 1998 (scale 0–6 from least to most restrictive)

	Britain	Rest of the EU	United States	Minima EU	Maxima EU
Air passenger transport	**2.2**	3.8	1.2	**2.2**	5.5
Road freight	**1.3**	2.8	1.5	**1.3**	4.6
Mobile telephony	**0.0**	2.9	n.a.	**0.0**	4.6
Fixed telephony	1.0	3.1	0.3	0.4	6.0
Electricity	**0.0**	4.1	4.3	**0.0**	6.0
Railways	**3.0**	5.1	1.5	**3.0**	6.0
Retail distribution	2.5	2.7	n.a.	1.2	4.7
Average	**1.4**	3.4	1.7	**1.4**	4.5

Source: Derived from table 5.2 of Messerlin (2001)

Table 6.A.2: Restrictiveness index scores (scale 0-1 from least to most restrictive)

	Index	UK	Rest of the EU	NAFTA	Rest of the world
Accountancy	Domestic	0.18	0.20	0.19	0.17
services	Foreign	0.19	0.36	0.37	0.43
Architectural	D	0.00	0.09	0.14	0.04
services	F	0.07	0.21	0.29	0.20
Engineering	D	0.03	0.09	0.09	0.04
services	F	0.07	0.16	0.23	0.17
Legal	D	0.18	0.19	0.25	0.16
services	F	0.31	0.40	0.50	0.47
Maritime	D	0.06	0.14	0.14	0.16
services	F	0.24	0.33	0.47	0.47
Telecommunications	D	0.00	0.12	0.13	0.25
	F	0.00	0.19	0.34	0.41
Banking	D	0.00	0.00	0.00	0.08
services	F	0.07	0.07	0.10	0.33
Distribution	D	0.05	0.09	0.02	0.08
services	F	0.19	0.24	0.15	0.21

Sources: Nguyen-Hong (2000), McGuire and Schuele (2000)

Table 6.A.3: Average gross operating margins of services firms, 1994–96

	EU	USA
Recreation	42.5	46.8
Business services	32.1	56.2
Construction	19.3	20.2
Consulting	22.1	−136.0
Finance	51.6	56.3
Health	22.3	37.0
Hotels	23.7	48.5
Retail trade	23.6	34.6
Wholesale trade	19.9	27.0
Transport/utilities	32.6	43.4

Source: Hoekman (2000)

Table 6.A.4: Price and cost effect measures (%)

	Foreign				Domestic		
	Price			Cost	Price	Cost	
	Banking	Telecoms	Engineering	Distribution	Telecoms	Engineering	Distribution
UK	5.32	0.00	2.54	2.76	0.00	0.00	1.39
US	4.75	0.20	7.38	2.26	0.20	0.00	3.79
Canada	5.34	3.37	5.31	3.09	1.07	0.98	2.68
Belgium	5.32	1.31	0.52	4.87	0.65	6.69	0.66
Denmark	5.32	0.20	1.14	n.a.	0.20	n.a.	0.69
Finland	5.32	0.00	2.28	n.a.	0.00	n.a.	0.73
France	5.32	1.43	0.92	5.16	0.34	7.10	0.69
Germany	5.32	0.32	10.17	n.a.	0.32	n.a.	2.93
Greece	5.32	4.52	n.a.	0.25	2.56	0.00	n.a.
Ireland	5.32	2.67	n.a.	2.70	1.46	0.00	n.a.
Italy	5.32	1.00	n.a.	n.a.	1.00	n.a.	n.a.
Luxembourg	5.32	1.05	n.a.	n.a.	1.05	n.a.	n.a.
Netherlands	5.32	0.20	3.67	2.73	0.20	0.00	5.25
Portugal	5.32	6.25	n.a.	n.a.	3.80	n.a.	n.a.
Spain	5.32	3.93	8.73	n.a.	2.03	n.a.	3.86
Sweden	5.31	0.65	6.76	n.a.	0.65	n.a.	0.74

Sources: Kalirajan et al. (2001), Warren (2000), Nguyen-Hong (2000) and Kalirajan (2000)

7 Evaluating the Costs and Benefits of EU Trade Arrangements

In this chapter we pull together the many figures from the preceding chapters on the trade arrangements made by the EU; and we use them to estimate their welfare implications for the UK and for the EU.

We use the best estimates we have been able to find of the overall tariff-equivalent of all the EU's protective regimes (including explicit tariffs, anti-dumping procedures, and state regulations). We then use our CGE world model (described in Chapter 2) to generate estimates of changes in trade that result from these. Here our method is to obtain the weighted tariff-equivalent produced by a given protected product (say high-tech manufacturing) for the relevant one of our three traded categories (primary/basic manufacturing/complex manufacturing and services) and apply it to the model; we take the trade changes to apply entirely to the subcategory on which the protection is levied (that is, here on high-tech manufacturing). The model also gives us the implied terms of trade changes. Finally we calculate from these changes the welfare effects in the normal manner: these consist of the terms of trade gains/losses of real income, the customs union transfers effected through trade-diversion of ROW sourcing to customs union partners, and finally of the consumer surplus lost through higher internal prices.

We decided to use the usual calculations of consumer surplus, measured in equivalent income variation, but applied to the general equilibrium results of our 4-bloc world trade model (see Appendix D for an account). For this purpose we disregarded all effects of in-

172

creased output and income, solely counting the substitution effects of protection; the reason for this is the standard one that income effects are compensated or compensatable, whereas the substitution effects cause costs via misallocation. We did also consider a calculation using the GE model alone as the basis. This incorporates the expansion effects in the model and allows for the cost of the extra resources used; because the GE model assumes (in line with realism) a high degree of interference both in the size of the agricultural sector and in the planning process for land there are material expansion effects as a result of the policy changes examined. The resource cost of the land used in expansion does not equal the income gain because the planning process is not entirely efficient. But as opportunities for land release in attractive uses become apparent its efficiency in effect increases. We discuss these welfare estimates carefully in Appendix C. In what follows we refer to them briefly in passing; the welfare gains are quite a lot larger on this basis but we rather emphasise the measures coming out of the conventional calculations which we now go on to describe in detail.

Our calculations fall into three parts for any given trade policy change:

1. The transfer effect of customs union protection whereby one partner pays more than the world price for imports from another partner.

2. The resource misallocation effect whereby output and demand is switched between sectors – this is the usual 'triangle' of lost consumer surplus. For this we use only the substitution effects predicted by the model.

3. The terms of trade effect whereby the changes brought about by the policy change in net world supplies alters world prices. For this calculation we use the full changes predicted by the model.

We present two sets of estimates. The first considers each product trade protection regime separately. From this we may estimate the effect of withdrawing that regime alone. The second set considers the full set of regimes together. Since plainly the regimes will each affect every part of the economy, effects of all regimes together will interact, either partly cancelling or possibly reinforcing each other. Hence in principle the second set gives the effect of withdrawing the whole set of regimes together.

We look at the net gains/losses to the UK and to the EU from two basic sets of policy changes:

1. If the UK withdraws from the EU trade arrangements in favour of unilateral free trade.

2. If the EU also moves to unilateral free trade.

We are interested in knowing whether it would pay the UK and EU for the UK to withdraw from the EU's trade arrangements; and whether it would pay the EU to liberalise its trade arrangements. In all our calculations we take the status quo, existing trade arrangements, as the benchmark.

What we will find is that it would indeed pay the EU to move to unilateral free trade in goods and services; the gain for the rest of the EU (REU) would be a substantial 2 per cent of REU GDP and for the UK an even larger 3.8 per cent of GDP. However, if we assume that because of the power of existing institutions and vested interests, the EU does not change from its existing protective set-up, then we find that the UK would still gain from withdrawing alone to unilateral free trade. The UK's gain would be a still substantial 2.5 per cent of its GDP, while the loss to the REU would be a small 0.2 per cent of its GDP. (Should the EU continue later to free trade too, then the UK would gain an extra 1.3 per cent of GDP because of resulting terms of trade effects. Hence the UK gains the same from moving to free trade whether the EU itself liberalises or not; but it also gains further if the EU liberalises.)

In these two estimates resides a dilemma for UK policy: does it stay within the EU and fight on in the hope of EU trade liberalisation from which it would derive the same benefits as from unilateral free trade and without the trauma of leaving the EU or does it leave in the expectation of the same gains but more certainly and immediately? There is also an interesting choice for the rest of the EU: does it benefit its citizens generally by going to free trade or does it accept that this is impossible because of the way that EU politics is conducted? If it assumes this impossibility, then should it welcome the departure (at rather small cost) of a UK that is fundamentally at odds with it over both the costs of the trade arrangements and the moves to a more federal politics? We return to these policy issues in our last chapter.

We now consider each product category in turn (the details are also tabulated in Appendix A). The calculations for the model are taken from Appendix B; this explains the model and shows the key simulations of tariff-equivalent changes.

7.1 AGRICULTURE

According to Bradford (2003) whose tariff-equivalent estimates we follow for all goods trade, EU agricultural protection is on average 36 per cent. The model, as we have implemented it, prevents agricultural land from responding to price change, in line with planning and CAP restrictions on planting. Also consumer spending on food is assumed to be highly inelastic. Hence we observe no effects on the terms of trade as net trade volumes are essentially unaffected. Thus the cost of the CAP consists purely of the transfer cost to the UK which is an equal gain of course to the rest of EU. (In addition there are administrative costs; but these are considered under separate headings in Chapter 3, Other Issues.)

As UK net imports of food are some 0.8 per cent of GDP this is 0.3 per cent of UK GDP and 0.06 per cent of EU GDP.

Other studies – see Chapter 3 – mostly allow for more trade volume effects; certainly our assumption stretches plausibility as undoubtedly farming interests have had ways of achieving acreage increases which must surely be partially reversed by a 26 per cent (36/136) fall in prices. However, because agriculture is a very small part of GDP – less than 1 per cent in the UK – even adding in more volume effects does not change the size of the estimate unduly as a fraction of GDP.

7.2 BASIC MANUFACTURING

Bradford's estimate (Bradford, 2003) here is of a 16 per cent average tariff-equivalent. The spread of tariff-equivalents across products is very high (see Chapter 5). But the reason the average is only 16 per cent is that many of these products (such as textiles) have been subject to competition from cheap-labour sources for so long that the domestic industries in the West have largely disappeared as their capital has depreciated; the vested interests pushing for protection have accordingly little power.

Here the UK is twice as big a net importer as it is of food, at 1.7 per cent of GDP. The model's estimated trade effect of the UK eliminating this tariff is that it would effectively eliminate this industry's production (14.4 per cent of GDP). There would be no terms of trade effect however, given the small size of this effect in terms of the world market. Thus UK withdrawal would save the customs union transfer effect of 0.3 per cent of GDP $(= 1.7 \times 0.16)$, which is worth 0.06 per cent of GDP to the rest of EU; and also the consumer surplus burden of 1.1 per cent of GDP $(= 14.4 \times 0.16 \times 0.5)$ – a total saving of 1.4 per cent.

Were the EU to liberalise, then its net exports would contract by 13.7 per cent of GDP against the current GDP share of basic manufacturing at 17.6 per cent. This is large in terms of the world market and induces a rise in world prices of basic manufactures by 4 per cent. Since both the UK and the REU would be, after liberalisation, large net importers of these, the terms of trade cost would be 0.6 per cent of GDP for the UK and 0.5 per cent of GDP for the REU. However the consumer surplus gain to the REU would be 1.1 per cent of GDP as for the UK. For the REU liberalisation would thus bring a net gain of 0.5 per cent of GDP $(= 1.1 - 0.5 - 0.06)$. For the UK the gain would be less than going to free trade on its own: because of the terms of trade effect, it would fall to 0.8 per cent of GDP.

7.3   HIGH-TECH MANUFACTURING

Bradford's estimate (Bradford, 2003) of protection for high-tech manufacturing (which includes the large transport equipment industry as well as electronics, both of them areas where emerging market countries in the far east and elsewhere have made recent penetration) is a very large 58 per cent. The model estimate of the trade effect of the UK withdrawing from this protection is the effective elimination of the UK's existing modest-sized industry, currently 3.6 per cent of GDP; of course with the decline of such industries as cars and computing equipment this has already contracted greatly. The consumer surplus gain to the UK from withdrawal would thus be 1.1 per cent of GDP (= $3.6 \times 0.58 \times 0.5$). The UK would also gain from not paying the customs union transfer on its net imports for the REU; these net imports run at 0.8 per cent of GDP hence the transfer is 0.5 per cent (0.58×0.8). Therefore the total gain for the UK from leaving the customs union in high-tech manufactures would be 1.6 per cent of GDP. For the REU the cost would be the loss of the UK's transfer, worth 0.1 per cent of REU GDP.

For the REU high-tech manufacture output constitutes 7.9 per cent of GDP, and net exports 1.5 per cent. Plainly certain of these industries have strong comparative advantage and require no protection while others are weak and under attack from emerging market competition. This latter portion, the model indicates, would be wiped out by the elimination of the protection; we have no good figures for what this portion is but we assume it to be the existing industry minus net exports (6.3 per cent of GDP). Thus the REU would make a consumer surplus gain of 1.8 per cent of GDP ($6.3 \times 0.58 \times 0.5$). However, it would lose the 0.1 per cent customs union transfer it gets from the UK. Furthermore, the model suggests (after allowing for the capping of the output effect at 6.3 per cent of GDP) that the prices of high-tech manufactures would rise by 4.2 per cent as REU supplies were withdrawn from world markets. Since both the REU and the UK would have become net importers after liberalisation (the REU to the tune of 4.8 per cent, the UK 4.4 per cent, of GDP) the terms of trade cost would be 0.2 per cent of GDP for both the REU and the UK. Thus for the REU the total net gain of moving to free trade would be 1.5 per cent of GDP (= $1.8 - 0.2 - 0.1$).

7.4 SERVICES

In this area our estimates of protection are particularly uncertain. The various pieces of evidence we looked at in Chapter 6 on service trade suggest that it is quite a lot higher in the REU than in the UK. This is supported by the net export figures. The UK's net exports are 3.4 per cent of GDP and 12.4 per cent of service production, suggesting that a large part of the industry must be competing on world markets and hence with no protection. The REU has a rough trade balance.

These studies, though largely qualitative, suggest that REU protection is rather high – we put it at 30 per cent which seems to be in line with these estimates. On the other hand, given its very large rate of net exports, UK prices are likely to be driven by competition to supply world markets down to world price levels; thus we assume that protection in the UK is effectively nil, We also assume in line with the studies cited in Chapter 3 that the protection is carried out by states not at the EU level; there has been very little penetration of common standards across the EU in services. In consequence the EU is assumed to have no customs union in services, with free trade inside the union; each country instead has the same barriers against all other countries including those in the REU.

Under these assumptions it is easy enough to work out the effect of the UK withdrawing from the EU protective system. Since the EU has only state-level protection and the UK is assumed to have no protection in the first place, the effect is simply nil. (Were we to have assumed that the UK had some protection in place, we would have found an additional gain from higher consumer surplus, as this protection was eliminated. However of course eliminating protection that is not due to the EU does not require withdrawal from the EU; so again we would not attribute this gain to 'withdrawal from the EU's protective system' as there is no such system in place.)

For the REU matters are different. Reducing each country's protection of 30 per cent on services would theoretically reduce output of services substantially; according to the model were the REU to do this service output (20 per cent of GDP) would fall to zero. However we must recall the assumption here that this policy is applied on its own; this is highly unlikely given that traded services are where most rich countries now think the future lies for their new industrial activity. Given this assumption however the estimate is not unreasonable, with internal prices falling by 23 per cent $(30/130)$ on this traded activity. On this assumption, the gain in consumer surplus is 32.3 per cent of GDP $(= 20 \times 0.23 \times 0.5)$. However the prices of services would rise on world markets by 6 per cent according to the model; with net imports now of 20 per cent of GDP, the REU would lose 1.2 per cent on the terms of trade, making its total gain 1.3 per cent of GDP. The UK as a net exporter would gain 0.2 per cent of GDP (3.4×0.06).

Services: Could the EU Create a Custom Union in Services using the Single Market Framework?

One might wish to consider the possibility that the EU will go on from here to extend its customs union to services, following a conceivable interpretation of the Single Mmarket agenda; in this case, the UK, as a large net exporter of services, would be better off while the EU would lose because it would have to pay the UK above world prices for imports of services.

The area of services is in flux within the EU because of the Single Market treaty. The purported aim of the EU is to create a single market across services. It has put in place many common standards across product markets (a relatively easy undertaking because these markets were already competing through free trade within the EU customs union; so all that had to be agreed were common regulations.) But in services it has faced the added problem of the lack of free trade in the EU. Thus in practice the test of the Single Market has become whether this can be done.

There are two main ways that one could think of such free trade being established. One would be simply to sweep away all state barriers and put no new barriers in their place; this would be unilateral free trade. Note that this could also be achieved by stimulating intense competition across the EU Single Market; in this case even though there might be barriers to non-EU companies they would not succeed in raising the internal price level since competition would have already driven it down to the world level. The other would be to set up a customs union as with goods: thus there would be one common barrier shielding EU producers from world producers but within that barrier free trade and competition. (Note again that as above, were the competition within the customs union to be intense, then prices could be driven by it down to the world level. This case is best thought of as equivalent to free trade; the customs union case we assume to be effective in raising internal prices by the extent of the common barrier.)

In terms of the politics of vested interests, both of these face great difficulties. Even if the common barrier were the same as the previous state barriers, national producers in less competitive regions would now face competition within the EU and would resist; yet EU consumers would get no gains if the new EU barrier were no lower. If the EU common barrier were to be reduced, consumers would gain but the resistance from producers would become more acute and more general across the EU. But the higher the common barrier is kept the bigger the transfer from the REU to the UK which has a large net export balance in services and this balance would get larger the higher the protection the UK would now get (in place of its existing zero protection).

It is therefore hard to predict what the EU might do in services as a result of the Single Market treaty. The most reasonable assumption seems to be nothing at all; this assumption is the one we make.

Another would be that the single market in services produces strong competition, equivalent to free trade. This is so far from the present reality that it is not of too much interest as yet. We investigate this as part of our EU liberalisation scenario; we find that it is beneficial to the UK because of its effects in improving our terms of trade. It makes no difference to the gain to the UK from leaving the EU's trading arrangements, since the UK obtains terms of trade gains whether it is in or out of the EU.

We now check the plausibility of the EU setting up a exemplar customs union, whose common barrier is half way between the UK's zero and the REU's 30 per cent – that is, a 15 per cent external tariff-equivalent. In our model we find that such a customs union in services would cause a sharp rise in service supply in the UK and contraction in the EU. The terms of trade would improve for services; and the UK would gain from trade diversion and getting much higher prices paid for its services exports to the REU. Thus the UK would obtain a large gain from both the customs union transfer and the terms of trade. The overall results are shown in Table 7.1.

For the REU to transfer such sums to the UK at the expense of its own consumers (line b in Table 7.1) seems a highly unlikely development. One prediction we can therefore make with some confidence is that were the EU to decide to reduce protection on services industries it would do so by general reduction in each state's protection (line c) rather than by moving to a customs union since the latter would in addition to the effects of liberalisation in the REU also transfer large resources sums to the UK. Hence our comparisons of trade policy changes are with the status quo, not with the case where some customs union in services is negotiated prior to the changes.

Table 7.1: Gain/loss (% cent of GDP) from the EU going to a customs union in services with 15% common tariff

		UK	REU
a)	Compared with the status quo of 30% state-level protection in REU and 0% in UK	+1.9%	+0.1%
b)	Compared with EU reducing all state protection to 15% without customs union	+1.5%	−0.5%
c)	Memo item: effect of EU reducing all state protection to 15% without customs union compared with status quo	+0.4%	+0.6%

7.5 GAINS AND LOSSES FROM SEPARATE ACTS OF POLICY COMPARED WITH THE STATUS QUO

We can now use these calculations to draw up a table of gains and losses were the UK to withdraw from various parts of the EU's trade arrangements (see Table 7.2).

Table 7.2: Net gains to the UK and to the REU if the UK withdraws from status quo trade arrangements and adopts unilateral free trade (% of GDP)

	UK	REU
Agriculture	+0.3	−0.06
Basic manufacturing	+1.4	−0.06
Hi-tech manufacturing	+1.6	−0.1
Traded services	−	−
Total	+3.3	−0.22

This table is relevant to the decision of the UK to withdraw or not from individual parts of the trade treaties. We note that the

UK has a strong incentive to withdraw. For the REU the UK's withdrawal creates marginally negative effects.

We can also ask whether the UK and REU have any incentive to liberalise EU markets and move to free trade, with the UK remaining a member of these common arrangements. For this we create Table 7.3 of net gains and losses for the UK and the REU, comparing a post-liberalisation situation with the assumed benchmark.

Table 7.3: Net gains to the UK and to the REU if the EU replaces status quo trade arrangements with unilateral free trade (% of GDP)

	UK	REU	REU if UK has already gone to free trade[*]
Agriculture	+0.3	−0.03	−
Basic manufacturing	+0.8	+0.54	+0.6
Hi-tech manufacturing	+1.4	+1.5	+1.6
Traded services	+0.2	+1.3	+1.3
Total	+2.7	+3.3	+3.5

Note: [*]this is column 2 plus transfer effects (these are already eliminated by UK liberalisation)

Here we can see that there is a strong incentive on welfare grounds for the REU to liberalise.

7.6 EXAMINING POLICIES AS A GROUP

Notice however that although we have added up the effects of the various acts of policy we cannot take this addition too seriously. If we want to know what the sum total is of doing all these things together we have to re-examine the estimates under that precise assumption. In practice UK withdrawal would occur across all the areas of trade; to leave one area would probably not be negotiable.

Essentially you must 'leave or not leave'; having left, certain treaty areas might be restorable under a completely new relationship.

Furthermore EU liberalisation would no doubt similarly occur as part of a general policy across all areas. The point here is that just liberalising one area could create very large changes in economic structure as we have seen. If by contrast all areas are liberalised at once, then relative prices between major sectors would not be so badly disturbed and structural changes would be far less. Thus it so happens that most EU traded sectors are highly protected; if all protection were to be withdrawn, then the least-protected sectors of services and (less relevantly as now so small) basic manufacturing would expand by a fair amount at the expense of agriculture and high-tech manufacturing. Such a joint policy would have beneficial effects and would also be less politically sensitive than piecemeal liberalisation. Thus one might conclude that if EU liberalisation is to occur at all, it will be as a joint package.

Thus in this section we examine the above policies in total, substituting the model estimates coming from their joint implementation.

Total Gain/Loss if the UK unilaterally moves to free trade (per cent of GDP)

UK: +2.5% REU: −0.22%

Cf sum of individual policies: UK +3.3% REU −0.22%

Estimates using the full GE model including large-scale expansion effects from land liberalisation (see Appendix C): UK +29% REU −0.22%

To calculate these we have taken the model's total predictions of sectoral change with the complete package. For the UK (referred to in Appendix B as 'Exercise 1') it predicts a reduction in the size of basic manufacturing by 7 per cent of GDP, with these resources going into services/high-tech. To obtain the surplus cost we multiply this by (half of) the relative effect on post-tariff relative traded prices of basic manufactures/services, − 10 per cent. Notice that we are valuing the switch of resources at the free trade relative prices of manufacturing – that is, in terms of manufacturing as the numeraire.

For the contraction of high-tech within services/high-tech due to the withdrawal of 58 per cent high-tech protection we take the same estimates as above, as this is the estimate from the model for the subsectoral switch effect.

The transfer costs are the same as in the disaggregated case. For UK unilateral moves there are no terms of trade effects.

We discuss in some detail in Appendix C the meaning of the full GE model simulation with full expansion effects. This simulation is carried out on two important assumptions, designed to reflect possible political realities – both of them made in all the simulations reported here with the model, including those for the individual tariff changes. We briefly alluded to them at the start of the chapter. The first is that agricultural production is maintained at existing levels whatever the changes in trade regime, by direct subsidy payments to farmers. The second is that as demand for land changes in other sectors the planning authorities release it (that is, allow its owners to sell it with the relevant use permission) at the market price. When one has the large-scale changes in tariffs all at once as in exercises 1 and 2, these assumptions permit the expanding sectors of the economy to use a large amount of additional land released onto the market by these authorities.

Plainly the gain of welfare to the UK here is dramatically larger at 29 per cent. What is going on is that with agricultural prices at home greatly lowered by the elimination of the CAP tariffs, land prices drop very substantially and this in turn is underpinned by the assumed willingness of the planning authorities to release land for industrial use, effectively in traded services and non-traded activity. These latter two sectors are therefore able to expand considerably, enriching the factors of production, including landowners, as a result of the higher factor prices paid to labour, the higher industrial usage of land (albeit at lower prices), and finally the lower consumer prices these factors pay on spending on consumption. One may legitimately have doubts about the political feasibility of this solution which is why we do not use it as our central estimate. However it does indicate that, in the presence of some planning flexibility, the central estimate we have used, based on substitution effects only, could be a significant underestimate – how much so depending naturally on the extent of such planning flexibility.

Total Gain/Loss if the UK and the REU Simultaneously Move to Free Trade (% of GDP)

UK: +3.8% REU: +2.0% REU if UK has already liberalised +2.2%
Cf sum of individual policies: UK +2.7% REU +3.8% REU if UK
already +4.0%

Estimates using full GE model including large-scale expansion
effects from land liberalisation (see Appendix C): UK +31%, REU
+12.4% (REU if UK has already liberalised +12.6%).

In this case of the EU as a whole, liberalising effectively eliminates the whole REU high-tech and traded services industry. Hence
no further effect within this industry from any subsectoral output
change in relative prices of high-tech versus services can be assumed; this implies no terms of trade effects either. For the UK
the effects are the same as liberalising unilaterally except for the
addition of terms of trade gains from the REU changes which raise
the world prices of high-tech and services.

Notice that it makes a considerable difference, as one would
expect from our earlier discussion, if we consider the liberalisation
programmes as a whole rather than as the sum of their parts. The
breakdown of the differences is shown in detail in Appendix A.

Again we should discuss the contrasting simulation of the full
GE model with expansion effects under land liberalisation – we
do so at some length in Appendix C. The discussion of the UK
situation is no different qualitatively from above, though in this
simulation the rewards are bigger due to the favourable movement
in the terms of trade. For the REU, it is harder to make the same
political case because it is manufacturing that is expanding owing
to the fact that pre-liberalisation tariffs are much the highest in
services. Planning in any case is a highly complex phenomenon in
the REU, differing both across countries and across regions within
countries. On the other hand, given the huge pressures to create
employment under the REU conditions of generally high unemployment, the popular pressure might be greater for liberalisation.
The essential point we make here is not that the full simulation
should be believed but that it reminds us that the central case
calculation based on substitution effects alone is a minimum which
could be added to depending on the extent of land liberalisation.

APPENDIX A   DETAILS OF BASIC CASE CALCULATIONS

Effects of Trade Policy Changes in Detail

Table 7.A.1: UK alone liberalises

	Agri-culture	Basic man.	Hi-tech man.	Services
UK Tariff equivalent (%)	36	16	58	0
UK net imports (% GDP)	0.8	1.7	0.8	−3.4
Gain/loss to UK (% of UK GDP)				
Transfer from UK to EU	+0.3	+0.3	+0.5	−
Consumer surplus gain	−	+1.1	+1.1	−
No terms of trade effect				
Gain/loss to REU (% of REU GDP)				
Transfer from UK to REU	−0.06	−0.06	−0.1	

Table 7.A.2: All sectors liberalised together ('Exercise 1' in Appendix B)

	Agriculture	Basic man.	Hi-tech man.	Services
Gain/loss to UK (% of UK GDP)				
Transfer from UK to EU	+0.3	+0.3	+0.5	–
Consumer surplus gain	–	+0.3	+1.1	–
Gain/loss to REU (% of REU GDP)				
Transfer from UK to REU	−0.06	−0.06	−0.1	–

Table 7.A.3: EU as a whole liberalises

EU Tariff-equivalent (%)	36	16	58	30 (UK 0)
Gain/loss to REU (% of REU GDP)				
Transfer from UK to REU	−0.06	−0.06	−0.1	–
Consumer surplus	–	+1.1	+1.8	+2.3
Terms of trade	–	−0.5	−0.2	−1.2
Gain/loss to UK (% of UK GDP)				
Transfer from UK to EU	+0.3	+0.3	+0.5	–
Consumer surplus gain	–	+1.1	+1.1	–
Terms of trade	–	−0.6	−0.2	+0.2

Table 7.A.4: All sectors liberalised together ('Exercise 2' in Appendix B)

	Agriculture	Basic man.	Hi-tech man.	Services
Gain/loss to REU (% of REU GDP)				
Transfer from UK to REU	−0.06	−0.06	−0.1	−
Consumer surplus	−	+3.2	−	−
Terms of trade	−	−	−	−1.0
Gain/loss to UK (% of UK GDP)				
Transfer from UK to EU	+0.3	+0.3	+0.5	−
Consumer surplus gain	−	+0.7	+1.1	−
Terms of trade	−	−	−	+0.9

APPENDIX B   THE 4-BLOC WORLD COMPUTABLE GENERAL EQUILIBRIUM MODEL

The model we have used for the evaluation of general equilibrium effects of trade policy is based on one we developed for assessing the effects of globalisation on the world economy – Minford et al. (1997). This model performed well empirically in accounting for the trade trends of the 1970–1990 period; we identified a group of major causal 'shocks' during this period which between them gave a good fit to the salient features of the period – including terms of trade, production shares, sectoral trade balances, relative wage movements and employment/unemployment trends.

The model adopts the key assumptions of the Heckscher–Ohlin–Samuelson set-up. Production functions are assumed to be Cobb-Douglas and identical across countries, up to a differing productivity multiplier factor; thus factor shares are constant, enabling us to calibrate the model parsimoniously from detailed UK data that we were able to gather. There are four sectors: non-traded and three traded ones, viz. primary, basic (unskilled-labour-intensive) manufacturing and services and other (skilled-labour-intensive) manufacturing. Three immobile factors of production are identified: unskilled and skilled labour and land. Capital is mobile. All sectors are competitive and prices of traded goods of each sector are equalised across borders.

This set-up gives rise to a well-known set of equations (see below for a full listing):

1. Given world prices of traded goods, price = average costs determine the prices of immobile factors of productions.

2. These factor prices induce domestic supplies of these factors.

3. Outputs of each sector are determined by these immobile factor supplies; non-traded sector output is fixed by demand, the traded sector outputs by the supplies of immobile factors not used in the non-traded sector.

4. Demands for traded goods are set by the resulting level of total GDP.

5. World prices are set by world demand = world supply.

The world is divided into four blocs: UK, REU (rest of EU), US + rest of NAFTA, ROW (rest of world). Data for the model base run is taken from 1998, the latest generally-available information that was comprehensive at the time we started this work.

In each country we assume that for the primary sector output is politically controlled (for example, by quotas) because of the high degree of protection on agriculture and the accompanying requirement to limit the extent of output response. The supply of land is adjusted (via planning and other controls) to adjust to this and other output requirements; in other words the supply of land is demand-determined. While this assumption is crude in overriding all incentive effects on output, the reality of agricultural production is closer to this than to the uncontrolled alternative: we were unable to implement any finer assumption.

Key Model Simulations

In what follows we detail the key simulations for this model which we have used to create the cost calculations reported in the text. The model effects are broadly proportional to the size of trade policy intervention, so we generally report results for a 1 per cent tariff-equivalent (t-e) and to obtain effects for x per cent tariff-equivalents these can be multiplied by x.

There are three tables.

1. Effects of 1 per cent tariff-equivalents imposed in the UK. (Notes: in these cases terms of trade effects are negligible owing to the UK being small in the world economy; hence internal prices rise by the full extent of the t-e. Transfer effects between the UK and REU are computed separately. World manufacturing prices are the numeraire.) Full effects reported but only substitution effects used in calculations of consumer surplus (tables 7.B.1–7.B.4).

2. Effects of 1 per cent tariff-equivalents imposed in the UK and REU simultaneously (Notes: in these cases terms of trade effects are negligible owing to the UK being small in the world economy; hence internal prices rise by the full extent of the t-e. Transfer effects between the UK and REU are

computed separately. World manufacturing prices are the numeraire.) Full effects reported but only substitution effects used in calculations of consumer surplus (tables 7.B.5–7.B.8).

3. Effects of Exercise 1 (where the UK eliminates its existing tariff-equivalents) and Exercise 2 (where both the UK and REU eliminate their existing tariff-equivalents). The figures show 10 per cent of the effect (tables 7.B.9–7.B.12).

Table 7.B.1: Effects on UK of 1% tariffs in UK

TARIFFS BY UK ALONE – 1%			
Effects of 1% tariffs in UK (NB the tariff on each sector is imposed on its own, other tariffs are held at zero.)			
Sector where tariff is imposed	Basic man.	Services & hi-tech	Primary
Output (% of base GDP)			
Primary	0.00	0.00	0.00
Basic manufacturing	1.49	−1.15	−0.29
Services and high-tech manufacturing	−1.11	1.22	−0.13
Non-traded	0.64	0.39	−0.99
Factor prices (% of base)			
Unskilled labour	2.26	−0.40	−0.84
Skilled labour	−0.58	2.24	−0.63
Land	−10.48	−3.01	16.33
Factor supplies (% of base)			
Unskilled labour	0.22	−0.04	−0.08
Skilled labour	−0.28	0.26	0.02
Land	12.95	3.76	−14.62
Demand (% of base)			
Primary	0.34	0.09	−0.41
Basic manufacturing	0.09	0.03	−0.12
Services and high-tech manufacturing	1.23	0.21	−1.35
Internal prices (% of base)			
Primary	0.02	−0.01	0.99
Basic manufacturing	1.00	0.00	0.00
Services and high-tech manufacturing	0.04	0.96	−0.01
Terms of trade (% of base)			
World primary/basic manufacturing	0.02	−0.01	−0.01
World service/high-tech/basic man	0.04	−0.03	−0.01

Table 7.B.2: Effects on rest of European Union of 1% tariffs in UK

TARIFFS BY UK ALONE – 1%
Effects of 1% tariffs in UK (NB the tariff on each sector
is imposed on its own, other tariffs are held at zero.)

Sector where tariff is imposed	Basic man.	Services & hi-tech	Primary
Output (% of base GDP)			
Primary	0.00	0.00	0.00
Basic manufacturing	−0.06	0.04	0.01
Services and high-tech manufacturing	0.05	−0.04	−0.01
Non-traded	0.00	0.00	0.00
Factor prices (% of base)			
Unskilled labour	−0.03	0.02	0.01
Skilled labour	0.09	−0.07	−0.01
Land	0.12	−0.03	−0.09
Factor supplies (% of base)			
Unskilled labour	0.00	0.00	0.00
Skilled labour	0.01	−0.01	0.00
Land	−0.11	0.01	0.09
Demand (% of base)			
Primary	0.00	0.00	0.00
Basic manufacturing	0.00	0.00	0.00
Services and high-tech manufacturing	−0.01	0.01	0.01
Internal prices (% of base)			
Primary	0.02	−0.01	−0.01
Basic manufacturing	0.00	0.00	0.00
Services and high-tech manufacturing	0.04	−0.03	−0.01
Terms of trade (% of base)			
World primary/basic manufacturing	0.02	−0.01	−0.01
World service/high-tech/basic man	0.04	−0.03	−0.01

Table 7.B.3: Effects on NAFTA of 1% tariffs in UK

TARIFFS BY UK ALONE – 1% Effects of 1% tariffs in UK (NB the tariff on each sector is imposed on its own, other tariffs are held at zero.) Sector where 1% tariff is imposed	Basic man.	Services & hi-tech	Primary
Output (% of base GDP)			
Primary	0.00	0.00	0.00
Basic manufacturing	−0.06	0.05	0.01
Services and high-tech manufacturing	0.05	−0.04	−0.01
Non-traded	0.00	−0.01	0.00
Factor prices (% of base)			
Unskilled labour	−0.03	0.02	0.01
Skilled labour	0.09	−0.07	−0.01
Land	0.12	−0.03	−0.09
Factor supplies (% of base)			
Unskilled labour	0.00	0.00	0.00
Skilled labour	0.01	−0.01	0.00
Land	−0.10	0.01	0.09
Demand (% of base)			
Primary	0.00	0.00	0.00
Basic manufacturing	0.00	0.00	0.00
Services and high-tech manufacturing	−0.01	0.00	0.01
Internal prices (% of base)			
Primary	0.02	−0.01	−0.01
Basic manufacturing	0.00	0.00	0.00
Services and high-tech manufacturing	0.04	−0.03	−0.01
Terms of trade (% of base)			
World primary/basic manufacturing	0.02	−0.01	−0.01
World service/high-tech/basic man	0.04	−0.03	−0.01

Table 7.B.4: Effects on rest of world of 1% tariffs in UK

TARIFFS BY UK ALONE – 1%
Effects of 1% tariffs in UK (NB the tariff on each sector
is imposed on its own, other tariffs are held at zero.)

Sector where 1% tariff is imposed	Basic man.	Services & hi-tech	Primary
Output (% of base GDP)			
Primary	0.00	0.00	0.00
Basic manufacturing	−0.05	0.04	0.01
Services and high-tech manufacturing	0.05	−0.04	−0.01
Non-traded	0.00	0.00	0.00
Factor prices (% of base)			
Unskilled labour	−0.03	0.02	0.01
Skilled labour	0.09	−0.07	−0.01
Land	0.12	−0.03	−0.09
Factor supplies (% of base)			
Unskilled labour	0.00	0.00	0.00
Skilled labour	0.01	−0.01	0.00
Land	−0.11	0.02	0.09
Demand (% of base)			
Primary	−0.01	0.00	0.01
Basic manufacturing	−0.01	0.00	0.01
Services and high-tech manufacturing	0.00	0.00	0.00
Internal prices (% of base)			
Primary	0.02	−0.01	−0.01
Basic manufacturing	0.00	0.00	0.00
Services and high-tech manufacturing	0.04	−0.03	−0.01
Terms of trade (% of base)			
World primary/basic manufacturing	0.02	−0.01	−0.01
World service/high-tech/basic man	0.04	−0.03	−0.01

Table 7.B.5: Effects on UK of 1% tariffs in UK and rest of EU

CUSTOMS UNION TARIFFS BY EU+UK − 1%

Effects of 1% tariffs in UK and rest of EU. In each sector the tariff is imposed on its own, other tariffs are held at zero.

Sector where 1% tariff is imposed	Basic man.	Services & hi-tech	Primary
Output (% of base GDP)			
Primary	0.00	0.00	0.00
Basic manufacturing	1.22	−0.94	−0.24
Services and high-tech manufacturing	−0.86	1.01	−0.17
Non-traded	0.65	0.37	−0.98
Factor prices (% of base)			
Unskilled labour	2.10	−0.30	−0.79
Skilled labour	−0.15	1.87	−0.70
Land	−9.97	−3.16	15.88
Factor supplies (% of base)			
Unskilled labour	0.21	−0.03	−0.08
Skilled labour	−0.22	0.22	0.01
Land	12.40	3.84	−14.29
Demand (% of base)			
Primary	0.33	0.09	−0.40
Basic manufacturing	0.09	0.03	−0.11
Services and high-tech manufacturing	1.17	0.23	−1.31
Internal prices (% of base)			
Primary	0.10	−0.05	0.96
Basic manufacturing	1.00	0.00	0.00
Services and high-tech manufacturing	0.25	0.80	−0.04
Terms of trade (% of base)			
World primary/basic manufacturing	0.10	−0.05	−0.04
World service/high-tech/basic man	0.25	−0.20	−0.04

Table 7.B.6: Effects on rest of the European Union of 1% tariffs in UK and rest of EU

CUSTOMS UNION TARIFFS BY EU+UK – 1%			
Effects of 1% tariffs in UK and rest of EU. In each sector the tariff is imposed on its own, other tariffs are held at zero.			
Sector where 1% tariff is imposed	Basic man.	Services & hi-tech	Primary
Output (% of base GDP)			
Primary	0.00	0.00	0.00
Basic manufacturing	1.23	−0.93	−0.26
Services and high-tech manufacturing	−0.86	1.00	−0.15
Non-traded	0.66	0.37	−0.98
Factor prices (% of base)			
Unskilled labour	2.10	−0.30	−0.79
Skilled labour	−0.16	1.88	−0.69
Land	−9.96	−3.17	15.88
Factor supplies (% of base)			
Unskilled labour	0.21	−0.03	−0.08
Skilled labour	−0.22	0.22	0.01
Land	12.43	3.83	−14.30
Demand (% of base)			
Primary	0.33	0.07	−0.37
Basic manufacturing	0.11	0.02	−0.12
Services and high-tech manufacturing	1.20	0.23	−1.33
Internal prices (% of base)			
Primary	0.10	−0.05	0.96
Basic manufacturing	1.00	0.00	0.00
Services and high-tech manufacturing	0.25	0.80	−0.04
Terms of trade (% of base)			
World primary/basic manufacturing	0.10	−0.05	−0.04
World service/high-tech/basic man	0.25	−0.20	−0.04

Table 7.B.7: Effects on NAFTA of 1% tariffs in UK and rest of EU

Sector where 1% tariff is imposed	Basic man.	Services & hi-tech	Primary
CUSTOMS UNION TARIFFS BY EU+UK – 1% Effects of 1% tariffs in UK and rest of EU. In each sector the tariff is imposed on its own, other tariffs are held at zero.			
Output (% of base GDP)			
Primary	0.00	0.00	0.00
Basic manufacturing	−0.34	0.26	0.07
Services and high-tech manufacturing	0.31	−0.25	−0.05
Non-traded	0.01	−0.03	0.02
Factor prices (% of base)			
Unskilled labour	−0.19	0.13	0.05
Skilled labour	0.52	−0.43	−0.08
Land	0.69	−0.18	−0.47
Factor supplies (% of base)			
Unskilled labour	−0.02	0.01	0.01
Skilled labour	0.07	−0.06	−0.01
Land	−0.57	0.07	0.47
Demand (% of base)			
Primary	−0.03	0.01	0.01
Basic manufacturing	−0.01	0.00	0.01
Services and high-tech manufacturing	−0.07	0.03	0.04
Internal prices (% of base)			
Primary	0.10	−0.05	−0.04
Basic manufacturing	0.00	0.00	0.00
Services and high-tech manufacturing	0.25	−0.20	−0.04
Terms of trade (% of base)			
World primary/basic manufacturing	0.10	−0.05	−0.04
World service/high-tech/basic man	0.25	−0.20	−0.04

Table 7.B.8: Effects on rest of the world of 1% tariffs in UK and rest of EU

CUSTOMS UNION TARIFFS BY EU+UK – 1%			
Effects of 1% tariffs in UK and rest of EU. In each sector the tariff is imposed on its own, other tariffs are held at zero.			
Sector where 1% tariff is imposed	Basic man.	Services & hi-tech	Primary
Output (% of base GDP)			
Primary	0.00	0.00	0.00
Basic manufacturing	−0.29	0.22	0.06
Services and high-tech manufacturing	0.28	−0.22	−0.05
Non-traded	−0.02	0.00	0.02
Factor prices (% of base)			
Unskilled labour	−0.19	0.13	0.05
Skilled labour	0.52	−0.43	−0.08
Land	0.69	−0.18	−0.47
Factor supplies (% of base)			
Unskilled labour	−0.02	0.01	0.01
Skilled labour	0.07	−0.06	−0.01
Land	−0.62	0.12	0.47
Demand (% of base)			
Primary	−0.04	−0.01	0.05
Basic manufacturing	−0.04	−0.01	0.04
Services and high-tech manufacturing	−0.02	0.00	0.02
Internal prices (% of base)			
Primary	0.10	−0.05	−0.04
Basic manufacturing	0.00	0.00	0.00
Services and high-tech manufacturing	0.25	−0.20	−0.04
Terms of trade (% of base)			
World primary/basic manufacturing	0.10	−0.05	−0.04
World service/high-tech/basic man	0.25	−0.20	−0.04

Table 7.B.9: Effect on UK of removal of trade barriers

REMOVAL OF TRADE BARRIERS SIMULTANEOUSLY		
Exercise 1: UK withdraws from all EU trade arrangements to free trade from existing arrangements		
Exercise 2: Both EU and UK move to free trade on all products from existing arrangements		
Results for two exercises	Ex. 1	Ex. 2
Output (% of base GDP)		
Primary	0.00	0.00
Basic manufacturing	−8.06	−16.63
Services and high-tech manufacturing	19.06	26.29
Non-traded	45.49	39.30
Factor prices (% of base)		
Unskilled labour	1.41	−3.54
Skilled labour	24.84	37.58
Land	−99.01	−99.60
Factor supplies (% of base)		
Unskilled labour	0.14	−0.36
Skilled labour	2.10	3.70
Land	10932.22	3912.00
Demand (% of base)		
Primary	10.69	9.68
Basic manufacturing	3.19	2.85
Services and high-tech manufacturing	35.24	30.86
Internal prices (% of base)		
Primary	−35.91	−34.73
Basic manufacturing	−16.00	−16.00
Services and high-tech manufacturing	−7.28	−1.77
Terms of trade (% of base)		
World primary/basic manufacturing	0.13	1.79
World service/high-tech/basic man	−0.30	5.54

Note: Exercise 2 was solved at 80% of the full shock and the results shown obtained by raising the simulated responses pro rata (convergence for the model could not be obtained for 100% of the shock).

Table 7.B.10: Effect on rest of European Union of removal of trade barriers

REMOVAL OF TRADE BARRIERS SIMULTANEOUSLY		
Exercise 1: UK withdraws from all EU trade arrangements to free trade from existing arrangements		
Exercise 2: Both EU and UK move to free trade on all products from existing arrangements		
Results for two exercises	Ex. 1	Ex. 2
Output (% of base GDP)		
Primary	0.00	0.00
Basic manufacturing	0.31	35.35
Services and high-tech manufacturing	−0.38	−27.26
Non-traded	−0.25	15.77
Factor prices (% of base)		
Unskilled labour	0.01	13.38
Skilled labour	−0.76	−44.29
Land	2.99	−98.70
Factor supplies (% of base)		
Unskilled labour	0.00	1.28
Skilled labour	−0.08	−6.56
Land	−3.17	1187.40
Demand (% of base)		
Primary	−0.07	7.18
Basic manufacturing	−0.02	2.35
Services and high-tech manufacturing	−0.25	26.33
Internal prices (% of base)		
Primary	0.13	−34.73
Basic manufacturing	0.00	−16.00
Services and high-tech manufacturing	−0.30	−34.15
Terms of trade (% of base)		
World primary/basic manufacturing	0.13	1.79
World service/high-tech/basic man	−0.30	5.54

Note: Exercise 2 was solved at 80% of the full shock and the results shown obtained by raising the simulated responses pro rata (convergence for the model could not be obtained for 100% of the shock).

Table 7.B.11: Effect on NAFTA of removal of trade barriers

REMOVAL OF TRADE BARRIERS SIMULTANEOUSLY
Exercise 1: UK withdraws from all EU trade arrangements to
free trade from existing arrangements
Exercise 2: Both EU and UK move to free trade on all products
from existing arrangements

Results for two exercises	Ex. 1	Ex. 2
Output (% of base GDP)		
Primary	0.00	0.00
Basic manufacturing	0.33	−7.30
Services and high-tech manufacturing	−0.40	6.83
Non-traded	−0.26	0.52
Factor prices (% of base)		
Unskilled labour	0.01	−3.77
Skilled labour	−0.76	11.88
Land	2.99	11.07
Factor supplies (% of base)		
Unskilled labour	0.00	−0.38
Skilled labour	−0.08	1.53
Land	−3.19	−7.65
Demand (% of base)		
Primary	−0.08	−0.47
Basic manufacturing	−0.03	−0.18
Services and high-tech manufacturing	−0.20	−1.31
Internal prices (% of base)		
Primary	0.13	1.79
Basic manufacturing	0.00	0.00
Services and high-tech manufacturing	−0.30	5.54
Terms of trade (% of base)		
World primary/basic manufacturing	0.13	1.79
World service/high-tech/basic man	−0.30	5.54

Note: Exercise 2 was solved at 80% of the full shock and the results shown
obtained by raising the simulated responses pro rata (convergence for the
model could not be obtained for 100% of the shock).

Table 7.B.12: Effect on rest of world of removal of trade barriers

REMOVAL OF TRADE BARRIERS SIMULTANEOUSLY		
Exercise 1: UK withdraws from all EU trade arrangements to free trade from existing arrangements		
Exercise 2: Both EU and UK move to free trade on all products from existing arrangements		
Results for two exercises	Ex. 1	Ex. 2
Output (% of base GDP)		
Primary	0.00	0.00
Basic manufacturing	0.26	−6.36
Services and high-tech manufacturing	−0.35	5.99
Non-traded	−0.23	0.05
Factor prices (% of base)		
Unskilled labour	0.01	−3.77
Skilled labour	−0.76	11.88
Land	2.99	11.07
Factor supplies (% of base)		
Unskilled labour	0.00	−0.38
Skilled labour	−0.08	1.53
Land	−3.10	−8.54
Demand (% of base)		
Primary	−0.24	−1.00
Basic manufacturing	−0.21	−0.87
Services and high-tech manufacturing	−0.10	−0.42
Internal prices (% of base)		
Primary	0.13	1.79
Basic manufacturing	0.00	0.00
Services and high-tech manufacturing	−0.30	5.54
Terms of trade (% of base)		
World primary/basic manufacturing	0.13	1.79
World service/high-tech/basic man	−0.30	5.54

Note: Exercise 2 was solved at 80% of the full shock and the results shown obtained by raising the simulated responses pro rata (convergence for the model could not be obtained for 100% of the shock).

APPENDIX C   WELFARE CALCULATIONS USING THE GENERAL EQUILIBRIUM MODEL

So far in this chapter we have used the GE model solely to provide estimates of output substitution effects and price effects. These have been combined with (a) standard formulae for consumer surplus gains and losses (b) direct calculation of the transfers between UK and REU, to provide an overall estimate of welfare losses. Note that in principle income effects are ignored because it is assumed that they do not increase the population's welfare: thus the expansion in output of one sector other than at the expense of another is offset in value by the use of resources in that expansion.

However we can also use the full GE model to provide an estimate. In this there is a complete accounting for all incomes and resource use and we may compute the total welfare measure in income equivalent. The GE model used here makes two important constraining assumptions: (a) that agricultural output is held (by government subsidies directly to producers, financed by lump sum taxes on households) at its original level (b) that land supply is controlled via planning/zoning procedures to equal demand for it from productive sectors of the economy. Implicit in this last assumption is that private use of land is only permitted in 'job creating' use, and otherwise is 'marginal' in reservation use (perhaps for leisure or low-value agricultural, for example subsistence, use). These assumptions were made to mirror the reality of government policies around the world. Governments are notoriously reluctant to allow agricultural output to vary with market conditions. They also generally do place substantial constraints on land use; land is often not allowed to be used for maximum private gain but rather is allocated for 'job creation' (with its implicit appeal to the community in which the land is being used).

The alternative, more standard, assumptions would have been to assume land to be brought into use in response to its market price and to assume agricultural output would adjust to market forces. However, we found that the commercial policy changes considered here produced very large fluctuations in agricultural output, which appeared totally unrealistic. Indeed so great are the relative price changes introduced when the UK is assumed to leave the EU that agricultural output is driven to zero in the free market solution (with no constraints at all). In fact there is some doubt whether one can get the model to solve at all because this is a 'corner solution' (that is, one where some relationships are frustrated by the absence of further resources to accommodate the expansion of other industries as agriculture disappears; in effect the model would like agriculture to go negative).

Plainly such a disappearance of agriculture would be unlikely to be permitted politically. One could accompany the assumption that agricultural production was somehow preserved by the assumption that a producer subsidy rate is paid to farmers sufficient to induce them to continue producing the same amount as before; however such a rate would have to be very high in order to allow farming to compete for land with the now-more-profitable service industries. Again, this falls foul of likely political reality.

Hence our adoption of our two assumptions above. What these amount to is that land is made available through the planning process in sufficient quantity to accommodate its expanding use in services, as well as its existing use in agriculture. This keeps the price of land down; as a result no ('deficiency') payments to farmers are needed to keep them producing at existing rates, at least in principle. In political terms one can think of the release of unused farming land as the 'compensation' to farmers for their lower prices; in economic terms however what is happening is that the price of 'planning land' is coming down towards the price of unused farming land.

In the chapter and main text we have used our general equilibrium results to support a conventional calculation of the trade costs – viz. one that ignores 'expansion' or 'income' effects. These are typically ignored because in general equilibrium existing resources can only support so much output; any expansion of one industry must therefore be offset by the contraction of another. The 'substitution' effect calculation done in the text calculates the increase in the efficiency of the use of resources from this substitution but obviously does not count any gain from the expansion of one industry. Similarly if resources are expanded by factor price changes, it is typically assumed that such expansion must come at the cost of extra effort or the loss of alternative uses (for land, for example, perhaps in private leisure use). Thus any expansion in overall GDP would come at an equivalent cost in resource utilisation and should not be counted.

Following this method, our calculations in the main text use the GE model only to provide estimates of the substitution of one industry for another and additionally of the world terms of trade effect of policy changes. These are then inserted into a standard trade efficiency calculation to obtain our main estimates. It is approximately as if we were assuming in the GE model not merely that agricultural output was fixed but that total non-agricultural output was fixed too.

This approach is highly conservative in calculating the trade costs for the following reason. Under our two 'political' assumptions made above the GE model in fact permits substantial overall expansion. Because the land used in the expansion is over-priced via the planning process, the extra availability permits extra value to be generated from available UK resources. What occurs is that the planning process, by making much extra land available, permits its price to fall sharply, allowing UK households to produce much more with their labour and capital without corresponding extra cost.

How realistic is this large extra supply of land? Some might argue that Nimbyism (the 'not-in-my-back-yard' protests that stalemate the supply of planning land) makes it entirely unrealistic. However it is worth reflecting on the nature of the industrial expansion in question in the UK, where the price changes unleashed by EU exit induce a massive expansion in services and a contraction in manufacturing, with agriculture unchanged. Services expansion can generally be accommodated in an environmentally friendly manner; the basic requirements of services being office buildings and capital such as computers. One can imagine a sprouting of stylishly-structured industrial parks in the countryside which might, because of the extra jobs provided, turn out to be generally popular to planners' constituencies.

In the case of the REU liberalising as well, the above analysis does not apply as it turns out that within the REU services are more highly protected than manufacturing and that it is therefore manufacturing and non-traded that expand massively at the expense of traded services. Whether the politics of providing more land for manufacturing and non-traded is attractive within the REU planning systems is beyond our ability to predict. The population density of the REU is much lower in most countries than in the UK. Also the unemployment rates are much higher, suggesting that there would be popular pressure for more land availability to support more jobs. However, the politics of land supply is complex and differs from country to country and even region to region. Thus there must be even more of a question mark about the practicality of the solution with expansion effects in Exercise 2 than there already is in Exercise 1.

Plainly we would not wish to put forward a calculation on this basis as a central one. However it is of some interest to take the GE model under these assumptions at face value and see what the welfare implications would be. Notice that in this case we are looking at not merely a structural transformation of British industry towards traded services but also a very large expansion in the economy, as traded services not merely expand beyond the mere substitution extent but also generate matching expansion in non-traded industries, also mostly of the service type.

The raw material of these calculations is in the attached tables. The welfare formula in general equilibrium is then the extra real spending power of UK households (= their factor incomes deflated by the consumer price index) minus the economic value of the extra input they contribute. For land this value is calculated as the extra land times the final price paid for it (once planning has released it): thus it is being assumed that planners' constituents value land at this new price once the new opportunities are presented to them (by implication the value of land to them cannot be greater than this as they have willingly given up all the extra land for only this price). For labour it is in standard manner the extra supply times the original price plus half the change in price induced by the policy changes (the latter being the 'surplus' cost).

The figures are, perhaps unsurprisingly, much larger than the cautious ones of the text:

Table 7.C.1: Welfare gains from Table 7.B.9

	UK	EU	NAFTA	ROW
UK leaves EU for unilateral free trade				
Welfare gains (% of GDP):	29.0	$(-0.2)^a$	neg	neg

	UK	EU	NAFTA	ROW
Both UK and EU move to free trade				
Welfare gains (% of GDP):	31.0	12.4^b	neg	neg

Notes:

a.   As given in the main text; the spillover effects of UK departure are negligible, apart from the loss of EU customs union revenue from the UK, as calculated in main text.

b.   Net of the loss of Customs Union revenue from UK as in main text.

APPENDIX D   LISTING OF THE GENERAL EQUILIBRIUM 4-BLOC TRADE MODEL

1–4 Prices, UK, Rest of EU, NAFTA, Rest of World p_M, p_S, p_A, p_D
p_M, p_S, p_A, p_D, domestic prices, solve for w, h, l and p_D respectively.

$$p_M = w^{0.52234} \cdot h^{0.14366} \cdot l^{0.035} \cdot (p_M \cdot r)^{0.299} \cdot \pi_M^{-1}$$

$$p_S = w^{0.21168} \cdot h^{0.51832} \cdot l^{0.033} \cdot (p_M \cdot r)^{0.237} \cdot \pi_S^{-1}$$

$$p_A = w^{0.147} \cdot h^{0.132} \cdot l^{0.079} \cdot (p_M \cdot r)^{0.642} \cdot \pi_A^{-1}$$

$$p_D = w^{0.38024} \cdot h^{0.17576} \cdot l^{0.113} \cdot (p_M \cdot r)^{0.331} \cdot \pi_D^{-1}$$

$$\ln(w) = \left(\frac{1}{0.52234}\right) \cdot \left\{ \begin{array}{c} \ln(p_M \cdot \pi_M) - 0.14366 \cdot \ln(h) - 0.035 \cdot \\ \ln(l) - 0.299 \cdot \ln(p_M \cdot r) \end{array} \right\}$$

$$\ln(h) = \left(\frac{1}{0.51832}\right) \cdot \left\{ \begin{array}{c} \ln(p_S \cdot \pi_S) - 0.21168 \cdot \ln(w) - 0.033 \cdot \\ \ln(l) - 0.237 \cdot \ln(p_M \cdot r) \end{array} \right\}$$

$$\ln(l) = \left(\frac{1}{0.079}\right) \cdot \left\{ \begin{array}{c} \ln(p_A \cdot \pi_A) - 0.147 \cdot \ln(w) - 0.132 \cdot \ln(h) \\ -0.642 \cdot \ln(p_M \cdot r) \end{array} \right\}$$

5–7 Factor demands, UK, Rest of EU, NAFTA, Rest of World N, H, L:

$$N = w^{-1} \cdot \left(\begin{array}{c} 0.38024 \cdot p_D \cdot y_D + 0.52234 \cdot y_M \cdot p_M + 0.21168 \cdot \\ p_S \cdot y_S + 0.147 \cdot p_A \cdot y_A \end{array} \right)$$

$$H = h^{-1} \cdot \left(\begin{array}{c} 0.168 \cdot p_D \cdot y_D + 0.14366 \cdot y_M \cdot p_M + 0.51832 \cdot p_S \\ \cdot y_S + 0.132 \cdot p_A \cdot y_A \end{array} \right)$$

$$L = l^{-1} \cdot \left(\begin{array}{c} 0.113 \cdot p_D \cdot y_D + 0.035 \cdot y_M \cdot p_M + 0.033 \cdot p_S \cdot y_S \\ +0.079 \cdot p_A \cdot y_A \end{array} \right)$$

$$y_M = \left(\frac{1}{0.52234 \cdot p_M}\right) \cdot \left\{ \begin{array}{c} N \cdot w - 0.38024 \cdot p_D \cdot y_D - 0.21168 \cdot \\ p_S \cdot y_S - 0.147 \cdot p_A \cdot y_A \end{array} \right\}$$

$$y_S = \left(\frac{1}{0.51832 \cdot p_S}\right) \cdot \left\{ \begin{array}{c} H \cdot h - 0.168 \cdot p_D \cdot y_D - 0.14366 \cdot p_M \cdot \\ y_M - 0.132 \cdot p_A \cdot y_A \end{array} \right\}$$

$$y_A = \left(\frac{1}{0.079 \cdot p_A}\right) \cdot \left\{ \begin{array}{c} L \cdot l - 0.113 \cdot p_D \cdot y_D - 0.035 \cdot p_M \cdot y_M \\ -0.033 \cdot p_S \cdot y_S \end{array} \right\}$$

When y^A is exogenised (as it is in these simulations), the last equation is solved for L and the exogenous values used for y^A are from the base run, viz.:

$$y_A^{\text{UK}} = 71.00$$
$$y_A^{\text{EU14}} = 306.00$$
$$y_A^{\text{NAFTA}} = 503.00$$
$$y_A^{\text{RofW}} = 3460.00$$

8 K

$$K = 0.2 \cdot \frac{1}{(p_M \cdot r)} \cdot \left\{ \begin{array}{l} 0.331 \cdot p_D \cdot y_D + 0.299 \cdot p_M \cdot y_M \\ +0.237 \cdot p_S \cdot y_S + 0.642 \cdot p_A \cdot y_A \end{array} \right\} + 0.8 \cdot K_{t-1}$$

9–11 Factor supplies:

$$N = a_N \cdot \left(\frac{w}{b}\right)^{0.1} \cdot POP^{0.5} \cdot G^{0.5}$$
$$a_N^{\text{UK}} = 0.486815$$
$$a_N^{\text{EU14}} = 1.105789$$
$$a_N^{\text{NAFTA}} = 1.309601$$
$$a_N^{\text{RofW}} = 71.594820$$

$$H = a_H \cdot \left(\frac{h}{w}\right)^{0.1} \cdot G^{0.5}$$
$$a_H^{\text{UK}} = 1.273294$$
$$a_H^{\text{EU14}} = 3.789872$$
$$a_H^{\text{NAFTA}} = 5.157474$$
$$a_H^{\text{RofW}} = 84.815077$$

$$L = a_L \cdot \left(\frac{l}{w}\right)^{0.1} \cdot POP^{0.5}$$
$$a_L^{\text{UK}} = 2.93624328$$
$$a_L^{\text{EU14}} = 14.232869988$$
$$a_L^{\text{NAFTA}} = 22.38231873$$
$$a_L^{\text{RofW}} = 1311.358098$$

If y^A is exogenised (as it is in these simulations) then factor supply for L is determined by equation 7 above, as noted earlier so that:

$$L = l^{-1} \cdot \left(\begin{array}{c} 0.113 \cdot p_D \cdot y_D + 0.035 \cdot y_M \cdot p_M + 0.033 \cdot p_S \cdot y_S \\ +0.079 \cdot p_A \cdot y_A \end{array} \right)$$

12   y_D
$$y_D = 0.50 \cdot E^{1.0} \cdot \left(\frac{p_D}{p_T} \right)^{-0.5}$$

13   y
$$y = y_D + y_M + y_S + y_A$$

14   E
$$E = y$$

15   C
$$C = E - \Delta K$$

16   E_T
$$E_T = E - y_D$$

17   E_M
$$E_M = E_T - E_S - E_A$$

18   E_S

$$E_S^{\text{UK}} = 0.9 \cdot E_T^{\text{UK}} - 238.90 - 12.0 \cdot \left(p_S^{\text{UK}} - p_T^{\text{UK}} \right)$$
$$E_S^{\text{EU14}} = 0.9 \cdot E_T^{\text{EU14}} - 1180.30 - 12.0 \cdot \left(p_S^{\text{EU14}} - p_T^{\text{EU14}} \right)$$
$$E_S^{\text{NAFTA}} = 0.9 \cdot E_T^{\text{NAFTA}} - 1335.00 - 12.0 \cdot \left(p_S^{\text{NAFTA}} - p_T^{\text{NAFTA}} \right)$$
$$E_S^{\text{RofW}} = 0.212 \cdot E_T^{\text{RofW}} + 1757.60 - 3.0 \cdot \left(p_S^{\text{RofW}} - p_T^{\text{RofW}} \right)$$

19   E_A

$$E_A^{\text{UK}} = 0.05 \cdot E_T^{\text{UK}} + 47.95 - 5.0 \cdot \left(p_A^{\text{UK}} - p_T^{\text{UK}} \right)$$
$$E_A^{\text{EU14}} = 0.05 \cdot E_T^{\text{EU14}} + 217.65 - 5.0 \cdot \left(p_A^{\text{EU14}} - p_T^{\text{EU14}} \right)$$
$$E_A^{\text{NAFTA}} = 0.05 \cdot E_T^{\text{NAFTA}} + 247.00 - 5.0 \cdot \left(p_A^{\text{NAFTA}} - p_T^{\text{NAFTA}} \right)$$
$$E_A^{\text{RofW}} = 0.413 \cdot E_T^{\text{RofW}} - 1168.35 - 15.0 \cdot \left(p_A^{\text{RofW}} - p_T^{\text{RofW}} \right)$$

20 p

$$p = p_M \cdot \left(\frac{E_M^{base}}{E^{base}}\right) + p_S \cdot \left(\frac{E_S^{base}}{E^{base}}\right) + p_A \cdot \left(\frac{E_A^{base}}{E^{base}}\right) + p_D \cdot \left(\frac{E_T^{base}}{E^{base}}\right)$$

21–23 p_M, p_S, p_A

$$p_M = p_M^{World} \cdot (1 + T_M)$$
$$p_S = p_S^{World} \cdot (1 + T_S)$$
$$p_A = p_A^{World} \cdot (1 + T_A)$$

24 p_T

$$p_T = p_M \cdot \left(\frac{E_M}{E_T}\right) + p_S \cdot \left(\frac{E_S}{E_T}\right) + p_A \cdot \left(\frac{E_A}{E_T}\right)$$

World prices. Sums are over four blocs.
Variables without superscripts are bloc variables.
p_A^{World} is derived from the relationship :

$$\sum y_A = \sum E_A$$

The RHS is expanded using the expression for E_A in Equation 19 and the expression for p_A in Equation 27.
a_1, a_2 and a_3 are the coefficients from the RHS of the equation for E_A

$$\sum y_A = \sum \{a_1 \cdot E_T + a_2 + a_3 \cdot (p_A - p_T)\}$$
$$\sum y_A = \sum \{a_1 \cdot E_T + a_2 + a_3 \cdot (1 + T_A) \cdot p_A^{World} - a_3 \cdot p_T\}$$
$$\sum y_A = \sum \{a_1 \cdot E_T + a_2 - a_3 \cdot p_T\} + p_A^{World} \cdot \sum a_3 \cdot (1 + T_A)$$
$$p_A^{World} = \frac{\sum y_A - \sum \{a_1 \cdot E_T - a_2 + a_3 \cdot p_T\}}{\sum a_3 \cdot (1 + T_A)}$$

p_S^{World} is derived similarly.
b_1, b_2 and b_3 are the coefficients from the RHS of the equation for E_S :

$$\sum y_S = \sum E_S$$

and

$$p_S^{\text{World}} = \frac{\sum y_S - \sum \{b_1 \cdot E_T - b_2 + b_3 \cdot p_T\}}{\sum b_3 \cdot (1 + T_S)}$$

Glossary

Subscripts
i	Sector
M	Manufacturing
S	Services
A	Primary
D	Non-traded
y	Output

Factor prices
w	Unskilled
h	Services and high-tech
l	Land

Factor supplies
N	Unskilled
H	Skilled
L	Land
E	Demand
p_i	Internal prices
p	GDP deflator

K	Capital
C	Consumption
r	Interest rate
π	Productivity
POP	working population
T	Tariff

Part 3

OVERALL CONCLUSIONS OF THE ANALYSIS

8 Last Thoughts: What is to be done?

In this chapter we consider this question in the context of the politics of our relationship with the EU. Some people say that the overriding reason for our membership of the EU is political: to ensure the unity of Europe and to prevent future wars. There is no doubt, given the ferocious history of our continent in the twentieth century, that this is a crucial aim. The expansion of the EU to include the ex-Soviet countries of eastern Europe is a major contributor to this aim. The EU is therefore plainly an important institution alongside others that govern inter-country relations in the twenty-first century including NATO, the UN, the WTO, the IMF and the World Bank.

However, the political aims of the EU as a community of nations do not need to be achieved by the exaction of huge economic costs from members of that community. We have argued in the preceding chapters that these costs are large also for other members of the EU. That is of course a matter for them; our focus has primarily been on the costs for the UK, which are of great size, as we have seen. Indeed, quite obviously the costs are unacceptably high by a large margin. Hence inevitably the UK is being forced to a reconsideration of its relationship with the EU in such a way that the political aims of peace and amity in Europe are not jeopardised. Nevertheless we must pause first to consider the wider issues for the whole of the EU.

8.1   THE LOGIC OF REFORM IN EUROPE

What is striking in what we have gone through is the huge costs for
the citizens of continental Europe, as well as those for UK citizens.
In fact of course we have been unable to measure the costs of
the heavy taxation and regulation already in place in continental
Europe; we measured the costs of protection but as far as these
other costs went we merely measured the cost of imposing them
on the UK. However, it is unlikely that their costs in continental
Europe are much less than those of imposing them on the UK,
that is, of the order of more than 10 per cent of GDP and more
than 10 per cent unemployment. When one adds these costs to
the measured costs of protection (some 3 per cent of GDP); it is
plain that the citizens of Europe are suffering under an intolerable
burden of inefficiency and waste.

Why is this? Plainly there is no space here to consider such a
weighty issue in detail. However the broad answer is clear enough:
the power of minorities to prevent, in their own narrow interests,
improvement and growth for the majority. These minorities include unions (which work for the benefit of their senior members
through the retention of restrictive practices and barriers to job
entry), the churches (which conspire to prevent Sunday shopping
and work to protect their attendance rolls), various single-issue
groups (including environmental, religious and 'social' in various
respects), large-scale industry that is no longer economic, and the
political groups that represent them and are paid for by them.
What nevertheless is puzzling is how the climate of opinion permits these groups to wield power with impunity. Here one is driven
to consider the role of education in economic matters – or rather
the lack of it. Thus most informed opinion has no idea of the costs
of the restrictive practices conceded to these groups; their agendas are considered in an economic vacuum, even though it is the
economics that is ruinous.

If one looks around the EU today, one is also struck by how different the situation is already in many of the smaller and also in the
less developed continental countries. Thus Spain has made considerable strides in reform, as have Austria and the Netherlands, to
take three examples. It is the three large economies at the centre
of the continent geographically that not only show no sign of serious change and adamantly resist change at the European level,

but also do their best to export their backward approach up to the European level and outwards to the parts of the EU that do not follow them – most especially of course to the UK.

This monstrous conspiracy by a few in Germany, France and Italy in short to defraud not only their own citizens but also those of their neighbours is an astonishing thing to contemplate. In one major sense this book is an attempt to draw attention to this conspiracy among its victims, not just in the UK but across Europe. It can be read as a call to arms to these victims, to put Europe right and to dethrone these few conspirators.

For it is obvious that just as these costs are huge so by the same token the potential for improvement and greater prosperity are as large. The problem is also the opportunity. Given that politically the expansion and consolidation of Europe is an exciting project with great benefits for many peoples, why cannot the economics catch up? Why must economic structures remain shrouded in an economically-illiterate 'social-democratic' fog?

The main answer to the question posed in this book (viz. what is to be done about the huge economic costs created as a by-product of the 'European Project'?) is therefore plain. It is that these costs are unnecessary, imposed by narrow interest groups on the wider public; and that they should be assaulted by a serious reform process. So far, reform in Europe has been essentially non-serious, a matter of what progress could be made by doing things that do not address the main tax and regulative restrictions at the heart of the problem. For example we have heard a lot about ALMs (active labour market measures), about subsidies to this and that (technology, small business and so on), about 'empowerment' of minority groups (women, young people, the elderly). Yet some of these are counter-productive (for example, subsidies raise taxes even further and the net effect is likely to be negative) and certainly they are all useless in the absence of measures to deregulate and open up markets (including the elimination of protection), to reduce the powers of anti-competitive agents like unions, and above all to lower marginal tax rates and business costs.

How likely is this? Lip-service has now been paid to these ideas for well over a decade – taking form in various 'agendas', Lisbon, Luxembourg, Cardiff and so forth – by the very people who never had any intention of carrying them out and indeed were responsible for the original problems; such men as Kohl, Schröder, Chirac,

Mitterrand and Prodi. Now we have seen the accession of several ex-Soviet states of eastern Europe, with more shortly to join – states that having experienced these regulative excesses in severe form have given their citizens a crash course in modern economics. Possibly the politicians from these states will help to swing the centre of gravity within the EU towards genuine reform. A new Commission has just been appointed under a Portuguese ex-prime minister, whose composition gives some hope that reform will be high on the agenda. However, in the face of the opposition from the three large countries' leaderships, one naturally wonders what hope it and its sympathisers among other governments really have.

At any rate, after so many years in an EU that has been unrelentingly hostile to its ideas of economic organisation and imposed such costs on it, it would be foolish of the UK to assume that reform will succeed. As matters stand the EU has in place a series of policies that appear well set to stay and that have the extremely damaging effects described above in the pages of this book. It is only prudent to plan for the worst. We now go on to consider what form that planning might take.

8.2   THE UK'S RELATIONSHIP WITH EUROPE ASSUMING EUROPE DOES NOT REFORM

The logic of this situation points to the UK doing one of two things. It can renegotiate a relationship within the Rome Treaty, a 'UK protocol' let us call it. Or it could leave the treaty altogether and achieve its political aims through other avenues – much as other friendly countries outside the EU, such as Norway or the US, do.

It may seem that the idea of renegotiation is a hopeless one, since why should other EU members agree to it? Yet in the present context where a dominant coalition of EU members is bent on creating a federal structure and the UK is largely isolated in its opposition to such a structure, the renegotiation offers an opportunity of universal progress. Under the terms of the Rome Treaty agreement on a new structure must be unanimous; thus the UK has the power of stalemate. This power has been greatly enhanced by this government's agreement to a UK referendum on the new draft EU constitution; it seems fairly likely that any structure remotely like the draft constitution would get the UK popular assent in a referendum. However, by renegotiation the UK could agree to allow others who so wished to proceed to a new federal structure within the treaty.

Of course, such a renegotiation would no doubt cause other countries unhappy with aspects of the treaty to consider asking for renegotiation also. This would be a matter for them; many would in all probability rather settle to join the dominant coalition for a variety of reasons of national interest.

Thus it seems reasonably likely that this coalition of the EU majority would be happy to agree on a UK protocol as the price of using the treaty to forge a federal union. However, one cannot be sure; such inter-national bargaining is inherently unpredictable. Suppose they refused and did one of two things. First, they could accept a stalemate and rely on the forces of gradual pressure to achieve the same federalist objectives over a longer period of time. Or second they could decide to proceed en bloc to recreate the desired federal union outside the EU institutions, creating in effect a duplicate structure; though this would pose practical difficulties as well as difficulties in the process of obtaining a completely fresh agreement on all previously agreed areas, it is not to be ruled out.

What should the UK do in these two cases? In the second the UK would de facto have left the EU since the existing treaty would be without practical content. In the first, the UK could wait and see, meanwhile resisting the pressure from the federalist agenda. However, given the extensive and subtle powers conceded already to the EU's central bodies, this resistance would be likely to fail. It is likely that before long the same crisis that has currently arisen with the draft constitution would reappear. It would therefore be an attractive option in this stalemate case to leave, given the lack of desire for accommodation.

In all this it needs to be remembered that the other EU members could react to the genuine threat of UK departure by becoming more accommodating. This is possible precisely because these members see the EU primarily in political terms and the loss of the UK would diminish the political weight of the EU.

There is a further point: that the present policy arrangements of the EU damage the welfare of the other EU country citizens just as they do that of UK citizens. With the UK threatening to leave over these policies, there could be a strengthening of the voices of those demanding change within the rest of the EU. The EU could reform in the direction of free trade, non-interventionism and competition, removing the arguments with the UK. However, we do not think anyone should hold their breath: this prospect looks remote.

Some people fear a different reaction: where either the EU as a whole or individual EU member states erecting discriminatory barriers against UK exports, whether special tariffs or other arrangements such as onerous customs requirements – all in retaliation against what they see as the UK's unreasonable departure or renegotiation. But such fears can be dismissed, for three main reasons. First of all, the changes the UK would ask for would not end a high degree of mutual cooperation in a variety of economic and political areas; any such retaliation would put such other areas of cooperation at risk and be against EU and individual EU members' interests. Second, the EU exports far more food and manufactured products to the UK than the UK does to the EU; the UK is a net importer of both and a war of trade retaliation would be damaging to the EU. Third, once the UK had opted for free trade in food and manufactures, such barriers would not affect the prices we paid for our imports or obtained for our exports, they would merely lead to a diversion of trade away from the EU. (The same applies to services where in any case the UK faces high barriers.) The only cost in this case would be temporary disruption as trade patterns were changed. But last and most important, such actions would be illegal under WTO trade law, and since the EU is a signatory to the WTO by implication under EU law. It is absurd to imagine that the EU, which relies so heavily on WTO law for large numbers of trade disputes, would put itself at risk by ignoring WTO law in its dealings with the UK, a state involved with it in friendly cooperation across so many areas, including the development of the single market in services.

What form finally therefore should a renegotiation of the UK's relationship take? We suggest here that it should be:

1. The UK should leave the EU's protective agreements altogether – the CAP, tariffs and anti-dumping and all else – and resume unilateral free trade. The agreement would place the UK outside the EU's protective arrangements; non-discrimination would be agreed, so that we would have the

same access to the EU market as any WTO non-EU member and EU members would have the same free access to the UK market as any WTO member.

2. If there were genuine concern about the EU pursuing discriminatory trade policies against the UK, then the UK could also join NAFTA to create countervailing power in the event of traded disputes. NAFTA allows each member to pursue its own trade agenda, provided it allows other NAFTA members free access in agreed trade areas. It would therefore be entirely consistent with the UK's free trade policy. However, as noted in our discussion above, there should be no concern on this score: joining NAFTA is unnecessary.

3. In the area of services, the UK already largely has free trade and free market entry. Here the Single Market could bring about competition within the EU through the discussions going on area by area. The UK has nothing to lose by participating in these discussions; and to the extent that residual UK barriers could be dismantled in particular areas, the UK would actually gain. Therefore, the UK should stay in the discussions on the Single Market for services, cooperating on a case-by-case basis to create new agreements. Existing competition agreements as for airlines would be kept to.

4. Freedom of movement of capital and labour has already been established and brought benefits. The UK should continue in these arrangements.

5. In other areas – such as competition policy, economic consultations, coordination of anti-terrorist policies – the UK would continue to participate but by specific and limited agreements in each area.

6. The 'social dimension' of the EU, including the Working Time Directive imposed for 'health and safety' reasons under the Single Market laws, would be abrogated in the UK.

7. Finally, EU law would no longer be binding on the UK. Instead, only those agreements explicitly made with the EU would be, as any treaty obligation, incorporated into UK law.

As already extensively discussed above, the UK would under these circumstances be outside the EU's customs union in food and manufacturing and would enjoy world prices. The EU could not reasonably be expected – nor would it be likely – to extend to the UK preferences in EU markets for our food and manufactured exports. Instead the UK would be treated like any other world trading country outside the customs union. It would have to pay any tariffs and anti-dumping duties and be subject to any other non-tariff barriers imposed on external suppliers. In whatever markets EU prices are kept up by the operation of an implicit cartel forcing potential low-price exporters to raise their EU prices – an arrangement we have suggested could be the most widespread of all the non-tariff mechanisms in EU use – then UK exporters too would be subject to this cartel. Ironically, this would benefit them considerably, just as it benefits other low-price participants in the cartel, provided they have a good market share. UK exporters are well established in the EU market and could well find that they continue to do well in it after UK exit to free trade. Since this situation would be costly to the EU and would draw wide attention to the existence of such cartel arrangements, the result could be greater pressure for EU competition, which would be beneficial to EU members. Such a development would bring about greater harmony in the long term in relations between the UK and the EU, making possible closer cooperation in trade policy, a key area from which the UK would have withdrawn.

Inside the UK either this new relationship, or total departure from the EU, would lower the prices received by farmers and by manufacturers previously protected by the EU customs union barriers. Transitional assistance should be given to them by the UK taxpayer (who of course will reap substantial gains from the new set-up). The whole issue of farm support and support of the rural environment will have to be visited afresh; in broad terms a long-lasting package that rewarded farmers for preserving the rural environment and freed them to carry out entrepreneurial development of their business and their assets (especially their land) could be devised, an arrangement such as this would make sense for both farmers and the taxpayer. For manufacturers however any assistance should only be transitional, since the UK's comparative advantage implies that resources should be shifted from this sector into the service sector.

8.3   CONCLUSIONS

In the course of this book we have examined the current functioning of EU economic policies and found them to be massively costly, to UK citizens in the first instance but in the second to EU peoples generally. Thus though the main focus of this book has been narrowly on the UK's interests it has inevitably taken in the much wider perspective of the EU as a whole. Additionally it should not be forgotten that other parties too lose out from the EU's policy failures in the trade area especially – these trade costs for others were also briefly reviewed above.

The only really satisfactory solution to this EU policy failure is for the EU itself to change its policies. This option, that of the 'reform agenda', has been pressed upon it from all sides (most recently again in reports from the IMF and the OECD), and has in principle been adopted by the EU in a series of summits – Lisbon, Luxembourg and so on.... However, one must be realistic; progress has been minimal, indeed in material respects matters have regressed. Most importantly the forces that support existing policies have gone on the rampage in recent months by adopting the draft constitution which is a document entrenching existing approaches and in many ways strengthening them.

Thus it seems only prudent to adopt the realistic view that these forces show no loss of power, no sign that they will permit meaningful reform and furthermore every sign that they will attempt to generalise their approach more effectively to recalcitrant elements in the EU such as the UK. Our argument in this book therefore amounts to this: the UK must protect itself against this situation as it threatens immense economic costs to the UK. Plainly at the very least the UK must resist new incursions into its economic policies – notably the draft constitution, the euro, new efforts at harmonisation and any demands for bail-out. However this essentially defensive posture would still leave the UK not only paying large existing costs but also vulnerable to opportunistic ambushes establishing elements of the above. Hence it is inadequate to safeguard the UK's interests. Our suggestion therefore is that of a 'UK protocol' under which the UK would withdraw from elements of these EU policies – essentially to unilateral free trade while maintaining the underlying freedoms of movement of labour and capital of the EU and also aspects of the Single Market, notably in services as they come to be deregulated over time. It is hard to judge in the end whether other EU members would go along with this. Should there be no willingness to do so, then it would be in the UK's interests to leave the EU and unilaterally pursue liberal policies, including towards members of the EU. We have shown in these pages that on the assumption that the EU would impose on the UK all the external barriers it now levies on other non-members the UK would be considerably better-off by following this course.

In conclusion, the UK and the EU have had a seriously troubled relationship for some two decades. Those troubles have concerned not merely the obvious irritations of rising political interference by the EU in UK affairs, but also the major costs of the EU's use of its steadily-increasing powers in economic affairs; the latter are the focus of this book since they are of a technical nature and therefore not at all widely understood and appreciated. Since our analysis suggests that the EU generally is damaged by current policies, we must hope that these policies would change in a way that would progressively also reduce the UK's costs arising from the EU, making formal changes in the UK's treaty with the EU unnecessary. However in the event that this does not occur, as the tendencies of the last two decades suggest it will not, then such formal changes are inevitable. We have shown that they are possible and highly beneficial to the UK. We have also argued that they are likely to help the forces of change within the EU since they will highlight the problems there by the very fact that they will no longer be present here; institutional competition between countries is a potent force in world affairs. Thus in the long term it is in all EU members' interests that the UK puts an end to what we have shown are the intolerable economic costs of its relationship with the EU.

Bibliography

Ackrill, R. (1999), 'CAP Reform 1999: Crisis Management in Search of a Crisis?' University of Leicester Discussion Papers in European Economics 99/1.

ACNielsen (2000), 'A Report into International Price Comparisons', Prepared for the Department of Trade and Industry, UK, 13 February. http://www.dti.gov.uk/CACP/cp/ipr/.

Amatori, F. (1999), 'European Business: New Strategies, Old Structures', *Foreign Policy* (summer), pp. 78–9.

Ark, B. van, R. Inklaar and R.H. McGuckin (2003), 'Changing Gear: Productivity, ICT and Service Industries: Europe and the United States', in J.F. Christensen and P. Maskell (eds) *The Industrial Dynamics of the New Digital Economy*, Edward Elgar, Cheltenham, UK and Northampton, USA, pp. 56–99.

Arthur Andersen (1999), 'Study for Dixons', Press Release 19 July.

Artis, M.J and N. Nixson (2001), *The Economics of the European Union*, Third Edition, Oxford University Press, Oxford.

Bacchetta. M. and B. Bora. (2003), Industrial Tariff Liberalization and the Doha Development Agenda, World Trade Organisation, DP No. 1.

Basu, S. and J. G. Fernald (1995), 'Are apparent productive spillovers a figment of specification error?', *Journal of Monetary Economics* **36**, pp. 165–88.

Batavia, B., N. Lash, A. G. Malliaris and E. Elgar (2001), 'The Impact of Agricultural Policies of EU and NAFTA on World Trade', in C. C. Paraskevopoulos, A. A. Kintis, and A. J. Kondonassis (eds), *Globalization and the Political Economy of Trade Policy*, APF Press, Ontario, Canada, pp. 225–36.

BBC (2003), US steel tariffs 'cost thousands of US jobs', 5 February. http://news.bbc.co.uk/1/hi/business/2726521.stm.

Beaureau of Economic Analysis (2004), *US International Services: Cross-Border Trade 1986–2002, and Sales Through Affiliates, 1986–2001.* International Economic Account, Washington D. C.

Belderbos, R. (2003), 'Antidumping and Foreign Divestment: Japanese Electronics Multinationals in the EU', *Weltwirtschaftliches Archiv*, 139 **(1)**, pp. 131–60.

Berger, N., W. C. Hunter. and S. G. Timme (1993), 'The Efficiency of Financial Institutions: A Review and Preview of Research Past, and Future', *Journal of Banking & Finance*, **17** (2–3), pp. 221–49.

Blake, A.T., A.J. Rayner and G.V. Reed (1998), 'A CGE Analysis of Agricultural Liberalization: The Uruguay Round and CAP Reform', First Annual Conference on Global Economic Analysis, Purdue University, USA.

Blake, A.T., L.J. Hubbard, G. Philippidis, A.J. Rayner and G.V. Reed (1999), 'General Equilibrium Modelling of The Common Agricultural Policy'. Report to the MAFF and HM Treasury.

Blonigen, B. A. and T. J. Prusa (2001) 'Anti-dumping'. *NBER Working Paper No. w8398*, July

Blonigen, B. A. and T. J. Prusa (2003), 'The Cost of Antidumping: The Devil is in the Details', *Journal of Policy Reform*, **6**(4), pp 233–246.

BLS (Bureau of Labor Statistics) (1999), Consumer Expenditure Survey,
United States Bureau of Labor Statistics, Washington D. C.

Borrell, B. and L.J. Hubbart (2000), 'Global Economic Effects of the EU Common Agricultural Policy', *Economic Affairs: Reforming the CAP*, **20**, pp. 18–26.

Bradford S. C. (2003), 'Paying the Price: Final Goods Protection in OECD Countries', *Review of Economics and Statistics*, **85**(1), pp. 24–37.

Bradford. S. and R. Z. Lawrence (2004), *Has Globalization Gone Far Enough? The Costs of Fragmented Markets*, Institute for International Economics, Washington D. C.

Brown, D. K., A. V. Deardorff and R. M. Stern (1996), 'Modeling Multilateral Liberalization in Services', *Asia-Pacific Economic Review*, **2**, pp. 21–34.

Brown, D. K. and R. M. Stern (1999), 'Measurement and Modelling of the Economic Effects of Trade and Investment Barriers in Services', Paper prepared for the Coalition of Services Industries (CSI) World Services Congress Atlanta, Georgia, 1–3 November.

Brown, D. K. and R. M. Stern (2000), 'Measurement and Modeling of the Economic Effects of Trade and Investment Barriers in Services', School of Public Policy Discussion Paper No. 453, University of Michigan.

Brown, D. K., A.V. Deardorff and R. M. Stern (2002), 'CGE Modeling and Analysis of Multilateral and Regional Negotiating Options', in R. M. Stern (ed.), *Issues and Options for US-Japan Trade Policies*, University of Michigan Press, Ann Arbor, pp. 23–76.

Buckwell, A.E., D.R. Harvey, K.J. Thomson and K.A. Parton (1982), *The Costs of the Common Agricultural Policy*, Croom Helm, Canberra and London.

Burniaux, J.M., and J. Waelbroeck (1985), 'The Impact of the CAP on Developing Countries: A General Equilibrium Analysis', in Stevens, C. and J. Verloren van Themat, (eds), *Pressure Groups, Policies and Development*, Hodder and Stoughton, London. pp. 123–140.

Burniaux, J. M. and J. Waelbroeck (1992), 'Preliminary Results of Two Experimental Models of General Equilibrium with Imperfect Competition', *Journal of Policy Modelling*, **14**, pp. 65–92.

Caballero, R. J. and R. K. Lyons (1990) 'Internal versus external economies in European industry', *European Economic Review* **34**, pp. 805–30.

Caballero, R. J. and R. K. Lyons (1991) 'External effects and Europe's integration', in L.A. Winters and A.J. Venables (eds), *European integration: trade and industry*, (CEPR), Cambridge University Press, Cambridge.

Caballero, R. J. and R. K. Lyons (1992) 'External effects in U.S. procyclical productivity', *Journal of Monetary Economics*, **29**, pp. 209–25.

CIE (Centre for International Economics) (2002a), Opportunity of a Century to Liberalise farm Trade, CIE, Canberra & Sydney, October.

CIE (Centre for International Economics) (2002b), Targets for OECD Sugar Market Liberalisation, CIE, Canberra & Sydney, October.

Chadha, R., D. Brown, A. Deardorff and R. Stern (2000), 'Computational Analysis of the Impact on India of the Uruguay Round and the Forthcoming WTO Trade Negotiations', School of Public Policy Discussion Paper No. 459, University of Michigan. Ann Arbor, Michigan.

Cecchini Report (1988), 'The Cost of Non-Europe', European Commission, Brussels.

Chadha, R. (2001), 'GATS and the Developing Countries: A Case Study of India', in Robert M. Stern (ed.), *Services in the International Economy: Measurement and Modeling, Sectoral and Country Studies, and Issues in the WTO Services Negotiations*, University of Michigan Press, Ann Arbor, Michigan, pp. 245–66.

Colecchia, A. (2001), 'The Impact of Information and Communications Technologies on Output Growth: Issues and preliminary Findings',
OECD STI Working Paper No 11, Geneva.

Colman, D. (ed.) (2002), Phasing out Milk Quotas in the EU. Report to DEFRA, SEERAD, NAW, and DARDNI. Centre for Agricultural Food and Resource Economics, Manchester.

Consumers Association (2001), Scrap the Cap! Consumers' Association Says Abolish the Common Agricultural Policy, as Research Shows UK Food Prices are Artificially High, 11 December.

Cox, D. and Harris, R. (1985) 'Trade Liberalization and Industrial Organization: Some Estimates for Canada', *Journal of Political Economy*, **93**, pp. 115–45.

Dang T T, P. Antolin and H. Oxley (2001), 'Fiscal implications of ageing; projections of age-related spending', Economics Department Working Paper No 305, OECD, Paris.

De Boer, J. (2002), The Sustainability of Japanese and EU Agricultural Policies, Japanese Institute of Global Communications Europe Report No. 17, July 25.

Dee, P. and K. Hanslow (1999), Modelling Liberalisation of Services, Paper presented at Productivity Commission and Australian National University Joint Conference, Australian National University, Canberra, 26–27 June.

Dee, P. and Hanslow, K. (2000), 'Multilateral Liberalisation of Services Trade', Productivity Commission Staff Research Paper, Ausinfo, Canberra.

Dee, P. and K. Hanslow (2001), 'Multilateral Liberalisation of Services Trade', in R Stern (ed.) *Services in the International Economy*, University of Michigan Press, Ann Arbor, pp. 117–39.

DEFRA (2003a), 'A New Direction for Agriculture: An Economic Note', http://www.defra.gov.uk/farm/agendtwo/stage3/econote.pdf.

DEFRA (2003b), Assessment of the Economic Impact of the Commission's Long Term Perspective For Sustainable Agriculture, March

DFAT (Department of Foreign Affairs and Trade, Australia) (1999), 'Global Trade Reform: Maintaining Momentum', Canberra

Diao. X., T. Roe and A. Somwaru (2001), 'What is the Cause of Growth in Regional Trade: Trade Liberalization or RTAs? The Case of Agriculture', *The World Economy*, **24**(1), pp. 51–79.

DigiTimes (2001), 'EU Decides Anti-Dumping Tariffs for CD-R Disc Companies', 20 December, http://www.digitimes.com/.

Dihel, N. (2002), 'Measuring the Benefits of Services Trade Liberalisation'. Background Paper, OECD–World Bank Services Experts Meeting, OECD, Paris, 4–5 March.

Dimaranan, B, T. Hertel and R. Keeney (2003), 'OECD Domestic Support and Developing Countries', World Institute for Development Economics Research Discussion Paper No. 2003/32.

Dobson, W. and P. Jacquet (1998), *Financial Services Liberalization in the WTO*, Institute for International Economics, Washington D. C.

DTI (Department of Trade and Industry) (2000), 'The Service Sector in France and UK: Addressing Barriers to the Growth of Output and Employment. An Anglo-French Report', http://www.dti.gov.uk/europe/servicesector.pdf.

DTI (Department of Trade and Industry) (2004) 'Industrial tariffs and non-tariff barriers (NTBs)' http://www.dti.gov.uk/ewt/tarrifs.htm.

DTI (Department of Trade and Industry) (2004) 'Partial Regulatory Impact Assessment (RIA) of the Directive of the European Parliament and of the Council on Services in the Internal Market', http://www.dti.gov.uk/ccp/topics2/pdf2/servicesria.pdf.

EC (European Commission) (1994), 'EC Agricultural Policy for the 21st Century', European Economy Reports and Studies.

EC (European Commission) (2001) 'Ninth Survey on State Aid in the European Union', Brussels.

EC (European Commission) (2002a), 'The Agricultural Situation in the European Union 2000, Report, European Commission, Brussels.

EC (European Commission) (2002b), 'Report on the State of Internal Market for Services', Brussels.

EC (European Commission) (2002c), 'The European Airline Industry: From Single Market to World-wide Challenges', Brussels.

EC (European Commission) (2003a), 'Agriculture in the European Union. Statistical and Economic Information 2002', Brussels.

EC (European Commission) (2003b), '9th Report on the Implementation of the Telecommunications Regulatory Package', Brussels.

Elbehri A. and S. Leetmaa (2002), 'How Significant are Export Subsidies to Agricultural Trade? Trade and Welfare Implications of Global Reforms'. Presented as a selected paper at the 5th Annual Conference on Global Economic Analysis, June 5–7, Taipei, Taiwan.

Electricity Association (2003), *International Electricity Price*, Preliminary Issue 27, London.

Emerson, M., M. Aujean, M. Catinat, P, Goybet and A. Jacquemin (1988), 'The Economics of 1992: The E.C. commission's assessment of the economic effects of completing the internal market', Oxford University Press, Oxford.

European Communities (1997), 'Dismantling of Barriers: Public Procurement', *The Single Market Review*, Office for Official Publications of the European Communities, Kogan Page-Earthscan: Luxembourg.

European Union (2000), 'Impact of Agenda 2000 Decisions for CAP Reform on Consumers', in *Impact Analyses of the Agenda 2000 Decisions for CAP Reforms*, Directorate-General for Agriculture of the European Commission, Brussels, February, pp. 85–90.

Folmer, C., M.A. Keyzer, M.D. Merbis,, H.J.J. Stolwijk and P.J.J. Veenendaal (1995), *The Common Agricultural Policy Beyond the MacSharry Reform*, Elsevier, Amsterdam.

Forbes Global (2004), 'The Tax Misery Index', May 24.

Francois, J.F., B. MacDonald, H. Nordström (1995), 'Assessing the Uruguay Round,' in W. Martin and A. Winters (eds), *The Uruguay Round and the Developing Economies*, The World Bank, Discussion Paper 201.

Francois, J. F. and H. K. Hall. (1997), 'Partial Equilibrium Modelling', in J. F. Francois and K. A. Reinert (eds), *Applied Methods for Trade Policy Analysis: A Handbook*, Cambridge University Press. Cambridge.

Francois J. F. and B. Hoekman (1999), *Market Access in the Services Sector*, Tingerben Institute.

Francois, J. F. and H. Glismann (2000), 'The Cost of EU Trade Protection In Textiles and Clothing'. Kiel Institute of World Economics Working Paper No. 997, Kiel.

Frandsen, S.E., B. Gersfelt and H.G. Jensen (2003), 'Impacts of Redesigning European Agricultural Support', *Review of Urban & Regional Development Studies*, **15** (2), pp. 106–31.

Gallaway M. P., B. A. Blonigen and J. F. Flynn (1999), 'Welfare Costs of US Anti-dumping and Countervailing Duty Laws', *Journal of International Economics*, **49** (2), pp. 211–44.

Gasiorek, M., A. Smith and A. J. Venables. (2002), 'The Accession of the UK to the EC: A Welfare Analysis', *Journal of Common Market Studies*, **40** (3), pp. 425–47.

Gasiorek, M., A. Smith and A. J. Venables (2002) 'The benefits to the UK of joining the EU: An Imperfect Competition CGE Analysis', *Journal of Common Market Studies*, **23** (4), pp. 425–47.

Gersfelt, B., S.E. Frandsen and H.G. Jensen (2002), *Decoupling the EU Direct Support*, 10th Congress of the European Association of Agricultural Economists, Spain, August.

Gohin A., and C. Meyers. (2002), 'The Phasing out of Export Subsidies: Impacts on EU Agriculture', International Conference on Policy modeling, 2002/07/04–06.

Guardian (2002), 'End Farming Subsidies. Europe Should Take the Lead', October 26.

Gulbrandsen, O. and A. Lindbeck (1973), 'The Economics of the Agricultural Sector' O. Industriens Utredningsinstitut, Stockholm. (Swedish ed. 1969).

Gyllenhammar Report (2002), *The Benefits of a Working European Retail Market for Financial Services*, European Commission, Brussels.

Haaland, J. and T.C. Tollefsen (1994), 'The Uruguay Round and Trade in Manufactures and Services. General Equilibrium Simulations of Production, Trade and welfare Effects of Liberalization', CEPR Discussion Paper 1008.

Hardin, A. and L. Holmes (1997), 'Services Trade and Foreign

Direct Investment', Staff Research Paper, Industry Commission, Australian Government Publishing Services, Canberra

Harrison, G.W., T.F. Rutherford and I. Wooton, (1995), 'Liberalising Agriculture in the European Union'. *Journal of Policy Modelling*, 17, pp. 223-55.

Harvey, D.R. and K.J. Thomson, (1981), 'Costs, Benefits and the Future of the Common Agricultural Policy', *Journal of Common Market Studies*, **24**, pp. 1-20.

Haskel, J., and H. Wolf (2002), 'From Big Macs to iMacs: What do International Price Comparisons tell us?', *World Economics*, **1** (2), pp. 167–78.

Henriksen, E., K.H.M. Knarvik and F. Steen (2001), 'Economies of Scale in European Manufacturing Revisited', CEPR Discussion Paper No. 2896, July.

Hertel, T. W. (ed.) (1997), *Global Trade Analysis: Modelling and Applications*, Cambridge University Press, Cambridge.

Hertel, T.W. (2000), 'Potential Gains from Reducing Trade Barriers in Manufacturing, Services and Agriculture', *Federal Reserve Bank of St. Louis Review*, **82** (4), pp. 77–99.

Hertel, T. W, K. Anderson, J. F. Francois and W. Martin (2000), 'Agriculture and Non-Agricultural Liberalization in the Millennium Round', Policy Discussion Paper No. 0016, Centre for International Economic Studies University of Adelaide.

Hindley, B. (1991) 'The Economics of Dumping and Anti-Dumping Action: Is there a baby in the bathwater?' in Tharakan, P.K.M. (ed.), *Policy Implications of Antidumping Measures*, Elsevier-Science Publishers B.V., Amsterdam.

Hindley, B. and M. Howe (2001), *Better Off Out? The Benefits or Costs of EU Membership*, Institute of Economic Affairs, London.

Hindley, B. and P. Messerlin. (1996), *Antidumping Industrial Policy: Legalized Protectionism in the WTO and What to Do About It*, AEI Press (Washington)

Hoekman, B. (1995), 'Assessing the General Agreement on Trade in Services', in W. Martin and L. A. Winters (eds) *The Uruguay Round and the Developing Economies*, World Bank, Washington D. C., pp. 327–64.

Hoekman, B. (2000), 'The Next Round of Services Negotiations: Identifying Priorities and Options', *Federal Reserve Bank of St. Louis Review* (July/August), pp. 31–47.

Hoekman, B and P. Braga. (1997), 'Protection and Trade in Services: A Survey', *Open Economies Review*, **8**, pp. 285–308.

Hoekman, B., N. Ng and M. Olarreaga, (2002) 'Eliminating Excessive Tariffs on Exports of Least Developed Countries', *World Bank Economic Review*, **16**, pp. 11–21.

Hubbard, L.J. (1995a), 'General Equilibrium Analysis of the CAP Using the GTAP model'. *Oxford Agrarian Studies*, **23**, pp. 163–76.

Hubbard, L.J. (1995b), 'CGE Modelling of the CAP: Trade Elasticities, Structural Effects and Welfare', Department of Agricultural Economics and Food Marketing Discussion Paper No. 4/95, University of Newcastle upon Tyne.

Hufbauer, G. C. and K. A. Elliott (1994), *Measuring the Costs of Protection in the United States*, Institute of International Economics, Washington, D.C.

Hufbauer, G. C., E. Wada and T. Warren (2002), *The Benefits of International Price Convergence: Speculative Calculations*, Institute for International Economics, Washington, D.C.

IMF (International Monetary Fund) (2002a), *US Selected Issues*, Country Report No. 02/165, August, Washington D.C.

IMF (International Monetary Fund) (2002b), 'World Economic Outlook Trade and Finance', *World Economic and Financial Surveys*, September, Washington D. C.

Johnson, D. G. (1995), *Less than Meets the Eye: The Modest Impact of CAP Reform*, Centre for Policy Studies, London.

Kalirajan, K. (2000), 'Restrictions on Trade in Distribution Services', Productivity Commission Staff Research Paper, Ausinfo, Canberra.

Kalirajan, K., G. McGuire, D. Nguyen-Hong and M. Schuele (2001), 'The Price Impact of Restrictions on Banking Services', in C. Findlay and T. Warren (eds) *Impediments to Trade in Services: Measurement and Policy Implications*, Routledge, New York, pp. 215–30.

Kang, J. S. (2001), 'Price Impact of Restrictions on Maritime Transport Services', in C. Findlay and T. Warren (eds) *Impediments to Trade in Services: Measurement and Policy Implications*, Routledge, New York, pp. 189–200.

Karsenty, G. (2000), 'Assessing Trade in Services by Mode of Supply', in P. Sauvé and R. Stern (eds), *GATS 2000: New Directions in Services Trade Liberalisation*, Brookings Institution,

Washington D.C., pp. 33–56.

Kox, H, Lejour, A., and R. Montizaan (2004) 'The free movement of services within the EU', Report No 69, CPB Netherlands Bureau for Economic Policy Analysis, the Hague.

Krugman, P. (1980), 'Scale Economies, Product Differentiation, and the Pattern of Trade', *American Economic Review*, **70**, pp. 950–59.

Leach, G. (2000), 'EU Membership — What's The Bottom Line?', Institute of Directors Policy Paper, March.

Lindsey, B. and D. J. Ikenson. (2003) *Antidumping Exposed: The Devilish Details of Unfair Trade Law*. Cato Institute, Washington, D.C.

Lloyd, T., O. Morrissey and G. Reed (1998), 'Estimating the Impact of Anti-dumping and Anti-cartel Actions Using Intervention Analysis', *Economic Journal*, **108** (447), pp. 458–76.

Mattoo, A. (1999), 'Financial Services and the WTO: Liberalization in the Developing and Transition Economies', World Bank Working Paper 2184, World Bank, Washington D.C.

McGuire, G. (1998), 'Australia's Restrictions on Trade in Financial Services', Productivity Commission Staff Research Paper, Australia, Canberra.

McGuire, G. and M. Schuele (2000), 'Restrictiveness of International Trade in Banking Services', in C. Findlay and T. Warren (eds), *Impediments to Trade in Services: Measurement and Policy Implications*, Routledge, London and New York, pp. 201–14.

McGuire, G., M. Schuele and T. Smith (2000), 'Restrictiveness of International Trade in Maritime Services', in C. Findlay and T. Warren (eds), *Impediments to Trade in Services: Measurement and Policy Implications*, Routledge, London and New York, pp. 172–88.

Meijl, H. van and F. van Tongeren (2002), 'The Agenda 2000 CAP Reform, World Prices and GATT–WTO Export Constraints', *European Review of Agricultural Economics*, **29** (4), pp. 445–70.

Mercenier, J. (1993) 'On Intertemporal General-Equilibrium Reallocation Effects of Europe's Move to a Single Market', Federal Reserve Bank of Minneapolis, Working Paper Number 87, December.

Messerlin, P. (2001), *Measuring the Costs of Protection in Europe:*

European Commercial Policy in the 2000s, Institute of International Economics, Washington D. C.

Milne, Ian (2004), *A Cost Too Far? An Analysis of the Net Economic Costs and Benefits for the UK of EU Membership*, Civitas, London.

Minford, A. P. L. (1996), *Britain and Europe: The Balance Sheet*, MCB University Press, Bradford.

Minford, A. P. L, J. Riley and E. Nowell (1997). 'Trade, Technology and Labour Markets in the World Economy 1970–1990: A Computational General Equilibrium Analysis'. *Journal of Development Studies*, **34** (2), pp 1–34.

Minford, A. P. L (1998), *Markets not Stakes – the Triumph of Capitalism and the Stakeholder Fallacy*, Orion Publishing, London,

Minford, A.P.L. and B. Jamieson (1999), *Britain and Europe: Choices for Change*, Politeia, London.

Minford, A. P. L. (2002) 'Should Britain Join the Euro? The Chancellor's Five Tests Examined', Institute of Economic Affairs, Occasional Paper 126, London.

Morris, C.N. (1980), 'The Common Agricultural Policy', *Fiscal Studies*, **1**, pp. 15-35.

Neufeld, I. N. (2001), 'Anti-dumping and Countervailing Procedures – Use or Abuse? Implications for Developing Countries'. Policy Issues in International Trade and Commodities Study Series No. 9, UNCTAD, New York and Geneva.

Nguyen-Hong, D. (2000), 'Restrictions on Trade in Professional Services', Productivity Commission Staff Research Paper, Ausinfo, Canberra, August

Nicoletti, G, S. Scarpetta and O. Boylaud (1999), 'Summary Indicators of Product Market Regulation with an Extension to Employment Protection Legislation', OECD Economics Department Working Papers, No 226, Paris.

Nicoletti, G. and S. Scarpetta (2001), 'Interactions between Product and Labour Market Regulations: Do they Affect Employment? Evidence from OECD Countries', Paper presented at the Banco de Portugal Conference on 'Labour Market Institutions and Economic Outcomes', 3–4 June, Cascais.

NIESR (2000), 'Continent Cut Off? The Macroeconomic Impact of British Withdrawal from the EU', February

Normile, M. A, A.B.W. Effland and C. E. Young (2004), 'US and EU Farm Policy – How Similar?', in M. A. Normile and S.E.

Leetmaa (eds), *US–EU Food and Agriculture Comparisons*, Economic Research Service, USDA, WRS-04-04.

Notaro, G. (2002), 'European Integration and Productivity: Exploring the Gains of the Single Market', Working Paper, London Economics, London.

OECD (1992), *Agricultural Policies, Markets and Trade: Monitoring and Outlook*, Paris.

OECD (1997), The OECD Report on Regulatory Reform, II, Thematic Studies, Paris

OECD (1997a), *Indicators of Tariff and Non-tariff Trade Barriers*, Geneva.

OECD (1997b), *Assessing Barriers to Trade in Services: A Pilot Study on Accountancy Services*, TD/TC/WP(97)26, Working Party of the Trade Committee. Paris.

OECD (2000a), 'Small and Medium Enterprise Outlook', Paris.

OECD (2000b), 'Quantification of the Costs to National Welfare of Barriers to Trade in Services: Scoping Paper', TD/TC/WP(2000)32, Working Party of the Trade Committee, Paris, 4–5 December

OECD (2001a), 'Towards more Liberal Agricultural Trade', Policy Brief, *OECD Observer*, November, Paris.

OECD (2001b), *The Development Dimensions of Trade*, Paris.

OECD (2001c), 'The Characteristics and Quality of Service Sector Jobs', *Employment Outlook 2001*, Paris.

OECD (2001d), *Open Services Markets Matter*, Working Party of the Trade Committee. Trade Directorate, TD/TC/WP(2001)24 /PART1/REV1.

OECD (2001e), 'Fiscal Implications of Ageing: Projections of Age-related Spending', OECD Economics Department Working Papers No. 305, OECD Economics Department.

OECD (2002a), *Agricultural Policies in OECD Countries: Monitoring and Evaluation 2002*, Paris.

OECD (2002b), *Basic Statistics*, Paris.

OECD (2002c), *GATS: The Case for Open Services Markets*, Paris.

OECD (2003a), *Agricultural Policies in OECD Countries Monitoring and Evaluation 2003 Highlights*, Paris.

OECD (2003b), *Quantifying Benefits of Liberalising Trade in Services*, Paris.

OECD (2004a), 'Employment Outlook', Paris.

OECD (2004b), 'Earnings Structure Database', Paris.

OECD (2004c), *Producer and Consumer Support Estimates, OECD Database 1986–2003*, Paris.

ONS (Office of National Statistics) (2003), *United Kingdom's Balance of Payments — The Pink Book*, London.

Pacific Economic Co-operation Council (1995), *Survey of Impediments to Trade and Investment in the APEC Region*, APEC Secretariat, Singapore.

Pain, N. and Young, G. (2000), The Macroeconomic Impact of UK Withdrawal from the EU, *Economic Modelling*, Elsevier, **21**(3), pp. 337–408

Peridy, N. (2004), 'Trade effects of scale economies: evidence from four EU countries', *Economics Letters*, **83**:3 (6), pp 399–403

Philippidis, G. and Hubbard L.J. (2001), 'The Economic Cost of the CAP Revisited', *Agricultural Economics*, **25** (2), pp. 375–85.

Pratten, C. (1988), 'A Survey of the Economies of Scale', in *Research on the Cost of Non-Europe*, **2**, Commission of the European Communities, Brussels.

Roberts, I. (1985), 'Agricultural Policies in the European Community', Bureau of Agricultural Economics Policy Monograph No. 2, Canberra.

Robinson, S., Z. Wang and W. Martin (2002), 'Capturing the Implications of Services Trade Liberalization', *Economic System Research*, **14** (1), pp. 3–33.

Roland-Holst, D.W., K.A. Reinert and C.R. Shiells (1994), 'A General Equilibrium Analysis of North American Integration', in J.F. Francois and C.R. Shiells (eds.), *Modelling Trade Policy: AGE Models of North American Free Trade*, Cambridge University Press, Cambridge.

Roseveare, D., W. Leibfritz, D. Fore and E. Wurzel (1996), 'Ageing Populations, Pension Systems and Government Budgets: Simulation for 20 OECD Countries', Economics Department Working Paper No. 168, OECD, Paris.

Rother, P.C., M. Catenaro and G. Schwab (2003) 'Ageing and Pensions in the Euro Area: Survey and Projection Results', Social Protection Discussion Paper 0307, World Bank, Washington D.C.

Rural Migration News. (2002), *Farm Subsidies: US, EU*, Volume 8, Number 3, July.

Smith, A. and A.J. Venables (1988), 'Completing the Internal Market in the European Community', *European Economic Review*, **32**, pp. 1501–525

Spencer, J. (1985), 'The European Economic Community: General Equilibrium Computations and the Economic Implications of Membership'. in: J. Piggot and J. Whalley (eds.), *New Developments in Applied General Equilibrium Analysis*, Cambridge University Press, Cambridge, pp. 94–124.

Stoeckel, A.B. and J. Breckling (1989), 'Some Economy Wide Effects of Agricultural Policies in the European Community: a General Equilibrium Study', in A.B. Stoeckel, D. Vincent and S. Cuthbertson (eds.), *Macroeconomic Consequences of Farm Support Policies*, Duke University Press, Durham

Stoeckel, A. (2002), 'Opportunities of a Century to Liberalise Farm Trade', Rural Industries Research and Development Corporation, Canberra.

Swinnen, J. F. M. (2003), 'The EU Budget, Enlargement and Reform of the Common Agricultural Policy and the Structural Funds', Paper presented at the Land Use Policy Group (LUPG) Conference on 'Future Policies for Rural Europe' 12–14 March 2003, Brussels.

Tharakan, P. K. M. (1991) 'The Political Economy of Anti-Dumping undertakings in the European Communities', *European Economic Review*, 35, pp. 1341–59.

Thum, C. (2002), 'Trade Liberalisation Benefits to EU Member States', in C. Thum (ed.), *Globalization, Trade Liberalization and Benefits*, A Mark Twain Institute Publication.

TUC (Trade Union Congress) (2002a) 'UK has least bank holidays in Europe — TUC wants three more a year', Tuesday 30 April, http://www.tuc.org.uk/work_life/tuc-4809-f0.cfm.

TUC (Trade Union Congress) (2002b), '48,000 Manufacturing Jobs Lost in Yorkshire and Humberside in the last three years', Monday 1 June, http://www.tuc.org.uk/em_research/tuc-5152-f0.cfm

Turner, D. and P. Richardson (2003), 'The Global Business'. *OECD Observer*, July 12.

Tyers, R. (1985), 'International Impacts of Protection: Model Structure and Results for EC Agricultural Policy'. *Journal of Policy Modelling*, 7, pp. 219–52.

Tyers, R. and K. Anderson (1987), 'Liberalising OECD Agricultural Policies in the Uruguay Round: Effects on Trade and Welfare', Working paper on Trade and Development no. 87/10, Australian National University, Canberra.

Tyers, R. and K. Anderson (1992), *Disarray in World Food Markets: A Quantitative Assessment*, Cambridge University Press, Cambridge.

USITC (United States International Trade Commission) (2000), 'The Impact on the US Economy of Including the United Kingdom in a Free Trade Arrangement with the United States, Canada and Mexico', Investigation 332-409, pub. 3339, Washington, D.C.

USITC (United States International Trade Commission) (2002), *Recent Trends in US Services Trade 2002 Annual Report*, Publication No 3514, Washington D.C.

UNCTAD (2003), *Back to Basics: Market Access Issues in the Doha Agenda*, New York and Geneva.

USDA (United States Department of Agriculture) (2001), *The Agriculture Policy Reform in WTO – Summary Report*, Washington, D.C.

USDA (United States Department of Agriculture) (2004), 'US–EU Food and Agriculture Comparisons', Economic Research Service, Agriculture and Trade Report No. (WRS04-04), February.

USTR (United States Trade Representative) (2003), *Trade Policy Agenda*, March. Washington, D.C.

Venables, A. and A. Smith (1986), 'Trade and Industrial Policy Under Imperfect Competition', *Economic Policy*, 1, pp. 622–72.

Verikios, G. and X. Zhang. (2004), 'The Economic Effects of Removing Barriers to Trade in Telecommunications', *The World Economy*, **27** (3), pp. 435–58.

Wall, H. J. (1999), 'Using Gravity Model to Estimate the Costs of Protection'. *Federal Reserve Bank of St Louis Review*, January–February, pp. 33–40.

Wallis, K.F. (1995), 'Large-scale Macroeconometric Modelling', in H. Pesaran and M. Wickens (eds), *Handbook of Applied Econometrics*, Blackwell

Warren, T. (2000), 'Identification of Impediments to Trade and Investment in Telecommunications Services', in C. Findlay and T. Warren (eds), *Impediments to Trade in Services: Measurement and Policy Implications*, Routledge, London, pp. 71–84.

Warren, T. and C. Findlay (2000), 'How Significant are the Barriers? Measuring Impediments to Trade in Services', in Pierre Sauve and Robert M. Stern (eds), *GATS 2000: New Directions in Services Trade Liberalization*, Brookings Institution, Washington, D.C.

Weyerbrock, S. (1998), 'Reform of the European Union's agricultural policy: How to Reach GATT-Compatibility?', *European Economic Review*, 42, pp. 375-411.

Williams, F. and A. Cane (1997), 'World Telecoms Pact to Slash Cost of Calls'. *Financial Times*, February 17.

Winters, L.A. (2002), The Economic Implications of Liberalising Mode 4 Trade, Paper prepared for the Joint WTO–World Bank Symposium on 'The Movement of Natural Persons (Mode 4) Under the GATS, WTO, Geneva, 11–12 April.

World Bank (2002) Global Economic Prospects and the Developing Countries 2002, Washington, D.C.

World Bank (2003), *World Development Report 2004: Making Services Work for Poor People.* Washington, D.C.

WTO (World Trade Organisation) (2001), *Market Access: Unfinished Business Post Uruguay Round Inventory* (Special study No. 6), Geneva.

WTO (World Trade Organisation) (2002), *European Union: Trade Policy Review*, Geneva.

WTO (World Trade Organisation) (2003), Tables on Anti-dumping, http://www.wto.org/english/tratop_e/adp_e/adp_e.htm

WTO (World Trade Organisation) (2004a), *World Trade Report 2004*, June, WTO, Geneva.

WTO (World Trade Organisation) (2004b), Statistics on Anti-Dumping, Geneva, at http://www.wto.org/english/tratop_e/adp_e/adp_e.htm

Index